VisualAge for Smalltalk and SOMobjects

Developing Distributed Object Applications

Walter Fang
Raymond Chu
Markus Weyerhäuser

INTERNATIONAL TECHNICAL SUPPORT ORGANIZATION
SAN JOSE, CALIFORNIA 95120

PRENTICE HALL PTR
UPPER SADDLE RIVER, NEW JERSEY 07458

This edition applies to Version 3.0 of IBM VisualAge for Smalltalk product set, and to all subsequent releases and modifications until otherwise indicated in new editions.

Comments about IBM Redbooks may be addressed to:
IBM Corporation ITSO, 471/80-E2, 650 Harry Road, San Jose, California 95120-6099

For information about redbooks:
http://www.redbooks.ibm.com/redbooks

Send comments to:
redbooks@vnet.ibm.com

Published by Prentice Hall PTR
Prentice-Hall, Inc.
A Simon & Schuster Company
Upper Saddle River, NJ 07458

Acquisitions Editor: Michael E. Meehan
Manufacturing Manager: Alexis R. Heydt
Cover Design: Andreas Bitterer, Marc Carrel-Billiard, Design Source
Copy Editors: Laura Nystrom, Camie Goffi
Production Supervision: Patti Guerrieri

The publisher offers discounts on this book when ordered in bulk quantities. For more information, contact:
Corporate Sales Department, Prentice Hall PTR, One Lake Street, Upper Saddle River, NJ 07458
Phone: 800-382-3419; FAX: 201-236-7141; E-mail (Internet): corpsales@prenhall.com

For book and bookstore information

http://www.prenhall.com

Printed in the United States of America
10 9 8 7 6 5 4 3 2 1

ISBN 0-13-570813-3

Prentice-Hall International (UK) Limited, *London*
Prentice-Hall of Australia Pty. Limited, *Sydney*
Prentice-Hall Canada Inc., *Toronto*
Prentice-Hall Hispanoamericana, S.A., *Mexico*
Prentice-Hall of India Private Limited, *New Delhi*
Prentice-Hall of Japan, Inc., *Tokyo*
Simon & Schuster Asia Pte. Ltd., *Singapore*
Editora Prentice-Hall do Brasil, Ltda., *Rio de Janeiro*

To my wife, Susan, and to my two daughters, Jennifer and Christine, for their love and support.

Walter

To my wife, Doris, my daughter, Peony, and to my parents and parents-in-law; also to my brother, sisters and brothers-in-law. Their support and encouragement are invaluable to me.

Raymond

To my parents Klaus and Ute.

Markus

Contents

Figures

Special Notices

This publication is intended to help software development managers, software designers, and application developers design and develop distributed object-oriented applications with VisualAge and the SOMobjects Developer Toolkit. The information in this publication is not intended as the specification of any programming interfaces that are provided by VisualAge for Smalltalk, VisualAge for C++, or the SOMobjects Developer Toolkit version 2.1. See the PUBLICATIONS section of the IBM Programming Announcement for VisualAge for Smalltalk, VisualAge for C++, and SOMObjects Developer Toolkit for more information about what publications are considered to be product documentation.

References in this publication to IBM products, programs, and services do not imply that IBM intends to make these available in all countries in which IBM operates. Any reference to an IBM product, program, or service is not intended to state or imply that only IBM's product, program, or service may be used. Any functionally equivalent program that does not infringe on any of IBM's intellectual property rights may be used instead of the IBM product, program, or service.

Information in this book was developed using the equipment specified, and is limited in application to those specific hardware and software products and levels.

IBM may have patents or pending patent applications covering subject matter in this document. The furnishing of this document does not grant the reader any license to these patents. You can send license inquiries, in writing, to the IBM Director of Licensing, IBM Corporation, 208 Harbor Drive, Stamford, CT 06904 USA.

The information contained in this document has not been submitted to any formal IBM test and is distributed AS-IS. The use of this information or the implementation of any of these techniques is a customer responsibility and depends on the customer's ability to evaluate and integrate them into the customer's operational environment. While each item may have been reviewed by IBM for accuracy in a specific situation, there is no guarantee that the same or similar results will be obtained elsewhere. Customers attempting to adapt these techniques to their own environments do so at their own risk.

The following document contains examples of data and reports used in daily business operations. To illustrate them as completely as possible, the examples contain the names of individuals, companies, brands, and products. All of these names are fictitious, and any similarity to names and addresses used by actual business enterprises is entirely coincidental.

Reference to PTF numbers that have not been released through the normal distribution process does not imply general availability. The purpose of including these reference numbers is to alert IBM customers to specific information relative to the implementation of the PTF when it becomes available to each customer according to the normal IBM PTF distribution process.

The following terms are trademarks of the International Business Machines Corporation in the United States and/or other countries:

AIX	AIX/6000
DB2/2	DB2/6000
DRDA	DSOM
IBM	OS/2
OS/2 Warp	RISC System/6000
SOM	SOMobjects
VisualAge C++ for OS/2	VisualAge for Smalltalk

The following terms are trademarks of other companies:

OMG	Object Management Group, Inc.

Other trademarks are trademarks of their respective companies.

Preface

This book describes the process of building a distributed object application using VisualAge for Smalltalk, VisualAge C++, and the SOMobjects Developer Toolkit.

It contains:

❑ A description of the distributed object environment, as defined by the OMG's CORBA specifications, and its implementation through IBM SOM/DSOM

❑ The modeling process for developing a distributed object application using the Visual Modeling Technique (VMT) developed at the IBM ITSO San Jose Center

❑ The design and implementation of the sample Foreign Currency Exchange (FCE) application using VisualAge and SOMobjects

❑ Recommendations for building distributed object applications with VisualAge and SOM/DSOM.

This book is written for software engineers, application engineers, application programmers, software development managers, and object technology consultants.

This book also includes a diskette which contains the sample programs used throughout the book. To install the sample programs, at a command prompt, type:

```
A:\install
```

and follow the instructions in the readme files in the diskette.

How This Book Is Organized

The book is organized as follows:

Part 1: Introduction

• Chapter 1. Introduction to Distributed Systems

This chapter provides an overview of distributed systems, client/server computing, and emerging distributed object applications.

• Chapter 2. Distributed Object Applications

This chapter provides an introduction to distributed object systems. It shows the general trend moving toward distributed object computing. It explains how object technology can be used to develop distributed application systems.

- Chapter 3. Industry Standards

  This chapter provides an introduction to the CORBA standard defined by the Object Management Group, and SOM, the IBM implementation of CORBA.

- Chapter 4. IBM System Object Model

  This chapter describes the IBM SOM and DSOM technologies, as well as the SOMobject product.

- Chapter 5. IBM Distributed Smalltalk Technology

  This chapter describes the IBM Distributed Smalltalk technology, and its co-existence capability with DSOM.

- Chapter 6. Implementation Alternatives for SOM Objects

  This chapter describes the implementation of SOM servers by writing IDL statements and compares it with the direct-to-SOM facilities of C++ compilers.

- Chapter 7. A Quick Tour through the Distributed SOM Object Land

  This chapter describes how to develop a simple thermometer application using SOMobjects and VisualAge SOMsupport.

Part 2. Developing a Distributed Object-Oriented Application

- Chapter 8. The Foreign Currency Exchange (FCE) Case Study

  This chapter describes the objectives and requirements for building the FCE sample application.

- Chapter 9. Analyzing the FCE System

  This chapter reviews the analysis work done in a non-distributed FCE case study application. Much of the analysis work can be reused in developing a distributed solution.

- Chapter 10. Designing the FCE Application with Distributed Objects

  This chapter provides the design details that are instrumental in extending the FCE application using distributed objects.

- Chapter 11. Implementing the Distributed FCE Application

  This chapter describes the implementation of the distributed FCE sample application using VisualAge Smalltalk SOM support and the VisualAge C++ compiler.

- Chapter 12. Looking Ahead

  This chapter summarizes the requirements and trends in distributed object application development.

Appendixes

- Appendix A. Requirements Specifications

  This appendix describes the requirements for building the FCE application.

- Appendix B. Setting Up the Implementation Platforms

  This appendix describes the client/server environment and tools used for building the distributed FCE sample application.

- Appendix C. FCE Database Definition

  This appendix describes the definitions for the relational databases used in the sample FCE application.

- Appendix D. SOM IDL Interface Listings

  This appendix describes the definitions used to define the server components with DSOM.

- Appendix E. SOM Objects Implementation Files

  This appendix lists the SOM objects implementation code used for the FCE application.

Related Publications

The publications listed in this section are considered particularly suitable for a more detailed discussion of the topics covered in this book.

- *Object-Oriented Application Development with VisualAge in a Client/Server Environment*, GG24-4227. This publication will be replaced by the following book:

  Visual Modeling Technique: Object Technology using Visual Programming, by Daniel Tkach, Walter Fang, and Andrew So, Eddison-Wesley ISBN 0-8053-2574-3, IBM SG24-4227-01.

- *Client/Server Computing Application Design Guidelines: A Distributed Relational Data Perspective*, GG24-3727.

- *Developing Distributed Object Applications with VisualAge Smalltalk Distributed Feature*, SG24-4521.

- *Client/Server Computing Application Design Guidelines: A Transaction Processing Perspective*, GG24-3728.

- *VisualAge for Smalltalk User's Guide, Version 3.0*, SC34-4518.

- *VisualAge for Smalltalk User's Reference, Version 3.0*, SC34-4519.

- *VisualAge Programmer's Guide to Building Parts for Fun and Profit*, SC34-4496-1.

❑ *SOMobjects: A Practical Introduction to SOM and DSOM*, GG24-4357.

❑ *SOMobjects: Management Utilities for Distributed SOM*, GG24-4479.

❑ *Object Technology In Application Development*, Benjamin/Cummings ISBN 0-8053-2572-7, SG24-4290-01.

❑ *Object-Oriented Programming Using SOM and DSOM*, by Christina Lau, Van Nostrand Reinhold ISBN 0-442-01948-3.

❑ *SOMobjects Developer Toolkit Programmers Reference Manual*, 59G5228.

❑ *SOMobjects Developer Toolkit Users Guide*, 59G5464.

International Technical Support Organization Publications

A complete list of International Technical Support Organization publications, with a brief description of each, may be found in:

Bibliography of International Technical Support Organization Technical Bulletins, GG24-3070.

To get listings of ITSO technical bulletins (redbooks) online, VNET users may type:

```
TOOLS SENDTO WTSCPOK TOOLS REDBOOKS GET REDBOOKS CATALOG
```

> **How to Order ITSO Technical Bulletins (Redbooks)**
>
> IBM employees in the USA may order ITSO books and CD-ROMs using PUBORDER. Customers in the USA may order by calling 1-800-879-2755 or by faxing 1-800-445-9269. Almost all major credit cards are accepted. Outside the USA, customers should contact their IBM branch office.
>
> Customers may order hardcopy redbooks individually or in customized sets, called GBOFs, which relate to specific functions of interest. IBM employees and customers may also order redbooks in online format on CD-ROM collections, which contain the redbooks for multiple products.

International Technical Support Organization

The IBM International Technical Support Organization (ITSO) is a unique group within IBM. The ITSO consists of seven centers located at major product development sites:

- ❑ Austin
- ❑ Böblingen
- ❑ Cambridge
- ❑ Poughkeepsie
- ❑ Raleigh
- ❑ Rochester
- ❑ San Jose

The mission of the ITSO is to provide how-to technical support for IBM products worldwide. Each center works closely with the development organizations to provide support for the products developed at their locations. In addition, the centers work together to provide cross-product and cross-platform support with a total system solution perspective.

Technical bulletins such as the one you are reading, commonly known as redbooks, are produced by the ITSO centers as one of their primary vehicles for delivering technical product information to customers and IBM field personnel. These redbooks are typically the result of several months of effort involving multiple IBM residents from around the world. The residents bring their technical expertise and knowledge of their customer's environment to the ITSO centers and spend 6 to 8 weeks testing the product and documentation. Their experiences and findings are then published in a redbook.

Redbooks are not intended to replace product documentation; rather they supplement the documentation with actual user experiences. Because the residents work with development to better understand the products, the IBM development organizations are better able to understand user requirements.

The ITSO centers also produce workshops and other deliverables designed to provide technical information to those who use and support IBM products.

We hope you find this and other ITSO redbooks useful and that you will make them an integral part of your systems library. Please take the time to fill out the enclosed evaluation form and let us know what you think.

You can send comments or questions regarding this redbook by electronic mail to:

```
Walter Fang
ITSO-San Jose Center
Internet: fangw@vnet.ibm.com
IBM VNET: FANGW at WTSCPOK
```

About the Authors

Walter Fang is a Senior Consultant, Object Technology, at IBM's International Technical Support Organization (ITSO) - San Jose Center. Before joining ITSO, he was an Information Technology Architect at IBM Canada Client/Server Center, where he has helped customers develop object-oriented client/server architectures and solutions. He is a Certified IBM VisualAge for Smalltalk Developer, and holds a Master degree in Computer Science from Taiwan University.

Raymond Chu is an I/T Specialist in IBM Consulting and Service, IBM China/Hong Kong, Specialising in Object Technology. He holds a Bachelor Degree in Engineering from the University of Hong Kong. He has been working with object technology since 1989, and has designed and developed a number of OS/2 applications using C++ and Smalltalk. He can be reached via e-mail at churkm@hkgvm8.vnet.ibm.com

Markus Weyerhäuser is an Object Technology Consultant in IBM Germany, with main focus on IBM SOMobjects technology. He holds a Bachelor degree in Business Computer Science from the Berufsakademie in Mannheim, Germany. He has been working on Smalltalk since 1988, and has designed and implemented financial management information systems. Markus can be reached via e-mail at mweyerhaeusr@de.ibm

Acknowledgments

This book is the result of two residency projects conducted in San Jose by the International Technical Support Organization during 1994 and 1995. The preliminary work was done in the 1994 ITSO residency led by Daniel Tkach. We would like to thank our managers in our home countries— Andy Banaszak, John Bailey, Andrew So, and Carl Ludwig— for letting us work on the project and this book.

Thanks to John O'Keefe from the VisualAge for Smalltalk development department, IBM Software Solutions, Raleigh, North Carolina, who contributed invaluable advice and technical review for the projects and this book.

Many thanks to Jens Tiedemann, ITSO—San Jose Center Manager, who provided an empowering environment that enabled the project to succeed. Special thanks to everyone at the ITSO—San Jose Center, in particular Elsa Barron, Mary Comianos, Alan Tippett; Andi Bitterer for the cover design of the book and his tips on getting the book *framed*; Maggie Cutler and Shirley Hentzell for doing a great editing job. Finally, thanks to Barbara Isa of the Santa Teresa Lab; Mike Meehan, Patti Guerrieri and Jane Bonnell at Prentice Hall; and Lou Evart, Tamra Smith, and Doris Chen at Softline International Inc. for their support. Thanks also to the many other collaborators and reviewers who contributed to improve this book.

F.W.F.
R.C.
M.W.

Acknowledgments

Part 1

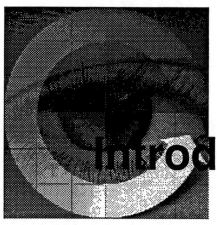

Introduction

Part 1 introduces distributed systems and explains the challenges of and approaches to developing them. Several options in the basic design of a distributed system are presented. We explain distributed object applications, what they are, and how they become the next wave of distributed computing.

Part 1 provides an overview of the Common Object Request Broker Architecture (CORBA) standard defined by the Object Management Group (OMG) and the IBM implementation of a CORBA-compliant object request broker through the Distributed System Object Model (DSOM). An overview of IBM distributed Smalltalk technology, including the VisualAge SOMsupport, is also provided to show how it relates to CORBA and DSOM.

We conclude Part 1 with a tutorial on how to develop a simple distributed object application with SOM objects.

1

Introduction to Distributed Systems

The computing industry is embarking on one of the most drastic technological transformations of the decade: the transition from a traditional computing infrastructure and its application development techniques to a new, distributed object computing infrastructure.

In this chapter we review the fundamental concepts of distributed systems and Client/Server computing. We explain the benefits and challenges associated with distributed application development.

Distributed Systems

A distributed system is a collection of autonomous computers connected by some type of network. Distributed systems offer a number of advantages over single-processor systems:

❑ Several computing elements are available in the system. If an application is decomposed into pieces that run concurrently, the application will run faster and yield more throughput.

❑ Fewer users compete for resources on different computers, thus reducing contention and response time variability during peak hours.

❑ Overall, availability is higher because the computers in a distributed system have independent failure characteristics. The failure of any single computer affects only the users of that computer. Availability of critical data can be ensured by replicating the data at server nodes.

❑ Scalability is improved. The total system can be configured with greater flexibility. Nodes can be:

➤ Added to or removed from the network.
➤ Reconfigured to meet changing requirements. For example:
  - Disks can be moved from one node to another.
  - Data can be moved from one node to another.
  - Data can be replicated at several nodes.
➤ Made more or less powerful. For instance, a node can be replaced by a multiprocessor node to increase its processing power.

The scalability of distributed systems is in sharp contrast to the limited growth potential of traditional mainframe computers.

The Client/Server Computing Model

The Client/Server computing model is widely used in a distributed system. The model defines two separate parts of a Client/Server application (see Figure 1 on page 5):

❑ The client (for example, an application running on a workstation) calls for services, such as data or processing functions.

❑ The server performs services on behalf of the calling client. The server can be a program, located on the same machine as the client, or it can run on a remote machine, or it can even run under a different operating system from that of the client machine.

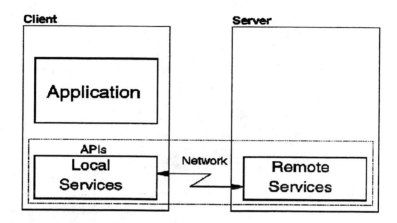

Figure 1. Client/Server Computing Model

In the Client/Server computing model, the client application does not have to distinguish between local and remote services. The programming complexities of network distribution are transparent to the client application, regardless of whether they are handled by the called service or the calling mechanism. Thus, the client application need not care about the location of services or the interconnection media.

The Client/Server model is inherently capable of providing resource sharing. A server can, for instance, provide access to data that reside on fast disks. It can improve data access further by using large cache buffers in memory. These expensive resources are made available to many client applications through Client/Server computing.

Client/Server Styles

Figure 2 on page 6 shows the distribution of the functional parts of an application. Everything from the presentation (the front end, that is, the GUI) to the business logic (the back end) can be flexibly placed on different nodes in a distributed environment. The Client/Server computing styles shown in Figure 2 have a direct impact on the complexity, portability, and reliability of a distributed application.

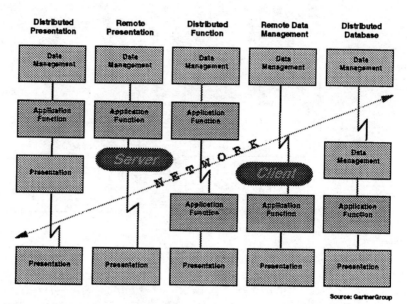

Figure 2. Client/Server Computing Styles

Challenges in Building Distributed Systems

Distributed systems present interesting functional capabilities. However, their implementation presents several challenges:

❏ **Partial and independent failures**

Because parts of an application run on different computers, it is possible that some parts will fail while others proceed. Partial failure leads to inconsistent states of the program. For example, when money is debited from an account on one computer to be deposited in an account on another computer, if the computer responsible for the deposit fails, what should be done with the money already removed from the source account? The application developer or administrator must be able to cope with such partial failures, possibly by stopping the functioning parts of an application and undoing some of their earlier effects.

❏ **Concurrent and independent events**

Many things that can be assumed in a single-processor environment do not apply to a distributed environment where independent computing entities are active. Concurrent and independent events have to be synchronized. A common way of ensuring atomicity of an action is that when one needs to update shared data, one must first obtain a lock, apply the update, and then return the lock to allow others to update the data. Overall, controlling access to shared resources is more difficult in a distributed computing environment.

❑ **Site autonomy**

There is a trade-off between making each node independent or integrating all modes in a "single system." The advantage of integrating nodes is that the user can continue to use the system even if other nodes fail. The disadvantage is that sharing and cooperation are harder to achieve. The advantage of integrating all nodes into one single system is that sharing and cooperation among users are facilitated, and one node can be used to provide such services as backup for another node. The disadvantage is increased interdependence of nodes on one another. If we introduce too much interdependence, the failure of one node may affect the rest of the system and its users. The extent of site autonomy can be determined by asking to what extent will a user taking his/her machine off the network affect the rest of the system and its users.

❑ **Heterogeneity**

The maximum advantage of scalability in distributed systems can be achieved only if the nodes on the network can be different from one another, and applications can use the most appropriate nodes for each function they perform. We can imagine having nodes with different system configurations (e.g., DASD, memory), which could be termed heterogeneous. More challenging is the integration of heterogeneous processors, operating systems, or programming languages. A distributed system could, for example, support nodes that are models of the same machine but run the same operating system. More difficult are systems that support nodes running different operating systems. Still more difficult are systems that could support an application written in multiple languages running on different processors and operating systems.

❑ **Security**

The geographical distribution of the nodes in a distributed system introduces security risks that do not exist with a time-shared system locked in a computer room. Approaches to solving these problems include password mechanisms and data encryption for stored data and messages, are being addressed. One approach to solving these problems is the OSF DCE environment.

Approaches to Building Distributed Systems

There can be many approaches to building distributed systems. Some of these are described below.

❑ **Distributed operating system**

The distributed operating system provides the programmer with a single-system image. A program running on top of a distributed operating system sees a collection of resources and services that it can use without any concern for whether the resources and services are actually available at the node at which it is running. The advantage of the distributed operating system approach is that the effort of dealing with distribution issues is paid only once, when the operating system is written. The disadvantage is that a distributed operating system requires the different nodes to be homogeneous nodes running the same level of the operating system.

❑ **Networked operating system**

In a networked operating system, each node runs an independent operating system. Each operating system, however, provides a network interface, which application programs can use to communicate with other nodes. Because the network interface is supported "on top" of the operating system, this approach can accommodate heterogeneous operating systems (and hence, processors).

❑ **Distributed file system**

In a distributed file system, a node can mount a file system from another node at boot time or upon request. In this way, the node can have access to the remote file system. The disadvantage of this approach is that each application program has to deal with issues of distribution.

❑ **Distributed programming language**

The distributed programming language approach supports the notion of distribution in the programming language. Here, the programming language implementation of the run-time system is responsible for dealing with distribution issues. If the abstraction of nodes and remote resources is provided in the programming language, the application can access remote resources directly. Alternatively, the programming language can try to make the network transparent, much like a distributed operating system makes it transparent. The advantage of this approach is that the language can be implemented on different operating systems and therefore can support a network of heterogeneous processors. The disadvantage is that it is complex to design a distributed programming language.

❑ **Distributed programming toolkit**

The distributed programming toolkit approach is somewhere between a networked operating system and a distributed programming language. It provides a library (toolkit) of routines that aid in the writing of distributed applications. These routines can provide mechanisms for communication, synchronization, failure detection, and recovery. This approach is at a higher level of abstraction than the networked operating system approach, but it is at a lower level than the distributed programming language approach. When there is no single appropriate abstraction for distributed programming, the toolkit approach is appealing because a toolkit can contain many different tools. Examples are IBM's Distributed SOM (DSOM), OSF's DCE remote procedure call (RPC), and Sun's Network Computing System (NCS).

Examples of Distributed Systems

The following are some examples of distributed systems:

❑ **Remote directories**

A user logged on to one node can see a global directory tree with directories maintained on different nodes. The Network File System (NFS) and OSF's DCE distributed file system (DFS) are examples of remote directories.

❑ **Distributed run-time library**

A distributed run-time library enables users to write applications without concern for the location of files and interprocessor communication. The library intercepts accesses to nonlocal files and forwards them to the correct destination node.

❑ **Specialized servers**

Users work at their personal workstations, which supply most of their computing needs. Specialized needs, such as file storage or gateway access, are provided by nodes on the network.

❑ **Processor pool**

Processing power is just another service; the user's need for such a service is variable over time. Most of the time, users are satisfied with the processing power available on their workstations. Sometimes, however, such as when they want to run a large simulation, they need a large amount of processing power. Thus, one or more processors from a pool can be allocated to a user and taken away when the processor-intensive application is finished. Processor pools are a good way of sharing processing power and distributing the computational load of the system.

Data and Function Placement

In designing distributed systems, a key design consideration is the placement and distribution of function and data. One important design aspect for distributed systems is how to share and manage data to ensure their integrity. Equally important is the placement of the control and processing functions in a distributed system to achieve optimal resource utilization and to maximize overall system performance.

We discuss basic data and function distribution strategies in the sections that follow.

Data Distribution

Data in a distributed environment can be managed through centralization, replication, or partitioning:

❏ **Centralized data management**

The data are placed at one node, and all accesses to those data are routed to that node.

❏ **Replicated data management**

Copies of data are made at various nodes. The nodes needing access to the data can access the "closest" node.

❏ **Partitioned data management**

The data can be partitioned into pieces, and the pieces can be placed at various nodes. Accesses to the data must be routed to the appropriate node according to which piece of data is being accessed.

These three techniques of data management in a distributed environment apply equally well to the management of processing and control functions. Thus, processing and control functions, as well as data, can be centralized, replicated, or partitioned.

Centralized Data

Consider the case of workstations connected on a Local Area Network (LAN) (see Figure 3 on page 11). A list of users is kept for authentication purposes. The list is accessed at login time. A single copy of the list is kept at a central location, such as a large computer that all workstations can access.

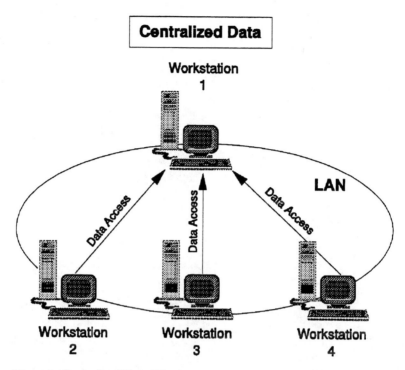

Figure 3. Centralized Data Management

The advantage of centralized data management is that, by maintaining a single copy of the data, the login information can be modified in one place. The disadvantage is that each login results in a message between the workstation and the host site where the login file resides. Furthermore, if the host site is nonoperational, users cannot log in at any of the workstations. There is both a performance and an availability disadvantage with maintaining a central login file.

Replicated Data

A circumvention of the problems of centralized data management is to have copies, or replicas, of the login file at multiple nodes (see Figure 4 on page 12).

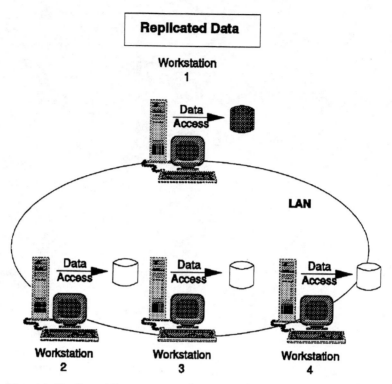

Figure 4. Replicated Data Management

Having multiple copies solves both the performance and availability problems of centralized data management. The performance problem is solved because accesses to the login file are local and not remote. The availability problem is solved because it is easier to find an available copy of the login file when several copies of it exist. In addition, concurrent accesses at multiple workstations improve throughput.

The disadvantage of replicated copies is the new problem (and cost) of ensuring the consistency of the replicated data. There are many different ways of solving the consistency problem. The level of difficulty and performance of the algorithm depend on the relative ratio of read operations to write operations against the replicated data. In our example of replicating the login file, accesses at login time pose no problem because they are read-only. If the login file is modified, however, one must ensure that the modifications are distributed to all copies and that inconsistent modifications are not made at different sites. If the number of read accesses is much larger than the number of write accesses, which is the case with the login file, replication is advisable.

One way of ensuring the consistency of replicated data is to lock all copies when an update is attempted. Only after all copies have been locked will an update to the file be allowed. After the update takes place, it is propagated to the different copies. This approach decreases the amount of concurrency, however, because logins are not allowed during locking and propagation of the update. The basic trade-off in replication techniques is to support the highest amount of concurrency while providing the highest availability of up-to-date data.

Partitioned Data

Instead of replicating the login file, another approach to solving the performance and availability problems of centralized data management is to partition or distribute the contents of the file (see Figure 5).

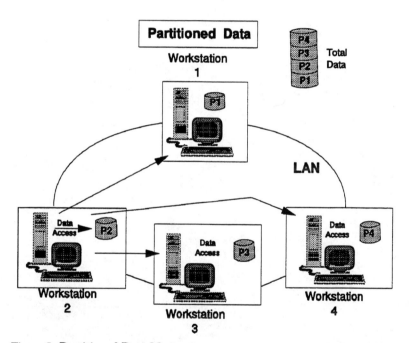

Figure 5. Partitioned Data Management

In the case of a network of, say, ten workstations, one could partition the login file into ten files, each one-tenth in size. The collection would be "the login file." This solution helps login performance because it is likely that user authentication will be distributed throughout the network rather than through the same node. This approach also supports partial availability because the unavailability of any single node only disallows one-tenth of the users from logging in. As in the case of data replication, there is some overhead both at data retrieval and at update time. The correct partition to address data retrieval and update needs must be determined. One possible way of partitioning the data is to have the data located near the nodes where they will be used most often. A typical example is a distributed database of bank accounts where the account information database is partitioned according to the geographical location of the owner of the account.

One can distinguish between horizontal and vertical partitioning. With horizontal partitioning, partitioning is on the unit of tables. With vertical partitioning, partitioning is within tables (that is, the customer table is divided into tables containing contiguous sets of customers).

Function Distribution

Processing and control functions can be centralized, replicated, or partitioned in much the same way as data.

Centralized Processing

With central processing of user login requests, the login service is at a single node (see Figure 6 on page 15).

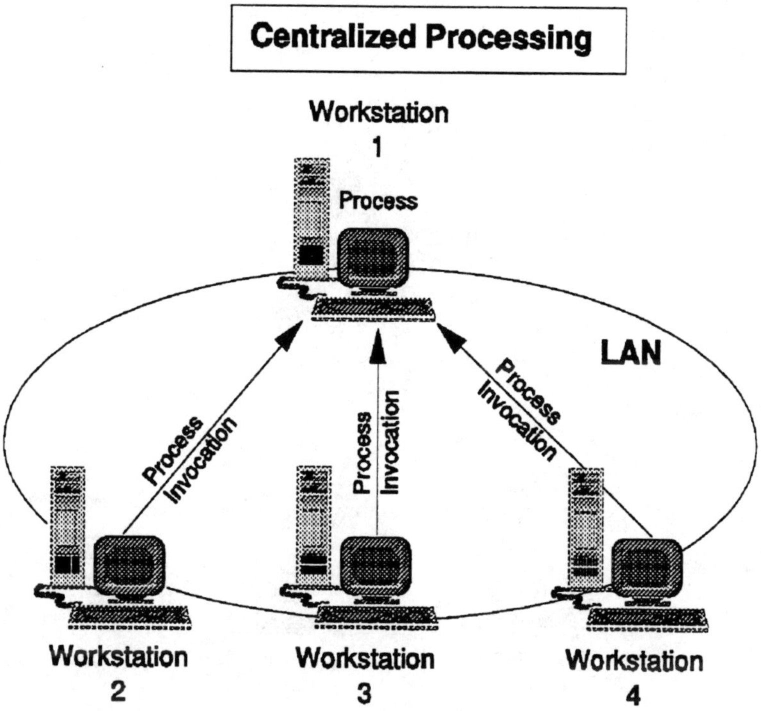

Figure 6. Centralized Processing

Replicated Processing
With replicated processing of user login requests, the login service is replicated at several nodes (see Figure 7 on page 16).

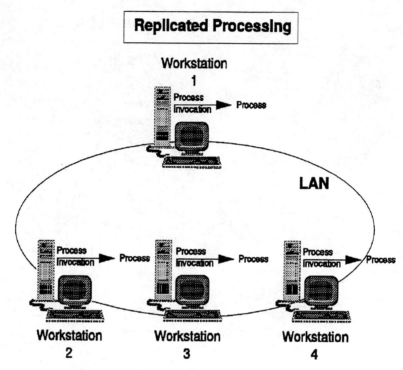

Figure 7. Replicated Processing

Partitioned Processing

With partitioned processing of user login requests, the login service is partitioned such that each node is capable of processing certain login requests (see Figure 8 on page 17)

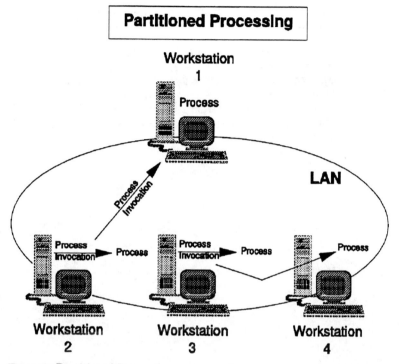

Figure 8. Partitioned Processing

Although centralized and partitioned login processing may not make too much sense, there are other examples where it is useful to consider replicating or partitioning functions independent of the data configurations. In a database application, a single node could be designated to process all functions to minimize the problems of dealing with contentions and locking; or some nodes might be allowed to perform lookup requests, while other nodes would be charged with permitting update requests. Also, one might consider replicating the function processing at several nodes to increase the concurrency-handling capabilities of the system.

In summary, if the main interest is a resilient service, centralization of the processing function is not the best approach. Instead, choose replication, partitioning, or a combination of both, depending on the amount of concurrency or availability in which you are interested. We have discussed the configuration of data and processing functions independently; in reality, however, the decisions regarding data and processing are closely related. For example, if you choose data partitioning, choose partitioned processing as well.

Although replication of data is the basis of providing data availability in distributed systems, and replicated processing is the basis of reducing contention and providing higher throughput, centralized data and centralized processing are easier to implement.

You may wonder why we discuss function and data placement here, while we, and this book, are mainly interested in distributed object applications. As functions and data are encapsulated in an object, it turns out that the design considerations for object distribution are similar to those considerations in data and function distribution in traditional distributed systems. Chapter 2 introduces the distributed object applications.

2

Distributed Object Applications

In this chapter, we explain the relationship of object-oriented techniques to distributed application development, with specific regard to the extent to which object-oriented techniques help distribution.

We show the shift in computing infrastructure, as well as how the development of distributed applications based on object technology exploits the latest distributed object computing technology. Generally, just as object-oriented design and programming have helped to improve productivity of nondistributed software development, they also help improve productivity in a distributed software development.

Distributed Object Computing

With the trend toward reducing computing costs by *rightsizing* (which implies distributed processing), developers must design their applications to run on networks of interconnected machines that share the processing load. Applications must make the best use of existing resources to meet the needs of business and achieve performance, scalability, security, usability, and maintainability objectives.

Today's businesses are also finding the traditional Client/Server approach to be inefficient. Typically, most application logic in a Client/Server environment is located on the client machines, with centralized or distributed database servers. This approach can lead to excessive network traffic and difficulty in maintenance. One solution to these problems is to put some of the application logic on the server where it can access the data locally. This requires an approach much more flexible than the traditional Client/Server approach.

The new approach is called *distributed object computing*, that is; objects are on the server as well as on the client machines. After all, object-orientation and Client/Server computing build on similar concepts:

❑ **Client/Server**

➤ Client requests a service.
➤ Server fulfills the request.

❑ **Object-orientation**

➤ Client (sender) object sends a message to request a service.
➤ Server (receiver) object responds and acts on the message.

Figure 9 shows an object model and the communication of objects through messages.

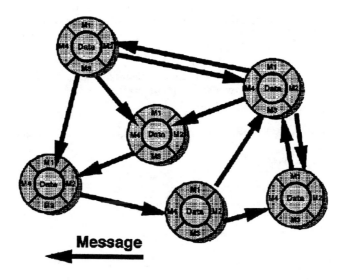

Message

Figure 9. The Object Model

Distributed object computing extends this model and enables developers to assemble applications from objects that run on disparate platforms distributed in a network. Objects communicate with each other through a message-passing mechanism. An object's role can change between client and server. A given object can act as a server to some objects and, at the same time, as a client of other objects. Furthermore, the client and server objects can be on the same machine and even in the same business process.

Distributed Objects

On the surface, object-oriented design seems ideally suited for distributed systems because the notion of objects provides a convenient mechanism for encapsulating data and function. Just as objects can be used as decomposition units, they also can be used as units of distribution. A problem arises, however, in the following case: if one were to cache data from a remote object and make it available to a local object, the encapsulation, as defined by object-oriented technology, is broken. A second problem is the handling of concurrency and concurrency control.

The configuration of data and processing with object-oriented technology are intimately related. Although processing and data could be looked at separately from a logical point of view, an object actually combines processing and data. When a database is used to store the state of the object, all data configurations mentioned above—centralized, partitioned, and distributed—apply equally. An object could be constructed from state (data) residing at a different node. In the case of using proxy objects (a proxy object is a stand-in object for another object), where the invocation of the process is replicated and the execution of the process is centralized, processing is in reality partitioned. Process invocation and method dispatching are executed locally, and the actual execution of the method is done at a different node.

Evolution of Client/Server Implementation with Objects

Figure 10 demonstrates the evolution of Client/Server implementation with objects. Object-oriented technology has started to move into the Client/Server realm, primarily on the client side. Eventually, we will reach the right-most configuration where objects are a common feature of client and server alike.

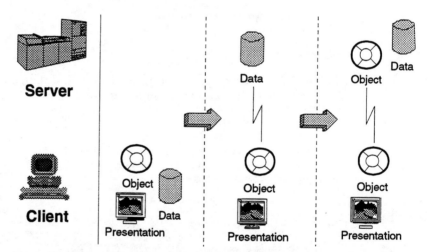

Figure 10. Evolution of Client/Server Implementation with Objects

The benefits that object-oriented technology has brought to client programming apply equally well to the server side. Perhaps most important is the ability to manage complexity and change. Multi-user requirements and the greatly magnified scale of the server side naturally lend themselves to complexity, which creates a need for the encapsulation, reusability, and close mapping between the problem and solution domains that object-oriented technology makes possible.

Data will be encapsulated in objects that will in some cases be able to roam to where they are most needed.

(Peter Wayner, Byte Magazine, 01/94)

Using encapsulation and reusability with object-oriented technology also helps to manage system changes. They enable server programmers to isolate changes and minimize maintenance costs. The close mapping between the problem and solution domains enables one to model the enterprise and then build an implementation that maps directly to the enterprise. This ensures that the changes are made quickly and correctly. Today's business environment creates pressure for information systems flexible enough to cope with the rapid pace of change. Such flexibility is difficult to manage on the server level, as evidenced by the pervasive IS backlogs. Benefits such as those offered by object-oriented technology are greatly needed.

Despite the potential advantages, however, to date there have been few successful object-oriented server implementations. One reason is an old story in the industry: critical mass. An organization cannot afford to maintain an entire proprietary object-oriented programming language or server environment just for its own use, and tool developers are hesitant to develop the needed tools until there is a proven market for them. However, as tool providers converge on architectural and language standards, costs can be spread among many users.

As Orfali [Orfali94] points out, we are within the third wave of Client/Server technology as shown in Figure 11. The first wave, which started in the early 1980s, came with network operating systems that allowed applications to share files, printers, and other networked devices. The second wave, which began in the mid-1980's, introduced SQL database servers into Client/Server applications. Along with that trend, groupware and Transaction Processing (TP) monitors, such as CICS OS/2, gained a solid piece of the Client/Server cake. The third wave, which began in the early 1990's, is the distributed objects wave. The distributed objects wave is still at a moderate height, but we should start to swim now so we can follow that wave up to its crest!

Distributed object computing represents a new and exciting trend to merge two powerful technologies in the information industry: Client/Server computing and object-oriented technology.

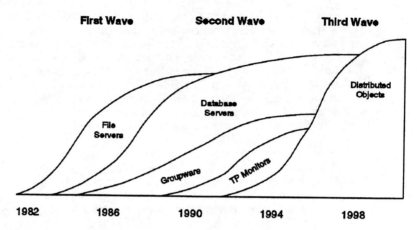

Figure 11. Waves of Client/Server Technology

This architecture holds significant promise for tomorrow's distributed applications.

Applicability of Distributed Objects

In this section, we describe three kinds of applications that are suitable for distributed objects: object server, active server, and peer-to-peer (see Figure 12 on page 25). These applications raise a new set of requirements that can be better addressed by a distributed object solution than by the traditional Client/Server approach.

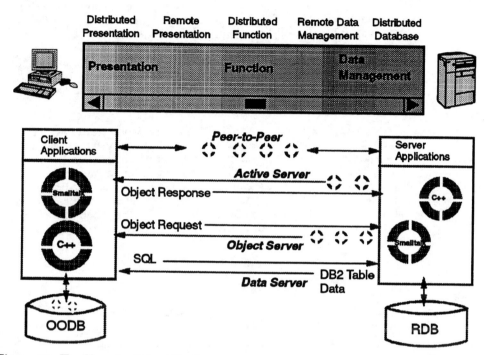

Figure 12. The Changing Role of the Server

Object Server

The most common Client/Server implementations today use the *remote data access* style, in which all of the business logic is on the client systems. The client systems become the so-called fat clients, accessing a remote relational database server.

Using the existing Distributed Relational Database Architecture (DRDA), client workstations can access a centralized database through the SQL interface across the network. However, this approach can lead to excessive network traffic between the clients and relational database server. This is especially true when we must retrieve many intermediate results from the database server to accomplish one task on the client.

In a *fat client* situation, the data server does not filter any information it retrieves from the databases, normally in the form of rows of data tables, before sending it to the client. Therefore, it generates unnecessary network traffic.

One way to reduce the network traffic is to use *stored procedures*, which many relational database products support. A stored procedure is a named collection of SQL statements and procedural logic that is compiled, verified, and stored in the database server. The problem with stored procedures is that there is no standard for them, and they only work for local databases. Each relational database vendor has its own implementation of stored procedures. Thus, it is very difficult, if not impossible, to use stored procedures to access multiple databases from different vendors in a single client task.

As shown in Figure 13, to avoid excessive network traffic, we could add more processing functions in the server. The server then becomes an *object server*. Instead of using the SQL interface between the client and server, the clients would issue a request to the server in the form of the required objects. By massaging the data and constructing the requested objects at the server before sending them to the client, we could reduce the network traffic, improve overall application performance, and potentially reduce the number of requests that the client must send to the server.

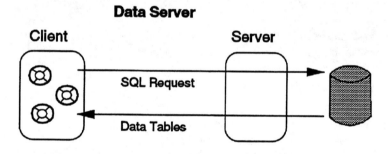

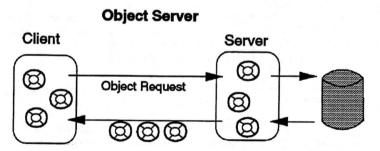

Figure 13. Object Server

A side benefit of this approach is that the relational database software does not need to be installed in the client workstations. In an operational environment with large numbers of clients, substantial savings could be gained from not having to pay license costs for client workstations.

Active Server

In a traditional Client/Server computing model, the client always originates the requests. The server is *passive* in the sense that it only reacts to the client's requests. We can change the way the server behaves in this model so that the server is an active party in the system. This is what we call an *active server*. The server can process data by itself and initiate the communication with clients.

We can look at an example of an active server in a publisher-subscriber scenario (see Figure 14). The server publishes events that it can handle, and clients can then subscribe to those events in which they are interested. Let us say that a stockbroker is interested in the current prices of some specific stocks. In an active server environment, the stockbroker can ask the server for the available (published) share prices and then choose (subscribe) those stocks that are needed. Whenever the price of a subscribed-to stock changes, the subscriber is notified automatically.

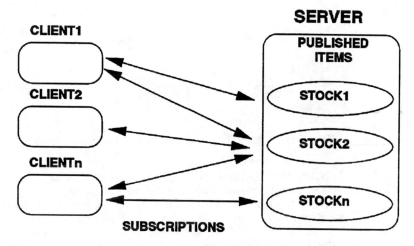

Figure 14. Active Server: Publisher/Subscriber Scenario

Another active server example is an auctioneer at an auction. The auctioneer starts the event and keeps track of the bidding. Bidders (clients) can send their bid to the auctioneer (server) who holds the current highest bid price and the name of the bidder. All bidders are notified whenever the situation changes.

Peer-to-Peer

In peer-to-peer applications (Figure 15), two client workstations communicate with each other directly, acting both as a server and a client at the same time. Peer-to-peer applications can be useful, for example, when two users on different client workstations must establish a session for consultation or negotiation on a certain subject matter.

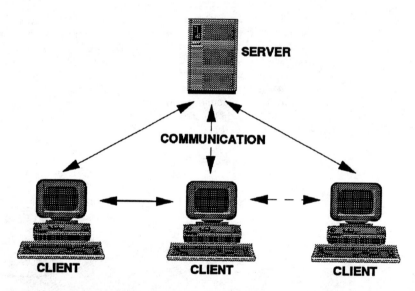

Figure 15. Peer-to-Peer Application

In a traditional Client/Server computing model, communication between two clients is through the server. Two separate concurrent sessions must be established between each client and the server, thus causing more overhead on the network and the server. Instead, we want to have a direct communication link between the two clients so that they can establish a session whenever they want and without going through the server.

3
Industry
Standards

In this chapter, we review the emerging standards and architectures for object-to-object communication and interoperability in a heterogeneous environment.

As with any new technology, standards are required for object-oriented server technology to gain widespread acceptance; such standards are increasingly evident. Object Management Group's (OMG's) Common Object Request Broker Architecture (CORBA) standard has come to provide the basis for the *Object Transaction Service* (OTS) distributed object architecture, also defined by the OMG. In addition, two distributed transaction standards with object-oriented implications are widely recognized: the X/Open Distributed Transaction Processing (DTP) model and the ISO Open Systems Interface Transaction Processing (OSI-TP) standard.

Standardization of programming languages is equally essential. In recent years, the industry has begun to converge on C++, Smalltalk, and object-oriented COBOL as standard industrial-strength object-oriented languages.

Standards can help to ensure that objects developed using different vendors' tools are mutually compatible. As software vendors develop object-oriented components that conform to these standards for the server, customer confidence will continue to grow and customers will increasingly adopt object technology.

The Object Management Group (OMG)

Object-oriented business applications and the promised benefits of mass customization of software, rapid implementation, and reusability are obvious industry goals. To achieve these goals, the complexities of distributing objects across networks must be solved. Most vendor implementations today primarily support objects implemented on a single system. Those customers who are beginning to work with objects across the network find that a background in Client/Server and wide-area transactional processing is essential. The basic design points for distributed objects are very similar to things learned from old online transaction systems. You want to minimize both the data that are transmitted and server processing time. Because many object approaches today were designed for a single desktop, they do not scale. The OMG is dealing with the technology issues related to distributing objects. Many of the design issues will be addressed as the collective experience base grows within the industry and as everyone learns from past lessons.

The OMG is an industry-wide, nonprofit consortium of more than 500 members, including Apple, AT&T, HP, IBM, Microsoft, and Sun. OMG was formed to help reduce the complexity, lower the costs, and hasten the introduction of new software applications. OMG does this by introducing its Object Management Architecture (OMA) with supporting detailed interface specifications. This single architecture and set of specifications based on commercially available object technology has been developed to enable the integration of distributed applications. Implementations are the domain of vendors, end-users, and those developing products and projects to solve a particular computing or business problem. Specifications are the domain of OMG membership.

The mission of OMG is to create a standard that realizes interoperability between independently developed applications across heterogeneous networks of computers. The goal is to achieve reusability of components, interoperability among heterogeneous platforms, and portability of applications based on open, standard, object-oriented interfaces. To that end, OMG has defined the architecture of an Object Request Broker (ORB) that enables interoperability. This architecture is known as CORBA.

Object Management Architecture (OMA)

The OMA (Figure 16) is the center of all activities undertaken by the OMG.

To support heterogeneous, distributed, networked environments, the OMA combines distributed processing with object-oriented computing. It provides a standard method for creating, preserving, locating, and communicating with objects, which can be anything from complete application systems to parts of applications. The OMA defines a layer above existing operating systems and communication transport mechanisms.

In the OMA's generalized object model, requests for object services are sent to the ORB. The requester can specify providers or alternative providers or leave the selection of a provider to the ORB. The model provides a common interface for objects of different origins. All client requests are issued in a standard format, improving modularity and decreasing coupling among modules. The OMA defines the mechanism that allows client objects to issue requests to and receive responses from OMA-conforming objects.

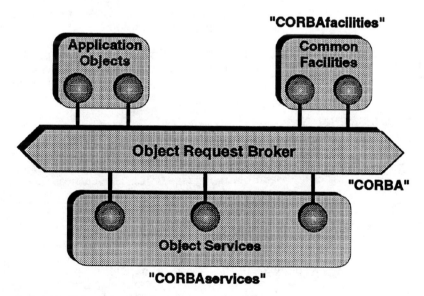

Figure 16. Object Management Architecture Components

OMA Reference Model

The OMA Reference Model partitions the OMG problem space into practical, high-level architectural components that can be addressed by technology proposers. It forms a conceptual roadmap for assembling the resultant technologies, while allowing for different design solutions. The Reference Model identifies and characterizes the components, interfaces, and protocols that compose the OMA, but does not in itself define them in detail.

The OMA can be viewed as two major segments consisting of four critical components (see Figure 16):

❑ **Application-oriented**

The OMA characterizes application objects and common facilities as solution-specific components that rest closest to the end-user.

❑ **System-oriented**

The ORB and object services are concerned with the system or infrastructure aspects of distributed object computing and management.

The ORB manages all communications among components. The ORB technology is now considered the most important approach for deploying open, distributed computing solutions.

The OMA assumes that underlying services provided by a platform's operating system and lower-level basic services, such as network computing facilities, are available and usable by OMA implementations.

OMA Components

Figure 16 shows the components of the OMA. Objects that belong to one of these components have their interface described with OMG's Interface Definition Language (IDL). This ensures that objects, which can be implemented by different vendors, can communicate. Interfaces for application objects, however, are not and will not be standardized by OMG. We can define the OMA components as follows:

❑ **The ORB** provides an infrastructure that enables objects to converse, independent of the specific platforms and techniques used to implement the objects. Compliance with the ORB standard guarantees portability and interoperability of objects over a network of heterogeneous systems. The official OMG name for the ORB is CORBA.

❑ **Object services** extend the ORB by standardizing additional services required to fulfill the general needs of object applications. An example of an object service is the Life Cycle Service, which is responsible for the life cycle management of objects. The Life

Cycle Service describes interfaces to create objects, control access to objects, keep track of relocated objects, and to control the relationship between styles of objects (class management). Also provided are the generic environments in which single objects can perform their tasks. Object services provide for application consistency and help to increase programmer productivity. The official OMG name for object services is CORBAservices.

❑ **Common facilities** provide a set of generic application functions that can be configured to the specific requirements of a particular configuration. The common facilities include printing, document management, database, and electronic mail. Standardization leads to uniformity in generic operations and better options for end-users for configuring their working environments. The official OMG name for common facilities is CORBAfacilities.

❑ **Application objects** are business objects that provide application logic (for example, a payroll system). Although not yet standardized by OMG, application objects are critical when considering a comprehensive system architecture. Application object components represent those application objects performing particular tasks for a user. An application is typically built from a large number of basic objects—some specific to the application at hand and some built from a set of common facilities.

The OMG Object Model

When any large body of contributors work together for a common technical good, it is necessary to work from a consistent basis of understanding and terminology. To this end, the OMG Object Model defines common object semantics for specifying the externally visible characteristics of objects in a standard and implementation-independent way. The common semantics characterize objects that exist in an OMG-compliant system.

The OMG Object Model is based on a few basic concepts: objects, operations, and types. An object can model any entity, such as a *person*, a *boat*, or a *document*. Operations are applied to objects and enable one to arrive at certain conclusions about an object, such as a *person's date of birth*. Operations associated with an object collectively characterize an object's behavior.

Objects are created as instances of types. One can view a type as a template for object creation. An instance of type *boat* could be *red boat, 38 feet long*, with a *seating capacity of 6*. A type characterizes the behavior of its instances by describing the operations that can be applied to those objects. A relationship can exist between types. For example, a *speedboat* could be related to a generic form of *boat*. The relationships between types are known as supertypes and subtypes.

The OMG Object Model defines a core set of requirements (based on the basic concepts of objects, operations, and types) in a Core Model, which can be supported in any system that complies with the Object Model standard. While the Core Model serves as the common ground, the OMG Object Model also allows for extensions to the Core to enable even greater commonality within different technology domains. The concepts, known as Components and Profiles, are supported by the OMA and are discussed at length in the *Object Management Architecture Guide* available from the OMG.

Common Object Request Broker Architecture (CORBA)

CORBA is the OMG's answer to the need for interoperability among the rapidly proliferating number of hardware and software products available today. Simply stated, CORBA enables applications to communicate with one another no matter where they are located or who has designed them. CORBA 1.1, introduced in 1991, defined the IDL and the Application Programming Interfaces (APIs) that enable Client/Server object interaction within a specific implementation of an ORB.

IDL provides a standardized way of defining the interfaces to network objects. IDL is a strongly typed declarative language based on the C language syntax. Strong typing is essential for building large, robust, long-lived systems. The IDL definition is the contract between the implementer of an object and the client. To support a given programming language, a mapping from IDL to the language is required. The CORBA 1.x specification defines such a mapping for the C language. However, work to provide further language mappings is in progress.

The ORB is the middleware that establishes Client/Server relationships between objects. Using an ORB, a client can transparently invoke a method on a server object, which can be on the same machine or across a network. The ORB intercepts the call and is responsible for finding an object that can implement the request, pass it the parameters, invoke its method, and return the results. The client does not have to be aware of where the object is located, its programming language, its operating system, or any other system aspects that are not part of an object's interface. The ORB provides interoperability between applications on different machines in heterogeneous distributed environments and seamlessly interconnects multiple object systems.

In fielding typical Client/Server applications, developers use their own design or a recognized standard to define the protocol to be used between the devices. Protocol definition depends on the implementation language, network transport, and a dozen other factors. ORBs simplify this process. With an ORB, the protocol is defined through the application interfaces by means of the IDL. ORBs also provide flexibility. They let programmers choose the most appropriate operating system, execution environment, and even programming language to use for each component of a system under construction. More importantly, they allow the integration of existing components. In an ORB-based solution, developers simply model the legacy component, using the same IDL they use for creating new objects, and then write wrapper code that translates between the standardized bus and the legacy interfaces.

CORBA is a signal step on the road to object-oriented standardization and interoperability. With CORBA, users gain access to information transparently, without having to know on which software or hardware platform it resides or where it is located on an enterprise's network.

Structure of an Object Request Broker (ORB)

Figure 17 shows the client and server components of an ORB. Communication between the client and server is accomplished through the *ORB core*, which is not defined by CORBA and is therefore implementation-specific. Instead, CORBA defines some components built on top of the ORB core. The interfaces to these components are defined in the CORBA IDL and are therefore the same for all ORB implementations.

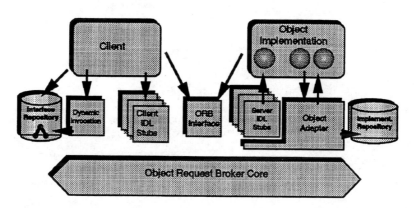

Figure 17. The Structure of a CORBA ORB

The ORB *client* is responsible for the following activities:

❑ *Client IDL stubs* define how clients invoke services on the servers. Services are declared using *IDL*, and client stubs are generated by the IDL compiler.

❑ The *Dynamic Invocation Interface (DII) APIs* facilitate the discovery of classes and their function at run-time.

❑ The *interface repository APIs* enable the acquisition of descriptions of registered classes and the methods they support with their respective parameters.

❑ The *ORB interface* consists of APIs to local services that may be of interest to an application.

The *server*, also known as "object implementation," is responsible for the following activities:

❑ *Server IDL stubs* provide interfaces to each service exported by the server. They are generated by the IDL compiler, in much the same way as the client IDL stubs.

❑ The *object adapter* interfaces with the ORB's core and accepts requests for service on behalf of the server's objects.

❑ The *implementation repository* provides run-time directory information about the classes a server supports.

As shown in Figure 18, the ORB establishes the Client/Server relationship between objects. It intercepts the call from the client object and is responsible for:

❑ Finding an object that can answer the call

❑ Passing all parameters to the server object

❑ Invoking its method

❑ Returning the results to the client.

The ORB must execute many functions to support this simple operation consistently and effectively, but the functions are hidden from the user.

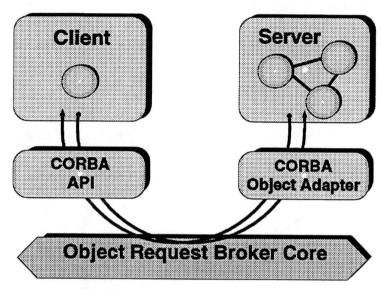

Figure 18. The Client, the Server, and the ORB

CORBA 2.0 Specification

CORBA 2.0, adopted in December 1994, defines true interoperability by specifying how ORBs from different vendors can interoperate. The CORBA 2.0 interoperability architecture, also known as Universal Networked Objects (UNO), specifies a simple, streamlined TCP/IP-based object messaging protocol. The OMG also allows vendors to provide ORBs that support additional protocols to provide higher-function, distributed object services. This opens the door to IBM, HP, DEC, and others to build CORBA 2.0 ORBs based on the DCE protocols and services.

Beside the interoperability issues, CORBA 2.0 clarifies some topics that were left open in the CORBA 1.2 specification. For example, the Interface Repository specification now defines the support for interface type equivalence checking, type codes, and IDL attributes.

The specification is a merged version of two responses to the OMG ORB 2.0 Interoperability and Initialization RFP. The first response to this RFP was submitted by BNR, Expersoft, IBM, ICL, IONA, and SunSoft. The interoperability of the first response was based on TCP/IP. A specification based on the DCE-CIOP protocol was submitted by DEC, HP, and IBM. OMG asked both groups to merge their specification and come back with a unified version. Therefore the final specification stands for a comprehensive, flexible approach to supporting networks of objects that are distributed across and managed by multiple, heterogeneous CORBA-compliant ORBs.

The CORBA 2.0 specification currently defines the following components:

Component	Contents
CORBA2/CORE	CORBA 1.2 minus IDL C mapping plus extensions required to support some object services plus interface repository extensions plus ORB initialization plus inter-ORB bridge support.
CORBA2/Interoperable	CORBA2/CORE as defined above plus CORBA2/Internet Inter-ORB Protocol (IIOP).
CORBA2/C	The IDL C language mapping, defined as a stand-alone specification.
CORBA2/C++	The IDL C++ language mapping, defined as a stand-alone specification
CORBA2/Smalltalk	The IDL Smalltalk language mapping, defined as a stand-alone specification.

Please note that each language mapping is defined as a single component.

ORB Interoperability Architecture

The *ORB Interoperability Architecture* provides a conceptual framework for connecting arbitrary ORBs. It describes bridging approaches both internal and external to ORBs. The architecture allows for flexible optimizations to ensure efficient bridging. It also covers several protocols, each allowing for a variety of IOPs.

OMG document 93-9-15 defines *interoperability* as "The ability for a client on ORB A to invoke an OMG IDL-defined operation on an object on ORB B, where ORB A and ORB B are independently developed."

The motivation factors for extending the current ORB architecture are numerous and vary with respect to scope, distance, and lifetime. Today, there are many different ORB products that address a variety of different user needs. Even when ORB implementations from a single vendor are used, there are reasons why some of the objects an application might use would be in one ORB, and others in another ORB. For example, there may be *security reasons*. Even if the ORB implementation is the same, the ORBs would be separate, so that access to objects could be easily controlled. Supporting multiple ORBs also helps with the difficult problems of testing and upgrading the object system. Just as networks are subdivided into domains to allow decentralized control of databases, configurations, and resources, the state of the ORB might also be managed by creating sub-ORBs.

❑ Interoperability with DCE During the evolution of the CORBA 2.0 specification, the role that the OSF's DCE played was not obvious. In fact, many people considered the standards to be mutually exclusive.

The OMG's decision to choose IIOP as the mandatory protocol for any ORB to be CORBA2-compliant has been viewed by some as evidence that in the object world, "DCE was a loser." The real story is that the DCE proposal did not die; it is an optional protocol that many vendors, including IBM, support. A case can be made that the OMG decision was a very prudent one, given the current state of distributed object computing in the marketplace. OMG chose the lightweight IIOP protocol that could meet the needs of many departmental and small-scale, distributed object implementations, while at the same time could provide a solution for DCE users who require common object naming and security mechanisms across their enterprise. From a customer's perspective this could only be considered a "win, win" strategy. The OMG did not turn its back on DCE as many would have you believe. DCE has a very strong place in the evolution of the world of distributed objects.

OSF's DCE tackles a broad scope of issues associated with a complete distributed computing environment. DCE is a highly robust, scalable architecture that provides a comprehensive set of services, including distributed security, directory, and time services, as well as a programming and run-time environment based on RPCs. OMG's CORBA 2.0, however, tackles the important issue of how distributed object systems interoperate with one another in a network. CORBA 2.0 also defines an optional protocol mapped to DCE RPC message formats.

IBM recognizes that different customers have different computing needs. Some customers need a basic interoperability solution for small-scale, minimally configured systems typical of many current PC-based application environments. Other customers have a need for the industrial-strength security, reliability, scalability, and flexibility characteristics required for large-scale distributed environments.

❑ **Domains**
A domain enables partitioning of systems into collections of components that have some characteristics in common. The CORBA 2.0 specification defines a domain as *"a distinct scope, within which certain common characteristics are exhibited and common*

rules are observed: over which a distribution transparency is pre-served." Interoperability, when crossing these domain boundaries, is a fundamental issue in interoperability architecture design.

CORBA distinguishes two different domains:

> **Administrative**
Includes naming domains, trust groups, resource management domains, and other *run-time* characteristics of a system.

> **Technology**
Identifies common protocols, syntaxes, and similar *build-time* characteristics of a system.

Examples of domains related to ORB interoperability issues are security domains, transaction domains, and referencing domains.

❑ **Interoperability Bridges**

Bridges, as defined in the CORBA 2.0 specification, enable requests from one ORB to be translated to requests on another ORB.

To ensure interoperability between domains, a well-defined mapping between the behaviors of the domains being joined is required. An ORB *"provides the mechanisms by which objects transparently make and receive requests and responses. In doing so, the ORB provides interoperability between applications."* The interoperability of ORBs extends this definition by defining protocols allowing client and server objects located in different ORBs to *"transparently make and receive requests."*

Figure 19 on page 41 shows the interoperability between different domains and possible different domain types. Note that every domain can use a different protocol.

ORB Domains   **ORB Domains**

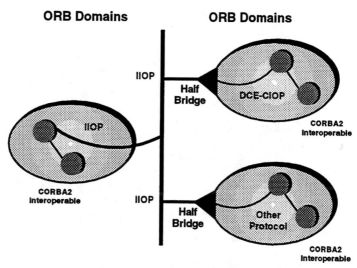

Figure 19. CORBA 2.0 Interoperability Architecture

The components of these bridges can be located in:

➤ **In-line bridges**
The necessary translations and mappings are done inside the ORB.

➤ **Request level bridges**
The translations and mappings are done outside the ORB by application code.

Request level bridges can be further distinguished:

Half bridge   The mediation is through a common protocol between distinct execution environments. The protocol that is used can be a network protocol, shared memory, or some other Inter-Process Communication (IPC) mechanism provided by the host environment.

Full bridge   The mediation is purely internal to one execution environment. Full bridges are usually built by using a shared programming environment's binary interfaces to CORBA IDL-defined data types.

CORBA 2.0 Interoperability Protocols

Figure 19 shows the protocols defined in the CORBA 2.0 specification.

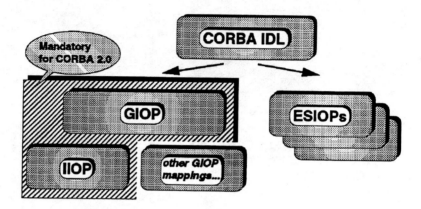

Figure 20. CORBA 2.0 Interoperability Protocols

The GIOP and IIOP are required for CORBA 2.0 interoperability. ESI-OPs are additional protocols which can be added to a future CORBA specification. Currently, DCE-CIOP is the only protocol based on the ESIOP.

We will explain all these protocols in the following sections.

General Inter-ORB Protocol
The motivation for the GIOP was to define a simple-to-implement protocol with low run-time costs. This new protocol can be used by an ORB internally, as well as when connecting different ORBs. The mapping from the GIOP can be done to any connection-oriented transport protocol. The GIOP makes only minimal assumptions about the architecture of the ORBs using it. A specific mapping of the GIOP, based on TCP/IP connections, is the IIOP. IIOP support is mandatory for every ORB product. This does not imply that the ORB has to use it internally, but that it at least provides a bridge to the protocol.

The design of the GIOP is based on the following objectives:

❑ Widest possible availability

❑ Simplicity

❑ Scalability

❑ Low cost

❑ Generality

❑ Architectural neutrality

Internet Inter-ORB Protocol
The IIOP is a specific implementation of the GIOP and is required by
a CORBA2-compliant ORB. The baseline transport specified for GIOP
is TCP/IP. The IIOP maps the GIOP message transfer specifically to
TCP/IP connections.

An Optional ESIOP—the DCE-CIOP
In addition to the GIOP and its specific implementation, the IIOP,
CORBA 2 architecture includes additional Environment-Specific
Inter-ORB Protocols (ESIOPs). There can be many different imple-
mentations of this protocol, each optimized for particular environ-
ments, such as DCE.

The DCE-CIOP was designed with the following goals in mind:

❑ Support of multi-vendor, mission-critical, enterprise-wide, ORB-
based applications

❑ Leverage services provided by DCE, wherever appropriate

❑ Efficient and straightforward implementation using public DCE
APIs

❑ ORB implementation freedom is preserved.

The DCE CIOP uses the DCE RPC to provide message support. It is
based on the wire format and RPC packet formats defined by DCE
RPC to enable independently implemented ORBs to communicate. It
also defines the message formats that are exchanged using DCE-RPC.
DCE-CIOP requires an RPC that is interoperable with the DCE RPC.

CORBA 2.0 Smalltalk Mapping

CORBA is independent of the programming language used to construct the implementation classes. However, to use the ORB, programmers must know how to access ORB functionality from the
programming language of their choice. CORBA 2.0 defines the mapping of OMG IDL constructs to programming languages, including C,
C++, and Smalltalk.

The following are highlights of the mapping of OMG IDL constructs to
Smalltalk language:

❑ The Smalltalk mapping has been designed with several vendors'
Smalltalk implementations in mind, including VisualAge, Visual-
Works, and Smalltalk/V.
❑ The Smalltalk constructs defined in the mapping rely primarily on
classes and methods described in the ITSO redbook, *Smalltalk
Portability: A Common Base* (GG24-3093).

- ❏ Whenever possible, OMG IDL types map directly to existing, portable Smalltalk classes.
- ❏ The Smalltalk mapping describes the public interface to Smalltalk classes and objects supporting IDL. It does not prescribe a specific implementation.

For complete specifications of CORBA 2.0 Smalltalk mapping, refer to the OMG *The Common Object Request Broker: Architecture and Specification*, Revision 2.0 (July 1995).

4

The System Object Model

IBM's System Object Model (SOM) is a software standard developed to ensure the portability of objects across platforms and development languages. It is an object packaging technology that is language-neutral, platform-independent, and supported by many third-party vendors.

Problems with Today's Object Models

Object-oriented programming is an important new programming technology that offers expanded opportunities for software reuse and extensibility. Object-oriented programming shifts the emphasis of software development away from functional decomposition and toward the recognition of units (called objects) that encapsulate both code and data. As a result, programs become easier to maintain and enhance. Object-oriented programs are typically more impervious to the "ripple effects" of subsequent design changes than their non-object-oriented counterparts. This, in turn, leads to improvements in programmer productivity.

45

Despite its promise, penetration of object-oriented technology to major commercial software products has progressed slowly because of certain obstacles. This is particularly true of products that offer only a binary programming interface to their internal object classes (that is, products that do not allow access to source code). The first obstacle that developers must confront is the choice of an object-oriented programming language.

So-called "pure" object-oriented languages (such as Smalltalk) presume a complete run-time environment (sometimes known as a virtual machine), because their semantics represent a major departure from traditional, procedure-oriented system architectures. As long as the developer works within the supplied environment, everything works smoothly and consistently. When the need arises to interact with foreign environments, however (for example, to make an external procedure call), the pure object paradigm ends, and objects must be reduced to data structures for external manipulation. Unfortunately, data structures do not retain the advantages that objects offer with regard to encapsulation and code reuse.

"Hybrid" languages, such as C++, require less run-time support, but sometimes result in tight bindings between programs that implement objects and their clients (the programs that use them). Implementation detail is often unavoidably compiled into client programs. If there is tight binding between class libraries and their clients, client programs often must be recompiled whenever simple changes are made in the library. Furthermore, no binary standard exists for C++ objects, so the C++ class libraries produced by one C++ compiler cannot (in general) be used from C++ programs built with a different C++ compiler.

The second obstacle developers of object-oriented software must confront is that software developed by using a particular language or toolkit is naturally limited in scope because different object-oriented languages and toolkits embrace incompatible models of what objects are and how they work. Classes implemented in one language cannot readily be used from another. A C++ programmer, for example, cannot easily use classes developed in Smalltalk, nor can a Smalltalk programmer make effective use of C++ classes. Object-oriented language and toolkit boundaries become, in effect, barriers to interoperability.

Ironically, no such barrier exists for ordinary procedure libraries. Software developers routinely construct procedure libraries that can be shared across a variety of languages, by adhering to standard linkage conventions. Object-oriented class libraries are inherently different in that no binary standards or conventions exist to derive a new class from an existing one, or even to invoke a method in a standard way. Procedure libraries also enjoy the benefit that their implementations can be freely changed without requiring client programs to be recompiled, unlike the situation for C++ class libraries.

For developers who must provide binary class libraries, these are serious obstacles. In an era of open systems and heterogeneous networking, a single-language solution is frequently not broad enough. Certainly, mandating a specific compiler from a specific vendor to use a class library might be grounds not to include the class library with an operating system or other general-purpose product.

A Solution

SOM is IBM's solution to the problems with today's object models. It provides an object-oriented programming technology for building, packaging, and manipulating binary class libraries.

Figure 21 shows the positioning of SOM in an object-oriented environment. With SOM, class implementers describe the *interface* for a class of objects (for example, names of the methods it supports, return types, parameter types) in CORBA IDL. They then *implement* methods in their preferred programming language (which may be either an object-oriented programming language or a procedural language, such as C).

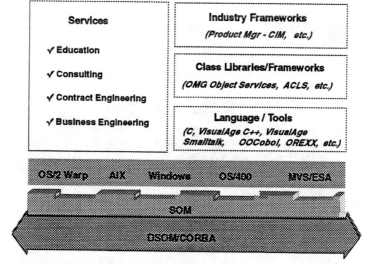

Figure 21. Positioning of SOM in an Object-Oriented Environment

The Object Model

The developers of SOM designed an advanced object model and implemented the object-oriented run-time engine necessary to support that model. SOM supports all of the concepts and mechanisms usually associated with object-oriented systems, including inheritance, encapsulation, and polymorphism. In addition, SOM provides a number of advanced object mechanisms, including support for metaclasses, three types of method dispatch with both static and dynamic method resolution, dynamic class creation, and user intercept of method dispatch.

SOM includes a run-time library, which provides a set of classes, methods, and procedures used to create objects and invoke methods on them. To use the SOM run-time library, a programming language must be able to:

❑ Call external procedures

❑ Store a pointer to a procedure and subsequently invoke that procedure

❑ Map IDL types onto the programming language's native types.

SOM classes are objects whose classes are called *metaclasses*. A class object differs from an ordinary object, because a class has (in its instance data) an instance method table defining the methods to which instances of the class respond. During the initialization of a class object, a method is invoked on it, informing the class of its parents. Thus, the class can build an initial instance method table. Once the class object is initialized, other methods are invoked on the class to override inherited methods or to add new instance methods.

When diagramming class hierarchies, we show metaclasses drawn with three concentric circles, ordinary classes (classes that are not metaclasses) drawn with two concentric circles, and ordinary objects (objects that are not classes) drawn with a single circle. Figure 22 depicts the initial state of a sample SOM program and shows the classes of which the SOM run-time environment consists.

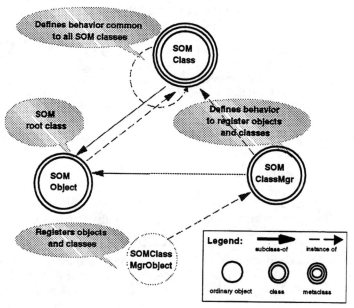

Figure 22. The SOM Run-time Model

Two relationships among objects must be understood. First, there is the *instantiation* or *instance of* relation between objects and classes, which is depicted by the dashed arrow line from an object to its class. When convenient, the inverse of instantiation, or class-of relation, is also used. In Figure 22, *SOMObject* is an instance of *SOMClass*, and *SOMClass* is the class of itself. An object's class is important because an object responds only to the methods that are supported by its class—the methods that the class introduces or inherits.

Second, there is a *inheritance* relationship between classes called the *subclass-of* relation, which is depicted by the solid arrow line from a class to each of its parents. *SOMClass* is a subclass of *SOMObject*. *SOMObject* has no parents.

SOMObject introduces the methods to which all SOM objects respond. In particular, *SOMObject* introduces the *somDispatch* method, which provides a single general dynamic dispatch mechanism for executing method calls on objects. Furthermore, a class can arrange its instance method table so that all method calls are routed through *somDispatch*. As a result, it is simple for SOM metaclass programmers to arrange for completely arbitrary processing in connection with method invocations on SOM objects.

As a subclass of *SOMObject*, *SOMClass* is an object, but it also introduces the methods to which all classes respond. For example, *SOMClass* introduces the *somNew* method, which creates instances of a class. Also, the methods responsible for creating and modifying instance method tables are introduced. All metaclasses in SOM are ultimately derived from *SOMClass*. The SOM API allows new abstractions to be created by programming metaclasses. The strength of this general approach is that new abstractions can be created after the object model is implemented. The before/after metaclasses are not part of the SOM kernel, but they are part of a framework for programming metaclasses that is built with the SOM API. By providing a metaobject protocol, we are able to add a new abstraction to SOM.

Interface Definition Language

SOMobjects Developer Toolkit Version 2.1 provides a SOM IDL compiler, which is key to language neutrality and supports the OMG standard IDL. IDL gives individual object implementations the means to tell potential clients which operations are available and how they should be invoked. By mapping the public and private types for a given SOM class to language-specific bindings, the compiler allows SOM objects to be used by different programming languages.

Interfaces to SOM objects are described by means of IDL. SOM IDL is a CORBA-compliant version of IDL that allows SOM class descriptions to be supplied in addition to object interface definitions. (The interface to a class is described by the IDL alone. SOM IDL allows additional information about the implementation to be added.) The SOMobjects Developer Toolkit has tools called *emitters* that translate SOM IDL into language-specific bindings for the corresponding classes of SOM objects. For example, to C and C++ programmers, this means that emitters produce header files for both the users and implementer of a class.

The following example shows the basic structure of an IDL definition for an object interface called *somAccount*.

```
┌─ Interface for somAccount ──────────────────────────
interface somAccount : SOMObject {
    // method and attribute declarations here
    #ifdef __SOMIDL__
     implementation
      {
         metaclass = SOMClass;
         // instance variable declarations here
      };
    #endif
};
```

The above example is also a SOM IDL description of the *somAccount* class that supports the somAccount interface. The *#ifdef* and *#endif* parts of the IDL language are used to hide the SOM class implementation section from non-SOM IDL compilers.

In the example, the *somAccount* interface inherits from the *SOMObject* interface, and at the same time, the *somAccount* class is declared to be a subclass of *SOMObject*. SOM supports multiple inheritance; additional parents of *somAccount* can be listed alongside *SOMObject* in a comma-separated list. The actual methods and instance variables of *somAccount* are not relevant to the current discussion.

As illustrated, the implementation section can explicitly indicate a metaclass to be associated with the class of objects that supports the interface being defined. This association is not necessarily direct. The actual class of the class described by any given SOM IDL is, in general, a subclass of the indicated metaclass.

Language-independence

One of the main advantages of SOM is the ability to describe the interface for a class of objects in a language-independent manner, namely within IDL. In addition to its programming interface to the SOM run-time classes, SOM provides *language bindings* as more convenient means of using and implementing SOM classes. Language bindings tailor the SOM programming interface to a particular programming language. They make SOM classes appear like ordinary constructs of the programming language as much as possible. The methods of a SOM class can be implemented, for instance, in C++, whereas a client program using the class can be implemented in C.

SOM can be used to provide object-oriented mechanisms for procedural languages (such as C or COBOL), or it can be used in conjunction with the capabilities of object-oriented programming languages like C++ or Smalltalk. In fact, several C++ vendors (including IBM) are currently incorporating SOM into their language run-time environment. SOM currently supports C and C++ implementation, with COBOL and Smalltalk implementation support to be available soon.

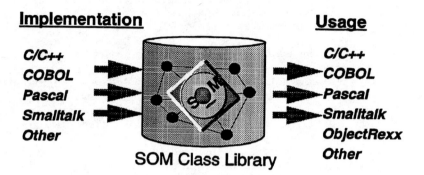

Figure 23. Implementation and Usage Options Available with SOM

Figure 23 illustrates the language-independence of SOM libraries. It shows that objects can be implemented by using one language and used by a totally different language.

Unlike the object models found in object-oriented programming languages, SOM is language-neutral. It preserves the key object-oriented programming characteristics of encapsulation, inheritance, and polymorphism, without requiring that the user of a SOM class and the implementer of a SOM class use the same programming language. SOM is said to be **language-neutral** for three reasons:

❑ All SOM interactions consist of standard procedure calls. On systems that have standard linkage conventions for system calls, SOM interactions conform to those conventions. Thus, most programming languages that can make external procedure calls can use SOM.

❑ The form of the SOM API can vary widely from language to language, as a benefit of the SOM bindings. Bindings are a set of macros and procedure calls that make implementing and using SOM classes more convenient by tailoring the interface to a particular programming language.

❑ SOM supports several mechanisms for method resolution that can be readily mapped into the semantics of a wide range of object-oriented programming languages. Thus, SOM class libraries can be shared across object-oriented languages that have differing object models. A SOM object can potentially be accessed with three different forms of method resolution:

➤ **Offset resolution**

Roughly equivalent to the C++ "virtual function" concept, offset resolution implies a static scheme for typing objects, with polymorphism based strictly on class derivation. It offers the best performance characteristics for SOM method resolution.

Methods accessible through offset resolution are called static methods because they are considered a fixed aspect of an object's interface.

➤ **Name-lookup resolution**

Similar to the method resolution used by Objective-C and Smalltalk, name-lookup resolution supports untyped (sometimes called *dynamically* typed) access to objects, with polymorphism based on the actual protocols that objects honor. Name-lookup resolution offers the opportunity to write code to manipulate objects with little or no awareness of the type or shape of the object when the code is compiled.

➤ **Dispatch-function resolution**

This technique is a unique feature of SOM that permits method resolution based on arbitrary rules known only in the domain of the receiving object. Languages that require special entry or exit sequences or local objects that represent distributed object domains are good candidates for using dispatch-function resolution. This technique also offers the highest degree of encapsulation for the implementation of an object, with some cost in performance.

Release-to-Release Binary Compatibility

SOM's Release-to-Release Binary Compatibility (RRBC) breaks the tight dependency between the code that implements a class and the client code that uses it. RRBC enables you to create and deploy a new version of a class without requiring that you recompile any unmodified application code. For example, you can add function or data members, or even inherit from additional base classes. In general, if you make a change to a SOM class that does not require a source code change in a client, that client will not have to be recompiled. By packaging your class in a Dynamic Link Library (DLL), you can replace the old DLL with the new one, and all the applications that used the old DLL will continue to run without modification.

RRBC is a prerequisite for subsequent modification of components (either applying fixes to or enhancing the components) without having to recompile preexisting clients that use them (upward binary compatibility). This is a key requirement because applications dependent on system libraries cannot be rebuilt each time a change is made to a component in the library.

Packaging Technology

Objects built with SOM can be distributed and subclassed in binary form. Class library developers do not have to supply source code to enable users to subclass their objects.

With SOM's RRBC, class libraries can be built that support robust binary interfaces. Client programs that are derived from the classes in the library can be constructed by using normal object-oriented inheritance techniques, without compromising the ability of the class library implementer to make evolutionary changes in the library's internals, and without requiring all client programmers to use the same development language. In short, SOM objects are similar to normal objects in an object-oriented programming language, except that their binary interfaces have been made more robust and replaced with language-neutral mechanisms.

Relationship Between CORBA and SOM

How does SOM fit into the OMG CORBA picture? SOM is IBM's language-neutral implementation of the CORBA architecture. What does this mean? It means that SOM classes are defined by using the CORBA IDL; SOM supports all CORBA data types; the C language bindings for SOM classes are CORBA-compliant; and, SOM provides an interface repository that supports the CORBA functionality and programming interfaces.

SOM enables language-independent sharing of libraries, classes, and objects across existing host/client networks, as well as future Client/Server networks.

With SOM, IBM is striving to achieve many of the same objectives as the OMG: To facilitate the interoperation of objects independent of their locations, the programming language in which they are implemented, or the operating system or hardware architecture on which they run.

Distributed Objects

SOM's distribution component lets programs share object libraries across address spaces. Thus programmers can use a single programming interface to develop applications using both local and remote classes. For enterprise-wide computing, this brings important flexibility to object-oriented programming, reuse, and sharing. The use and reuse of SOM objects depend on neither the original implementation language of the objects nor the location of the object on the network.

SOM fully conforms with the OMG CORBA standards. In particular:

❑ Interfaces to SOM classes are described in CORBA's Interface Definition Language (IDL) and the entire SOMobjects Toolkit supports all CORBA-defined data types.

❑ SOM bindings for the C language are compatible with the C bindings prescribed by CORBA.

❑ All information about the interface to a SOM class is available at run-time through a CORBA-defined "Interface Repository." The interface repository in SOM is a data store that contains all class information, method call definitions, and user-defined data.

IBM's Distributed SOM will support both the DCE and UNO protocols in a future version. IBM will provide DCE-based directory and security services for both protocols to facilitate an even closer link between CORBA and DCE.

IBM SOMobjects Developer Toolkit Version 2.1

The SOMobjects Developer Toolkit includes a compiler that generates bindings for a given target language from the IDL description. Bindings are language-specific macros and procedures that allow a programmer to interact with SOM through a simplified syntax that is more natural for the particular language. For example, C++ bindings enable SOM objects to be manipulated through C++ pointers to objects, using any C++ compiler. Direct-To-SOM support lets the programmer define and use SOM classes directly in C++ without the need for IDL definitions. In addition to tools like the SOM compiler, the SOMobjects Developer Toolkit Version 2.1 provides a set of object-oriented development frameworks.

A *framework* is a set of objects that work together to perform a specific task. Graphical user interface frameworks, for example, allow objects such as windows, menus, and dialogs to work together to provide an efficient way of building consistent graphical applications. There are also frameworks for business problems, such as hospital management or inventory control. Well-designed frameworks provide a general design and implementation for specific purposes and enable a developer to customize them to suit a particular situation.

Below we describe the various SOMobjects Developer Toolkit frameworks and then focus on the Distributed SOM Framework.

Framework	Description
Distributed SOM	The ability to access remote objects across address spaces and heterogeneous networks. Distributed SOM is a framework that implements a CORBA-compliant ORB.
Replication	A copy of an object can exist in multiple address spaces on a local machine or can be distributed over the network. The Replication Framework takes care of synchronizing updates on these copies.
Persistence	Saves and later restores object hierarchies from a persistent data store.
Event management	A central facility for registering all events of an application.
Interface Repository	CORBA-compliant run-time access to all information in the IDL description of a class of objects.
Emitter	Tools to write emitters.
Collection classes	Organizes objects into base data structures, such as queues, lists, and sequences.

Distributed SOM Framework

The power of Distributed SOM (DSOM) lies in the fact that it insulates the object client from the object's location. With DSOM, application programs can access objects across address spaces, that is, in other processes, and even on different machines. Both the location and implementation of an object are hidden from a client, and the client accesses the object (through method calls) in the same manner regardless of its location.

DSOM can be characterized in two ways:

❑ As an extension to SOM, enabling a program to invoke methods on SOM objects in other processes.

❑ As an ORB, that is, a standardized "transport" for distributed object interaction. In this respect, DSOM complies with the CORBA specification published by the OMG and X/Open.

Some of DSOM's more important features are:

- ❑ Uses the standard SOM Compiler, Interface Repository, language bindings, and class libraries. DSOM provides a growth path for nondistributed SOM applications.
- ❑ Enables an application program to access a mix of local and remote objects. The fact that an object is remote is transparent to the program.
- ❑ Supports both interprocess communication in the same system and remote transport across systems.

DSOM is extensible. Using a socket interface for communication services, it supports TCP/IP on AIX and TCP/IP, NetBIOS, and Netware on OS/2. In the future, it will support large-scale distributed environments, incorporating OSF DCE.

DSOM Workstation and DSOM Workgroup

DSOM supports the distribution of objects among processes within a workstation (DSOM workstation) and across a LAN consisting of OS/2 and AIX systems (DSOM workgroup).

A DSOM workstation supports Client/Server object interactions among processes on the same machine, using existing Interprocess Communication Facilities (IPCs) (see Figure 24). A DSOM workstation, as a highly optimized, single address space ORB, provides interlanguage interoperability and supports binary subclassing and upward binary compatibility.

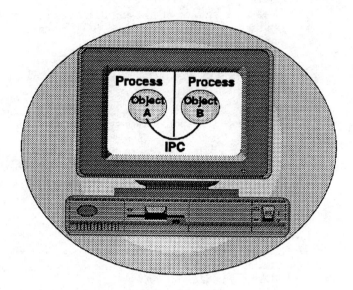

Figure 24. DSOM Workstation Environment

The DSOM workgroup supports Client/Server object exchanges across networks of Windows, OS/2, and AIX machines. It uses socket-based TCP/IP, IPX/SPX, and NetBIOS stacks, and it can be customized to other stacks (see Figure 25).

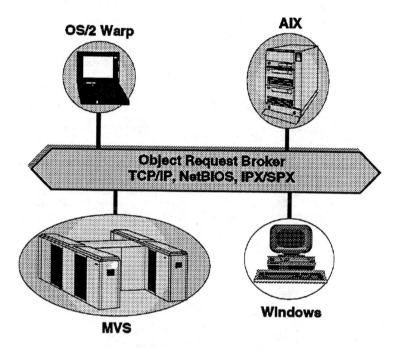

Figure 25. DSOM Workgroup Environment

DSOM Servers

In a DSOM environment, client programs can access one or more distributed objects. These objects reside on DSOM servers.

A DSOM server is a process that manages target objects on behalf of a client. It manages objects of a set of classes. In particular, the DSOM server takes care of the creation and destruction of instances of those classes. It handles messages passed to it from clients and passes them to the proper method of a target object.

The classes supported by a DSOM server usually implement business logic, that is, they represent a part of the application's problem domain. They usually also have to access data held in databases or files.

One or more class libraries provide the implementation of the classes the server must manage. They are built as DLLs that can be loaded by the server on demand.

A default server implementation (somdsrv) provided by DSOM can be used as a generic server program. The generic server simply receives request messages, executes them synchronously, and passes back the results to the client.

The DSOM server must be registered with DSOM in the Implementation Repository before it can be used. A DSOM server does not necessarily have to run on a machine different from the client program; it can also run on the same system in a separate process.

Simplified DSOM Environment

Using SOM objects in the FCE application as examples, Figure 26 shows a high-level view of some of the components in a DSOM environment. Actually, more classes are involved in the DSOM environment than shown, but this simplified view provides a starting point for a basic understanding of DSOM.

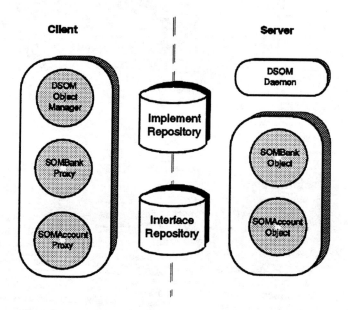

Figure 26. Simplified DSOM Environment

❑ DSOM Object Manager

The DSOM Object Manager assists the client application with locating object servers. An object server, simply called a *server* in DSOM, is the program (process) running on the remote machine (or if a DSOM workstation is used on the same machine in a different process). The server is the entry point into the application. It accepts requests on the objects that it controls. One could imagine the server to be a large program housing a large number of objects on behalf of many clients. The server waits within a request loop and executes requests on behalf of the various clients. It also provides high-level methods for creating and destroying remote objects.

❑ **Bank Server Proxy and SOMAccount Proxy**

A proxy is an object that is *a local representative for a remote target object*. A proxy inherits the target object's interface, so it responds to the same methods as the target object.

The client contains proxies for real objects located in the server. The local client makes method calls on these proxies as if they were the target object. DSOM then passes the method call to the server, where the method call is invoked on the actual objects, and the results are returned.

Operations invoked on the proxy are *not* executed locally; they are forwarded to the real target object for execution. The DSOM runtime environment creates proxy objects automatically whenever an object is returned as the result of a remote operation. A client program always has a proxy for each remote object on which it operates.

❑ **Daemon**

On any system that acts as a server, a separate daemon process called somdd.exe must be active. This process is instrumental in initializing server processes and creating the binding between the client process and server process.

❑ **Bank Server Object**

In DSOM, the process that manages a target object is called the object's server. Servers are implemented as programs that use SOM classes. When a client asks for a server, it is given a proxy to a server object that provides interfaces for managing the objects in server.

There is *one server object per server process*, which has the following responsibilities for managing objects in the server:

➤ Provide an interface to client applications for basic object creation and destruction services, as well as any other application-specific object management services that may be required by clients.
➤ Provide an interface to the SOM Object Adapter (SOMOA) for supporting the creation and management of DSOM object references (which are used to identify an object in the server) and for dispatching requests.

❑ **SOMAccount Object**

The SOMAccount is another server object of an implementation class that uses SOM.

❑ **Implementation Repository**

A server's implementation definition must be registered in the Implementation Repository before a server can be used. The implementation definition contains server information that includes:

➤ Name of the server program
➤ Host name of the machine for the server
➤ Classes that are associated with this server.

When a client wants to use any of the somdFindServer...() methods, the DSOM Object Manager consults the Implementation Repository to find a server that can satisfy the request.

The current implementation of the Implementation Repository consists of four flat files:

- somdimpl.toc
- somdimpl.dat
- somdcls.toc
- somdcls.dat

DSOM looks for these files in the directory to which the OS/2 SOM-DDIR environment variable points.

Although not strictly required, the Implementation Repository files, in most cases, should be located on a *shared file system to which all clients and servers have access*. If the Implementation Repository is static, it may be possible to copy the appropriate files from one system to another and function without the shared file system. However, this is a dangerous practice and should be avoided in environments where the Implementation Repository is not static. The more dynamic the Implementation Repository, the higher the risk and cost of attempting to maintain multiple copies of identical files across systems.

❑ **Interface Repository**

The Interface Repository provides *a mechanism for storing interface definitions*. Class interface definitions or signatures (a method's parameters and return value) are registered with the Interface Repository by compiling the IDL file with the ir emitter and the -u option that updates the interface repository.

DSOM makes extensive use of information stored in the Interface Repository. Before an object can be accessed remotely by DSOM, it is necessary to register the class interface and implementation (from the IDL) in the Interface Repository. DSOM uses interface information to drive the generic remote dispatch routine. Based on parameter type descriptions in the interface definition, the remote

dispatcher traverses the method call parameter list and copies
parameter data into a message buffer. A receiving process performs the symmetric operation when extracting parameter data
from a message buffer.

DSOM Architecture

Figure 27 illustrates the high-level architecture of DSOM. In the sections that follow, we provide an overview of the functions on both the
client and server sides.

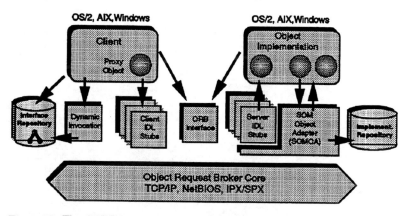

Figure 27. The CORBA-compliant DSOM Architecture

❏ **Client Side**

DSOM dynamically creates a proxy object (and its proxy class)
whenever a reference is made to a remote target object.

Users of a remote object can syntactically pretend that they have a
local object. Thus, method calls can be written as if the object were
local.

By default, each proxy class is constructed to forward all method
calls defined on the target class. This is accomplished by initializing the proxy class method table with pointers to SOM redispatch
stubs, which are functions that convert specific method calls into
calls to the generic dispatching method, somDispatch, and by
overriding the somDispatch implementation to forward the
method call (or request) to the remote object. Figure 28 illustrates
the dynamic creation of a proxy object during run-time.

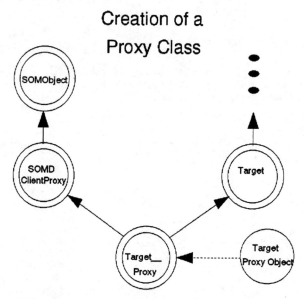

Figure 28. Proxy Object Creation

❏ **Server Side**

To activate an object, the object adapter consults the Implementation Repository which contains the information about the object implementation such as DLL name, process structure, etc. The Implementation Repository is a data store that is only needed by the server. To receive and dispatch each request, the object adapter must do the following:

➤ Obtain the request message

➤ Demarshal the request

➤ Invoke the request locally (using the default somDispatch implementations)

➤ Build a message to represent the response (marshaling)

➤ Send the response message to the client.

Replication Framework

The Replication Framework is a collection of SOM classes that enables a replica or copy of an object to exist in multiple address spaces while maintaining a single-copy image. In other words, an object can be replicated in several different processes while it logically behaves as a single copy. Updates to any copy are propagated immediately to all other copies. The Replication Framework handles locking, synchronization, and update propagation and guarantees consistency among the replicas.

The Replication Framework can be exploited only if the applications are structured appropriately. The recommended structure is similar to the Model-View-Controller paradigm that Smalltalk programmers use. The Replication Framework proposes a View-Data paradigm. The view object has no state, but it has methods to show a rendition of the state in the data object. In addition, it may have some data pertaining to the image that is displayed to the user. For example, in a visual presentation, the colors used for different regions are in the view object, and the content information comes from the data object. The data object has whatever state information the application wants to store in it.

The view and data objects must have a protocol between them so that when the data object changes, a signal is sent to the view object to note the change and refresh the display. This protocol can be extended to multiple views on the same data object, whereby an update to the data object is automatically seen in all visual presentations. Effectively, the views "observe" the data.

The Replication Framework is concerned with data objects only. Application developers must implement "observation" protocol between the views and data. The Replication Framework requires that data objects be derived from a distinguished framework class, *SOMRReplicbl*.

The Replication Framework enables multi-party applications, where the requirement is for each user to have access to his/her own copy of an object; that is, a single object with multiple shadows spread throughout the system or network. The framework provides all of the necessary functions for serializing the updates to the master object, as well as selecting a new master if the original master unexpectedly goes away.

Figure 29 on page 66 illustrates the basic facts about the Replication Framework, which are as follows:

❑ The Replication Framework is the first implementation of replicas using objects.

❑ The Replication Framework synchronizes multiple copies of a single object in the address spaces of several distributed processes, thus providing the foundation for collaborative online activities such as:
> Distributed whiteboards
> Group editing
> Games.

❑ Updates are communicated in real time, without the use of a secondary store.

❑ None of the participants knows how many replicas exist or where they are located, because replicas are totally transparent. In addition, any participant is free to join or leave the replica group at any time.

❑ Replica support is made possible through *multiple inheritance*. All replicable classes must be derived from the *SOMRReplicbl* class.

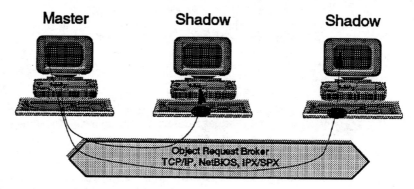

Figure 29. Replication Framework

Persistence Framework

The Persistence Framework is a series of classes enabling the state of an object to be easily stored and available after termination of the process that created it. This framework provides a generic interface so that the actual data store for an object is independent of the method calls used to make the object persistent. SOM provides a default facility using the standard file system. However, one can easily extend this to use object-oriented databases or other facilities based on the application requirements.

Figure 30 on page 67 shows the basic facts about the Persistence Framework:

❑ The Persistence Framework stores complex objects.
❑ Objects contain persistent pointers to other objects.

❑ The persistent store uses standard files. Objects can be grouped together in files or stored individually. Grouped objects are said to be *near* each other.

Although the Persistence Framework uses a standard file system, persistent framework classes managing the store can be overridden to make them work with an object or SQL database.

❑ Any IDL-supported data type can be declared persistent.

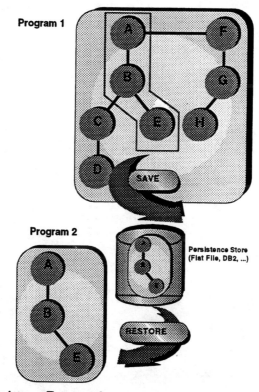

Figure 30. Persistence Framework

Event Manager Framework

The Event Manager Framework, also known as EMan, is a central facility for registering all the events of an application. This registration facilitates the grouping of various application events and waiting on multiple events in a single-event processing loop. The Replication Framework and DSOM use EMan to wait on their respective events. Any interactive application that uses DSOM or replicated objects must also use the EMan Framework.

EMan handles the sending and receiving of asynchronous events. It is particularly useful in a single-threaded environment, where an application would like to be notified when a particular event occurs elsewhere in the system.

Figure 31 shows the structure of the EMan Framework.

EMan is similar in design to many typical Graphical User Interface (GUI) environments where applications must respond to messages generated by external events or other components of the application:

❑ EMan loops forever to handle events and distribute them to callback methods. It is similar to the Presentation Manager (PM) event loop, except that events can be routed across the network.

❑ EMan currently supports four event types:

➤ Timer events
➤ Sink events, such as socket calls
➤ Client (for application-specific) events
➤ Work procedure events, which are background tasks that can be executed when the event loop is idle.

❑ EMan is extensible. Any special event can be managed by the application if the EMan classes are subclassed and personalized.

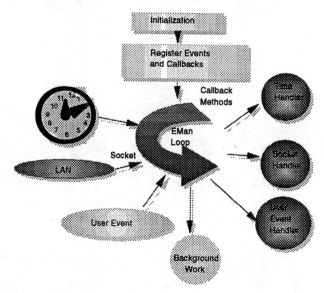

Figure 31. Event Management Framework

Interface Repository Framework

The Interface Repository Framework is a database that consists of the 11 classes defined in the CORBA standard for accessing the Interface Repository. The Interface Repository Framework provides run-time access to all information in the IDL description of a class of objects.

Figure 32 shows the inheritance hierarchy of Interface Repository objects.

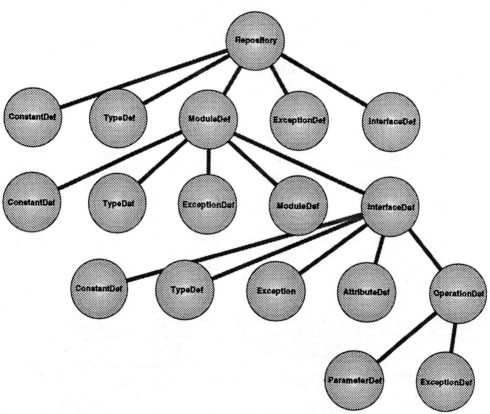

Figure 32. Inheritance Hierarchy of Interface Repository Objects

Emitter Framework

The Emitter Framework is a collection of SOM classes that allows programmers to customize the operation of the SOM compiler. The SOM compiler processes IDL files, which define class interfaces. The Emitter Framework simplifies the process of creating an emitter to generate language-specific bindings from an IDL file.

SOM provides a set of emitters that generate the binding files for C and C++ programming (header files and implementation templates). Figure 33 shows how the SOM compiler generates source files (such as C and C++ templates and the necessary language bindings) based on emitters defined by the user. In addition, developers can write their own special-purpose emitters. For example, an implementer could write an emitter to produce documentation files or binding files for programming languages other than C and C++.

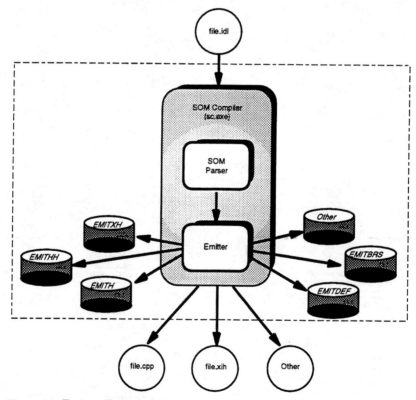

Figure 33. Emitter Framework

As you can see in Figure 33 on page 70, the emitter depends on some DLLs. Depending on the parameters by which the SOM compiler is called, a different emitter DLL is used. For example, if the SOM compiler is called with the following parameters:

```
─ Invocation of the SOM compiler with the XH emitter ──────────
sc -sxh somAccount.idl
```

it uses the emitxh.dll to generate the somAccount.xh usage bindings. You can find the emitters that are part of the SOMobjects Developer Toolkit in the %sombase%\lib\ directory.

Collection Classes

The SOMobjects Developer Toolkit provides a set of commonly required collection classes. These classes include:

Hash table A table of key and value pairs providing fast access by hashing on the key.

Dictionary A table of key and value pairs similar to the hash table. However, objects with equal keys can appear only once in the dictionary.

Set An unordered collection of objects where the objects can appear only once.

Queue A list of objects where objects are inserted and removed in First-In-First-Out (FIFO) order.

Dequeue A double-ended queue; insertion and removal can occur at either end of the list.

Stack A list of objects where objects are inserted and removed in Last-In-First-Out (LIFO) order.

Linked list A list of objects where each object is linked to the object in front of it and behind it.

Sorted sequence A collection of objects where the order is determined by how the objects relate to each other.

Priority queue A special case of sorted sequence, where ordering is based on priority.

Other collection classes are designed to facilitate the use of the above classes.

Outlook: SOMobjects Developer Toolkit Version 3.0

Versions of SOMobjects have been available for years. As a matter of fact, SOM Version 1.0 was shipped with OS/2 2.0 in April 1992. Since then, the SOM architecture has been improved in several areas.

SOM Version 2.0 made a significant leap in terms of new features and capabilities. It represented the first attempt of any commercial product to embrace the fledgling CORBA 1.1 standard. One major change was the move from IBM's *Object Interface Definition Language (OIDL)* to a version that fully complies with the OMG's standard. Another change was to the infrastructure of SOM to support distribution through an ORB.

The current version of the SOMobjects Developer Toolkit offers a powerful set of frameworks and IBM continues to extend this set with additional CORBA-compliant frameworks, which are based on the latest Object Services and Object Facilities specifications published by the OMG.

In the sections that follow we provide an overview of what you can expect of the SOMobjects Developer Toolkit in the future. We cover some general ideas that will lead to a new implementation of SOMobjects. Our discussion is not, however, an announcement or product plan. Nor do we claim to present a full list of features.

Object Request Broker Interoperability

Section CORBA 2.0 Specification on page 37, describes the various CORBA 2.0 interoperability protocols. The IIOP is mandatory for CORBA 2.0 interoperability and will therefore be part of SOMobjects Developer Toolkit Version 3.0. However, we expect implementation of the DCE interoperability protocol for a future version of SOM.

Programming Model

One of the design goals of the first version of SOM was support of release-to-release binary compatibility. This support will be maintained in all future versions of SOM. Thus, the programming model will remain the same as in previous releases of SOMobjects. Nevertheless, SOMobjects will be restructured to provide maximum flexibility for enhancements so that porting teams and other vendors can extend SOMobjects appropriately for their specific needs.

DSOM interoperability between Version 2.1 and 3.0 is not supported, however. Because the use of the IIOP for DSOM-to-DSOM, as well as DSOM-to-other-ORB communications, the old wire protocol could not be supported.

Requirements

To ensure portability and interoperability of objects developed on different hardware and software platforms, IBM supports the standards defined by the OMG. To establish SOMobjects as a ubiquitous object middleware, SOMobjects must be available on all major 32-bit platforms.

Because SOMobjects is used in totally different application areas, different implementations of SOMobjects must be provided. Large corporations, such as banks and insurance companies, have different needs regarding security, robustness, and performance compared to small software vendors implementing Personal Digital Assistant (PDA) commmunication software. Implementations can share the same architecture and use the same APIs, but they differ in terms of their scalability and network protocol support. For example, one implementation supports only a few objects, and another supports millions of objects. Corporate customers using mainframe computers tend to use the SNA protocol, whereas customers working in a workstation environment tend to use TCP/IP. A specific implementation should work with all protocols but be optimized for a particular one.

The management of systems is more challenging in a distributed environment than in a nondistributed environment. A distributed environment based on thousands of communicating objects must provide an infrastructure that enables multiple system management applications written by multiple, unrelated vendors to manage in a consistent way the objects created by an application programmer.

Local and Remote Transparency

Applications developed by using SOM objects only locally do not have to reimplement those objects when moving to a distributed environment. This is one of the biggest advantages of SOM. Currently, only the client that creates and destroys a SOM object must be changed. In the future version of SOM, the way in which a client creates and destroys objects will be transparent to programmers. Therefore, the APIs for local and remote object access will be almost the same.

Remember that objects must be constructed with distribution in mind. There are significant performance penalties when a local object is moved to a distributed node. Typically, the local object inefficiently moves data to the application. When a distributed communications protocol is added, the application experiences tremendous performance degradations.

The better approach is to design all objects as if they will be distributed. The system administrator can then decide whether the objects are local or remote, without having to change the code that uses the objects.

Service Provider Interfaces and Customization

Different users have different needs concerning performance, security, and robustness, among other requirements. Therefore, customization for all possible combinations of uses is one of the most desirable features of a next-generation SOMobjects version.

Implementing, testing, and supporting many customized versions is a costly undertaking, however. Based on the current requirements, we can think of three different levels of service provider interfaces (SPIs):

❑ **Porting SPIs:**

Available only to porting teams that have full access to the SOMobjects source code.

❑ **Value-added vendor SPIs:**

Sophisticated SPIs available only on a limited basis to vendors for adding significant functions to SOMobjects.

❑ **Customer SPIs:**

Extensively tested SPIs available in the SOMobjects Developer Toolkit. Vendors can use them to tie in other products; customers can use them to customize installations.

Implementation Repository Redesign

We can think of many requirements that should be considered for a redesign of the Implementation Repository. To enable the use of SOMobjects in a commercial distributed environment, the Implementation Repository must be able to hold information about a very large number of objects, without severe performance impacts. The Implementation Repository might, for example, be distributed across multiple administrative domains. Customization of the Implementation Repository is needed so that users can include domain- and application-specific information. The current Implementation Repository enables the use of a plain-file-based approach only. This approach might not be sufficient in all cases and raises the need for alternative storage mechanisms.

Interface Repository

Changes in DSOM marshaling have enabled type information to be moved from the Interface Repository to class DLLs. Although support of information in the Interface Repository is supported for backward compatibility, we do not expect to see great performance improvements of the actual Interface Repository implementation.

Object Services

The current version of SOMobjects Developer Toolkit provides a comprehensive set of powerful object services. The next version will extend this set of object services to speed up application development and enable application programmers to concentrate on their specific application domain.

Persistence Service

The OMG Persistence Service provides an architecture that supports Two-Level Store (TLS) objects. The architecture has a router mechanism called the *Persistent Object Manager (POM),* which finds the correct *Persistent Data Store (PDS)* to drive the data store mechanism indicated by the object's *Persistent Identifier (PID).* The PID describes how to find the object's persistent data. The PDS is responsible for getting the data in and out of the object and into and out of the data store. The PDS is the only entity that knows the data store's native interface.

To enable objects to persist beyond the process that created them, a persistence service is necessary. SOMobjects version 2.x offered such a service but was not CORBA-compliant. The next version will implement a CORBA-compliant service based on the specifications of the OMG Persistence Service. With the support of PDSs, it will be possible to use the persistence service in a commercial environment.

Naming Service

The OMG Naming Service provides a standardized way of storing and retrieving object references by name. It provides the ability to bind a name to an object reference relative to a *naming context.* A *naming context* is an object that contains a set of name bindings in which each name is unique.

Because naming contexts can be named in other naming contexts, the Naming Service supports hierarchical naming schemes for objects and naming contexts. Graphs of naming contexts can be supported in a federated fashion.

The Naming Service part of SOMobjects Developer Toolkit Version 3.0 provides a lightweight implementation of the OMG Naming Service that deals primarily with name and object bindings. Not included in the OMG specification is the binding of properties and the possibility of performing searches. IBM will implement these features as well.

Life Cycle Service

The OMG Life Cycle Service establishes conventions for creating, deleting, copying, and moving objects. Because objects can be networked, the service accommodates lifecycle operations on objects in different locations. The client program's model of creation is defined in terms of *factory* objects. A factory is an object that creates another object. As with any object, factories have well-defined IDL interfaces.

The Life Cycle Service provides a lightweight, concrete implementation of the abstract OMG Object Life Cycle Service that also addresses location transparency issues. The implementation is based on generalized factory objects that can be registered and searched in the Naming Service. It is proposed that interfaces of these factory objects will be the object creation interfaces for all SOMobjects applications.

Event Service

The OMG Event Service defines push-style and pull-style delivery models. An Event fan-in (collect) and fan-out (multicast) model is also supported.

The Event Service, as part of SOMobjects Developer Toolkit Version 3.0, provides a lightweight implementation of the OMG Event Service based on DSOM as the event transport mechanism. It is possible that future versions will add other types of transport to provide more flexibility.

Externalization Service

The OMG Object Externalization Service is the standard OMG way of getting data into and out of an object. This service can be used, for example, to copy and/or move an object across address spaces or store and/or restore an object's persistent state.

The implementation of the OMG Object Externalization Service is based on the IBM/SunSoft Object Externalization Service submission. (The OMG is still working on a final specification.)

Security Service

The upcoming OMG Security Service provides for secure object operations in a distributed system. Security is not only essential in a distributed environment; but, it is also far more challenging than in a nondistributed environment. Because the OMG Security Service has not reached its final state, IBM is implementing a first draft of the upcoming OMG specification. In the future, applications based on IBM's implementation might be changed in some areas when the OMG Security Service is standardized.

In general, security covers several elements, including authentication, authorization, audit, administration, and confidentiality. However, SOMobjects Developer Toolkit Version 3.0 will support authorization and authentication.

Object Transaction Service

The OMG Object Transaction Service provides normal two-phase commit coordination. A user creates a new transaction context relative to the current context. If the current context is not null, a nested transaction will be started.

Transaction monitors like CICS have a long tradition in IBM's history and are very important to customers. The Object Transaction Service, as part of SOMobjects Developer Toolkit Version 3.0, provides transactional capabilities to distributed objects. In addition, it supports inclusion in the two-phase commit protocol of procedural resource managers that support the X/Open DTP protocol. Object transactions based on the OMG Transaction Service specification can therefore be mixed with procedural transactions.

Concurrency Service

The OMG Concurrency Service provides a lock manager that can get locks on behalf of either transactions or threads in an object's address space. When getting locks for transactions, it correctly handles lock inheritance for nested transactions.

When speaking about the importance of transactions, the same is true for concurrency. Enterprise solutions depend heavily on the ability to process several tasks concurrently. For that reason, the Object Concurrency Service allows application writers to easily implement locking protocols.

5

IBM Distributed Smalltalk Technology

IBM Distributed Smalltalk technology provides a set of Smalltalk classes and tools that are designed to support the development of distributed applications in an IBM VisualAge Smalltalk environment. The IBM Smalltalk language is powerful, easy-to-learn, and well-suited to short development cycles. It lends itself to the development of GUIs, as well as to application business logic. IBM VisualAge for Smalltalk provides visual programming capabilities for the Smalltalk environment to further enhance programmer productivity.

IBM's Distributed Smalltalk technology provides a two-level solution for distributed programming that is available for both the VisualAge for Smalltalk and IBM Smalltalk environments (see Figure 34):

- Distributed Object Space, which takes advantage of "Smalltalk everywhere" applications to provide true local and remote transparency. Distributed object space technology is provided through the Distributed Feature available for both the IBM VisualAge for Smalltalk and IBM Smalltalk products.

- Support for IBM's CORBA-compliant SOM and DSOM. This support is provided through the SOMsupport feature in VisualAge for Smalltalk and IBM Smalltalk as part of the base products.

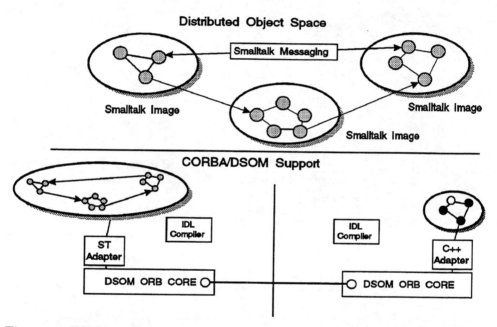

Figure 34. IBM Distributed Smalltalk Solution for Distributed Programming

The Distributed feature extends the basic Smalltalk model to support distribution of objects in different object spaces. These objects can send standard Smalltalk messages to one another, regardless of their physical location. They can also freely send other Smalltalk objects as arguments and receive objects as results. The different parts of an application can be located on any computer in the network that is running IBM Distributed Smalltalk.

The VisualAge Smalltalk SOMsupport feature provides a mechanism for distributed programming in heterogeneous environments where some parts of an application are written in languages other than Smalltalk. The SOMsupport feature is intended for distributed applications that are built with multiple programming languages for which SOM bindings exist. Currently, this includes C, C++, and IBM Smalltalk.

IBM Distributed Smalltalk technology offers flexible development alternatives that ease the transition to object-oriented, distributed application development.

VisualAge SOMsupport

The VisualAge SOMsupport is an installable feature provided with VisualAge and IBM Smalltalk. It provides an interface through which VisualAge applications can use objects implemented with SOM that actually exist outside the Smalltalk domain. These SOM classes can be developed in any language that has SOM bindings. With this interface, VisualAge applications can create instances of SOM classes and send messages to them (see Figure 35). This is made possible by letting you create SOM wrapper classes for the SOM classes from within Smalltalk.

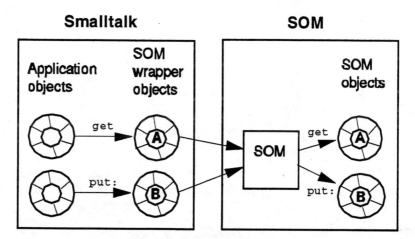

Figure 35. VisualAge SOMsupport Overview

The SOM wrapper classes make the SOM classes appear as if they are ordinary Smalltalk classes. In fact, most of the time the only interface differences between the Smalltalk classes and the SOM wrapper classes are the default icon with the SOM logo on it and the SOM prefix normally put in the class names for the SOM wrapper classes.

Interaction with the SOM wrapper classes seems as though the programmer is directly using the SOM classes they represent. When an instance of a wrapper class is created, an instance of the associated SOM class is also created. Interaction with the instance of the SOM wrapper is the same as with any Smalltalk class. The attributes and methods of the SOM class are represented by methods of the Smalltalk class.

The SOM wrapper classes can also be used visually in the VisualAge Composition Editor. A wrapper object added to the Composition Editor appears as a nonvisual part[1]. Attributes and actions on the part's public interface represent the attributes and methods of the SOM object. Of course, there are some other considerations that you have to consider when using the VisualAge SOMsupport. They will be dealt with later in this book.

The VisualAge SOMsupport capability also extends the classes that make up the SOM kernel. In effect, VisualAge applications can interact with the SOM run-time environment.

In summary, VisualAge SOMsupport consists of the following:

1. The SOM runtime library

   Provide the run-time support for the SOM environment.

2. The SOM frameworks

   Provide a subset of the SOM frameworks, including the Distributed SOM framework (workstation DSOM), the Interface Repository framework, as well as the Metaclass framework. [2]

3. SOM Smalltalk Constructor

   It is used to generate the Smalltalk wrapper classes.

4. SOM samples

   Provide SOM samples that you can run and examine.

5. SOMsupport Migration Facility

New in VisualAge Version 3.0 SOMsupport

VisualAge Version 3.0 SOMsupport includes a subset of the SOMobjects Base Toolkit, so no additional software is needed to create Smalltalk bindings to use SOM objects. SOMsupport is delivered with complete pregenerated bindings for all SOMobjects base components to simplify setup. SOMsupport provides both an API and visual interface for creating SOM bindings.

---

[1] However, a SOM wrapper class is not really a VisualAge nonvisual part. It does not inherit from AbtPart and does not have events in its public interface.

[2] To obtain full SOM frameworks, you have to install the (full) SOMObjects Toolkit which is not included in VisualAge Smalltalk.

Enhancements in Version 3.0 include:

- Conformance to OMG Smalltalk language mappings. This affects some of the SOM data representations in Smalltalk.
- Improved exception handling. SOM exceptions are now mapped to Smalltalk exceptions, thus providing complete user control of exception handling with default behavior.
- Support for SOM character output, such as somPrintf. Users can redirect SOM print output to a Smalltalk stream, such as the Transcript.
- Support for all SOM data types, including *float* and *pointer* data types.
- Improved data marshalling and demarshalling. Deep-nested, constructed data types are now supported.
- Availability of all SOM global information in the Smalltalk environment.
- Automatic memory management for SOM parameters. Users are not compelled to use SOMFree.
- Automatic environment management, which removes the need for users to supply setup code.

Expected Benefits

By integrating the strengths of the VisualAge development environment with IBM's SOM and DSOM technology, VisualAge developers and end-users of the resulting applications will benefit from the following enhancements:

- **Cross-language object classes**

  Using currently available development tools, object classes developed in one language environment cannot be effectively reused in another language environment.

  SOMsupport enables VisualAge Smalltalk developers to reuse and subclass object classes developed in other languages. This possibility of cross-language reuse of classes significantly increases the availability of object classes in VisualAge and other development environments, such as C or C++. In all, the support of SOM by VisualAge enables developers to reuse more code, thus resulting in less costly and risky development.

- **Support for CORBA distributed objects**

  Client/Server computing is quickly becoming a normal requirement for the development and deployment of new applications. The OMG's CORBA standard (as fully implemented in IBM's SOM/DSOM technology) was designed to provide a productive, flexible, and dynamic Client/Server solution by exploiting the power of distributed object services. IBM's DSOM is a scalable extension of SOM that provides local and remote distributed object services across a heterogeneous network.

VisualAge SOMsupport enables the development of CORBA-based distributed objects. VisualAge SOMsupport can significantly reduce the costs and risk associated with developing, deploying, and adapting Client/Server applications, while it enhances the migration path from local objects to distributed objects.

❏ **Support for SOM-based operating system services**

Over time, an increasing number of operating system services will be packaged as SOM object classes and frameworks. The first of these frameworks was the OS/2 Workplace Shell, which enabled developers to customize, extend, and integrate into the Workplace Shell desktop, as well as inherit behavior and characteristics (such as drag/drop) when developing new applications. OpenDoc, a compound document architecture supported by IBM, Apple, Novell, WordPerfect, and others, will be packaged as a framework of SOM classes that can be used in developing document-centric applications.

VisualAge SOMsupport is positioned to exploit these frameworks, which will help automate the design and development of a new wave of document-centric, collaborative, distributed object applications.

❏ **Industry-standard class definitions**

The SOM IDL and Interface Repository, which provide run-time access to class information and definitions, fully conform to the OMG's CORBA standard.

The VisualAge Version 3.0 SOMsupport Smalltalk bindings are compliant with the OMG standards as defined in the CORBA 2.0 Smalltalk mapping specifications. VisualAge SOMsupport classes therefore will adhere to industry standards (CORBA IDL), enabling customers to retain investments in skills and code, while providing a mechanism for interoperability with other CORBA-compliant object ORBs (such as Hewlett-Packard's HP ORB).

In summary, SOM, when integrated with the VisualAge development environment, can result in a more productive and powerful set of application development capabilities.

VisualAge Distributed Feature

The VisualAge Distributed Feature provides Distributed Object Space support. When all parts of a distributed application are written in Smalltalk, IBM Distributed Smalltalk takes advantage of this situation with a technology called the Distributed Object Space. In effect, the Distributed Object Space extends the Smalltalk model across a network.

❑ **IBM Smalltalk base**

IBM's Distributed Smalltalk technology is based on IBM Smalltalk, an industrial-strength, object-oriented development environment. The industry-standard Smalltalk language provides a smooth transition to object-oriented development. IBM Smalltalk provides an open and extensible programming environment that supports large-scale team development with version control.

IBM Smalltalk is the foundation of IBM's VisualAge, an object-oriented visual programming environment. IBM Smalltalk applications can be ported to any platform on which IBM Smalltalk runs. With VisualAge and IBM Distributed Smalltalk, Smalltalk programmers can quickly begin to build portable distributed applications.

❑ **Smalltalk development model**

Using IBM's Distributed Smalltalk technology, programmers can quickly develop applications that span networks, without having to learn the details of network communications, distributed application programming, or specialized interfaces. IBM Distributed Smalltalk extends the familiar Smalltalk tools—browsers, inspectors, debuggers, and workspaces—to the distributed environment.

❑ **High-level development paradigm**

IBM Distributed Smalltalk enables developers to focus on solving the business needs of the enterprise rather than on the mechanics of distributed programming. IBM Distributed Smalltalk is based entirely on the Smalltalk model, providing a very high level of programming abstraction and removing much of the complexity of distribution from the task of program design.

❑ **Flexible distribution approach**

The IBM Distributed Smalltalk model supports much more than a simple Client/Server approach. Applications can be "split" in many different ways, supporting both Client/Server and true peer-to-peer designs. The distribution of an application can be dynamically changed throughout the development cycle.

❑ **Security**

IBM Distributed Smalltalk uses the industry-standard Generic Security Service API (GSS-API), and currently supports the Network Security Program (NetSP) Version 1.2. Used with NetSP, IBM Distributed Smalltalk provides transparent support for client authentication, message verification, and message encryption.

❏ **True server programming**

IBM Distributed Smalltalk provides full support for true server programming:

➤ It is scalable to accommodate the demands of your business.

➤ Its security support provides for authentication of clients and servers.

➤ It supports concurrent execution of multiple client requests within a single server Smalltalk image.

Distributed Object Space

The Distributed Object Space is made up of multiple, individual *object spaces*. An object space is a single instance of a running Smalltalk image, and it can exist on any computer attached to a network and running IBM Distributed Smalltalk. With this technology, objects can:

❏ Send standard Smalltalk messages to one another regardless of physical location

❏ Send and receive other Smalltalk objects as arguments and results—even across the network— without having to "flatten" them into serialized data

❏ Reside in different physical locations from one application version to the next, without requiring any change to the Smalltalk code.

The Distributed Object Space enables developers to use the full power of the Smalltalk language, including high-performance messaging and efficient storage management through automatic garbage collection.

Because the Distributed Object Space is based on Smalltalk, you can send Smalltalk objects as arguments to remote objects just as you would pass them locally, without any conversion necessary. The Smalltalk code used to send messages to remote objects is the same standard syntax used to communicate with local objects. Therefore, at development time, the programmer need not be concerned with the physical location of the objects in the application. In fact, the physical location of the application modules can be dynamically changed throughout the development process, without any change to the Smalltalk code.

Distributed Object Space Run-time Environment

The Distributed Object Space run-time environment provides all of the support necessary to implement distributed execution of Smalltalk applications with true local and remote transparency. The run-time environment provides an additional layer on top of IBM Smalltalk (see Figure 36 on page 88). It provides the following distribution services:

❑ **Messaging**

IBM Distributed Smalltalk provides all of the communications logic necessary to send Smalltalk messages between object spaces. Once configured with the necessary location information, IBM Distributed Smalltalk handles the low-level task of passing Smalltalk objects across a network connection.

❑ **Distributed garbage collection**

IBM Distributed Smalltalk extends Smalltalk garbage collection so that it is distribution-aware. Unused memory is freed when it is no longer being used by other local or remote objects.

❑ **Activation support**

IBM Distributed Smalltalk provides the necessary support to start any remote Smalltalk images that are required by an application. If an object in one object space sends a message to an object space whose image is not currently running, the IBM Distributed Smalltalk activator automatically starts it.

❑ **Name server support**

A name server is a directory of objects in a network. A name server contains *object references*, which provide information about the physical location o objects used by an application. By changing the object references, developers can update location information for objects without having to change the Smalltalk code.

If the name server cannot resolve a particular object name, it has the ability to relay the request to a second-level name server. The IBM Distributed Smalltalk name server is designed to comply with the industry-standard OMG Naming Service specification. The name server is also designed to be adaptable to other naming services, such as the OSF DCE directory service.

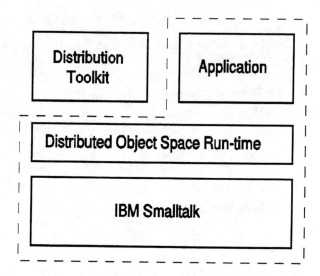

Figure 36. Distributed Object Space Run-time Environment

Distribution Toolkit

The IBM Distributed Smalltalk Distribution Toolkit is currently planned to be a set of tools to help developers and administrators design, develop, debug, optimize, and configure distributed applications from a single physical location. The Distribution Toolkit will itself be set of applications that run on top of the Distributed Object Space run-time environment (see Figure 36). The toolkit will include the following tools:

❑ **Remote Transcript and workspace windows**

A remote Transcript window is a local window that mirrors the System Transcript window of a remote object space, enabling developers to interact with a remote Smalltalk image as if it were local. Likewise, a remote workspace is a standard Smalltalk workspace from which objects in a remote object space are addressable.

❑ **Remote inspectors and browsers**

IBM Distributed Smalltalk extends the IBM Smalltalk inspectors and browsers to enable browsing and editing of remote objects and classes. Using these tools, you can browse other object spaces on the network, add, delete, and edit the classes that reside in those object spaces (provided you have authority to do so), and inspect and modify the contents of remote objects.

❏ Distributed debugger

IBM Distributed Smalltalk provides an enhanced Smalltalk debugger that shows distributed program execution as a single call stack. The debugger enables you to trace program execution that spans a network just as you would with an entirely local application. You can also make changes to remote code from within the debugger.

❏ **Name server GUI**

IBM Distributed Smalltalk provides a GUI you can use to browse and update the contents of the name server. Thus, you can add, delete, and change object references and other named objects.

❏ **Distribution configuration editor**

This editor enables a developer to partition and distribute the modules of an application to various object spaces on the network. Each module is a group of Smalltalk classes. [1] Using the distribution configuration editor, a developer can specify into which object spaces (images) each module should be loaded. After the location for each module is specified, the developer can also use this editor to automatically load the appropriate modules into the remote images.

The distribution design of an application—the designation of which applications are loaded into which object spaces—is saved, along with each version of the application. Developers can dynamically change the locations of the different modules of the distributed application to fine tune performance.

The distribution design of an application is always kept in synchronization with any corresponding code changes. You can freely modify the design of the application to use a different distribution design without having to keep track of which versions of the code belong with each design. Each version's code and distribution are stored together.

❏ **Remote message probe**

This tool profiles all messages traveling between object spaces. It shows you a stack containing every message sent from a particular object space. Thus, you can analyze your message traffic and evaluate the efficiency of your design.

❏ **Event profiler**

The event profiler enables you to analyze message traffic among the objects in your application. Such analysis helps you decide the best way to split your application. For example, if two objects have

---

[1] Each group of classes is actually called an *application* in IBM Smalltalk terms, although in fact it may only be a part of your complete distributed business application. This is based on the terminology of IBM Smalltalk Team environment.

a lot of traffic between them, they should probably be in the same object space, whereas two objects that seldom interact with each other can generally be remotely located.

❏ **Run-time configuration tool**

This tool is used to set up the components of a distributed application on the system upon which it will run. When an administrator installs a distributed application, the run-time configuration tool ensures that the IBM Distributed Smalltalk run-time environment can find all of the object spaces and objects that make up the application. Using this tool, the administrator configures the name server information to reflect the physical locations of the object spaces that make up the application.

6

Implementation Alternatives for SOM Objects

This chapter describes the development environment in which a distributed object application based on SOM could be implemented. It describes the tool set needed for implementation and explains the implementation steps a programmer shotldollow to work with the SOMobjects Developer Toolkit to implement objects based on the IDL and the Direct-To-SOM approach.

C++ programmers can define SOM classes in one of two ways: through the CORBA standard IDL, or directly in C++ using a Direct-To-SOM C++ compiler. IDL is a language-neutral means of describing object interfaces, thereby enabling different compilers and even different programming languages to manipulate shared objects. The IDL definition describes the interface to, but not the implementation of, a SOM class.

The server part of an application can be implemented using two different approaches. One approach centers around IDL as the main work product and uses the SOMobjects Developer Toolkit extensively. The other approach is based on the compiler supporting the Direct-To-SOM feature. Figure 37 shows the relationship between the two approaches.

VisualAge Smalltalk provides some tools that enable easy access to SOM objects implemented with either approach. The implementation of the client part described in this chapter is based on IBM's Visual-Age SOMsupport.

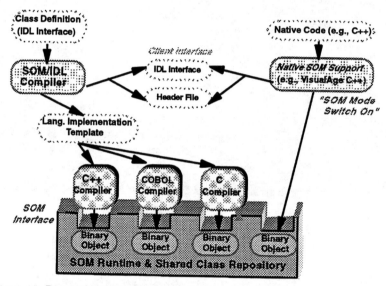

Figure 37. Direct-To-SOM and the IDL Implementation Approach

Interface Definition Language Approach

— Definitions ———————————————————

The *Free On-Line Dictionary of Computing* on the World Wide Web defines *server* and *client* as follows:

server: *A program which provides some service to other client programs. The connection between client and server is normally by means of message passing, often over a network, and uses some protocol to encode the client's requests and the server's responses.*

client: *A computer system or process that requests a service of another computer system or process.*

Distinguishing between these two terms is very important to understanding the development approach discussed below[4].

Together with a C/C++ compiler like IBM's VisualAge for C++, for example, the SOMobjects Developer Toolkit provides the necessary tools to develop SOM clients and servers.

IDL, as opposed to languages like C, C++, and COBOL where you implement your objects, was designed to describe the interface of your object. It is therefore only a declarative language; it has no syntax to describe the program logic. With SOM, class implementers describe the interface for a class of objects (names of the methods it supports, the return types, parameter types, and so forth) in CORBA IDL. They then implement methods in their preferred programming language (which may be either an object-oriented programming language or a procedural language such as C).

Because the server and client play completely different roles in the development process of a distributed object-oriented application, the implementation of a client and server also differs. .

Steps to create a SOM class library

❑ Use the SOM IDL compiler to compile the interface definitions written in IDL. The SOM IDL compiler generates the following:

➤ Object definitions in the Interface Repository

➤ A skeleton for implementation

➤ Language-specific implementation bindings (used by the implementer of the objects defined).

❑ Build the implementation by starting from the skeleton,

❑ Compile and link the implementation, together with the implementation bindings, to generate the binary class libraries for the defined objects. A class import library is also generated for use by the users of the class library.

Steps to use a SOM class library

❑ Use the SOM IDL compiler to generate a language-specific usage binding

❑ Write the client program with calls to the objects in the class library; consult the Interface Repository as needed

❑ Compile and link the client program with the class import library and usage bindings to generate the binary client program.

---

[4] Some literatures use the terms *class implementer* for the server, and *class user* for the client.

An important aspect of the object-oriented paradigm is the idea of reuse. For that reason, you probably want to focus more on the development of client programs than on the implementation of a server because you can reuse much more. In fact, we expect that the market for domain-specific class libraries, frameworks, or SOM-based components will rapidly grow within the next few years. This will give you the opportunity to *buy* the objects you otherwise would have to develop yourself. However, you probably want to build server programs that implement the specific flow of control of your business model. This should be the first step when building SOM class libraries. You should implement your business logic at least once afterward, you can reuse it. Therefore, we focus in the next section on the development of a SOM-based server.

Server Development

SOM server development consists of two steps. The first step is to develop the objects that will run in the server. These are usually the objects that implement the business logic and are therefore sometimes called "business objects." To provide a run-time environment, we also need an executable, like a SOM server program. The general executable that is part of the SOMobjects Developer Toolkit can be used in most cases.

For a detailed discussion of server development, refer to *SOMobjects: A Practical Introduction to SOM and DSOM* and the *SOMobjects Developer Toolkit Version 2.1 User's Guide.*

DSOM Server Program

A SOM class library is a class library packaged as an OS/2 DLL containing SOM objects. In a distributed environment, these objects will not run in the same address space in which the client program runs. We therefore must create a different address space. For that purpose, the SOMobjects Developer Toolkit includes a program called somdsvr.exe. This program is responsible for loading and activating objects from a library into memory. In most cases, this server program provides everything you need. The SOMobjects Developer Toolkit documentation describes how to write your own server program. Writing your own program might be necessary if you need more control over objects. For example, you could keep a list of objects in the server program that have been activated by the object. Because we use the generic server program that is part of the SOMobjects Developer Toolkit, we do not explain how to write a new server program here.

Developing a SOM Class Library

The implementation of SOM objects packaged in a class library has two major advantages over the development process with traditional compiler technology like C++, for example. The implementation is language-independent, so access to the library is possible not only from the language with which it is implemented, but also from several other languages. In addition, the objects in the SOM class library can be distributed without changing their design or implementation. Although the implementation of the SOM class library is almost transparent with regard to local and remote access, in your design of a distributed application, keep in mind the performance impact of accessing remote objects.

Figure 38 highlights the steps of the IDL-based server implementation process. Note that the sequence of the steps is not the only sequence to use to build a SOM library.

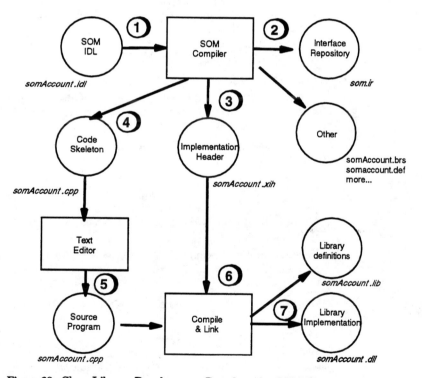

Figure 38. Class Library Development Based on the SOMobjects Developer Toolkit

1. Write the class descriptions in IDL.

   The design phase of a project results in an object-oriented design model that describes in detail the classes, their attributes, and their methods. The object-oriented design model also documents class relationships, such as inheritance, aggregation, and association.

   Starting with such a model, creation of IDL files really means mapping the details of the model to corresponding IDL constructs like attributes and methods.

2. Register the classes in the SOM Interface Repository.

   CORBA defines the concept of an Interface Repository and a set of methods to access it. As the name implies, the repository contains interface information about classes that have been registered with it. Basically, this information is equivalent to the information in an IDL file. At run-time, an application can access the Interface Repository to gain information about a class needed to interact with the class or its objects. DSOM requires that objects that will be accessed from another process have their interfaces added to the Interface Repository.

   The SOM compiler is used to register a class given as an IDL file with the Interface Repository.

   Once the Interface Repository holds the class information and VisualAge is used for the client code, the client development process can start with deriving the wrapper classes from these SOM classes.

3. Generate language bindings for C++ from IDL using the SOM compiler.

   C++ language bindings are actually header files containing flat C++ class definitions. The bindings are required not only to make use of the SOM classes in client programs written in C++, but also to implement the SOM classes themselves to make them available from a server.

   Because the SOM compiler generates binding files, the programmer need not be aware of their specific contents and should not modify them.

4. Generate C++ program skeleton code from IDL using the SOM compiler.

   The SOM compiler produces a C++ source file, which contains everything that the class implementer needs, except the actual logic of the methods. The class implementer can now add the required logic.

5. Add the logic of the class's member functions to the skeleton file.

   The class implementer modifies the generated skeleton file to add the actual logic to the method bodies that the SOM complier provides.

6. Compile the completed class source file using VisualAge for C++.

   The C++ compiler is invoked in the usual way, along with compiler options to ensure that it can find the SOM-specific header files.

7. Make SOM class implementation available as a class library.

   One of the principal advantages of SOM is that it makes binary reusability possible. This is why SOM classes are often packaged and distributed as class libraries. A class library holds the actual implementation of one or more classes. It can be dynamically loaded and unloaded as needed by applications. Furthermore, class libraries can also be replaced independently of the application that uses them.

8. Register class implementation with the Implementation Repository.

   Before an application can be run, the server implementation must be registered with the DSOM Implementation Repository, so that clients can find servers, and DSOM can activate those servers on demand. This registration must be effectively installed on every machine that is going to use the SOM classes

9. Generate the stub DLL to run in the client.

Client Development

Figure 39 on page 98 outlines the development process of a SOM client program.

1. Generate usage language bindings from IDL.

   The usage bindings for C++ supply functions for each method that uses the release order to map the method invocation to the appropriate slot in the method table for the class.

   Generate the usage bindings with the SOM included in the SOMobjects Developer Toolkit. The usage bindings define the public interface to a SOM class and are included by clients to create and manipulate objects of that class. Both the implementation and usage bindings files are regenerated completely by the SOM compiler when the class is modified, and they should not be modified directly.

2. Write the main program.

With the C++ bindings, SOM objects are declared and manipulated as pointers to the given class. You use the *new* operator to create instances of a class. The first time an object of any class is created, the SOM run-time environment will be implicitly initialized. The first time an instance of a given class is created, the associated class object will be created, along with any parent class objects. The initialization of the SOM run-time environment includes the creation of a class object and the allocation of storage for an instance of the class, which can be assigned to a variable. Methods on SOM objects are invoked as on every C++ object. The final line of your main program should deallocate storage for the object.

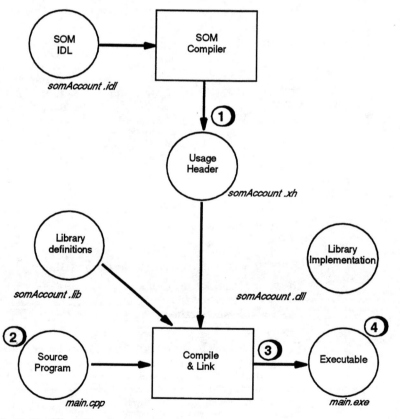

Figure 39. Client Development Process

One difference between a program accessing local SOM objects and a program accessing remote SOM objects is the way objects are created and destroyed. DSOM uses its own proprietary APIs for that task. With SOMobjects Developer Toolkit Version 3.0 the OMG Lifecycle service will be supported, allowing the almost transparent creation and destruction of objects in local and remote environments.

3. Compile and link using the VisualAge for C++ compiler.

   This program can be compiled and run with any C++ compiler. The C++ compiler is invoked in the usual way, along with compiler options, to ensure that it can find the SOM-specific header files.

4. Execute the client program.

   The executable is invoked as every other executable on OS/2 is invoked. When you execute a client that accesses remote objects based on the DSOM framework, make sure that you have started the DSOM daemon, somdd.exe, on every server machine. Also, make sure that the Implementation and Interface Repositories are up-to-date.

Direct-To-SOM Approach

This section introduces the Direct-To-SOM approach and describes how it can be used with C++. Object-oriented language compilers that utilize SOM as their run-time library are referred to as Direct-To-SOM compilers.

Figure 40 on page 100 illustrates the fact that Direct-To-SOM users can compile C++ source code to create SOM-compatible binaries without having to write interface descriptions. The resulting objects can interoperate with SOM objects written in any other language. Moreover, the compiler can automatically generate IDL for C++ classes so that other SOM-supported languages that use IDL can interface with your classes. You can even subclass the OS/2 Workplace Shell just by writing C++ code.

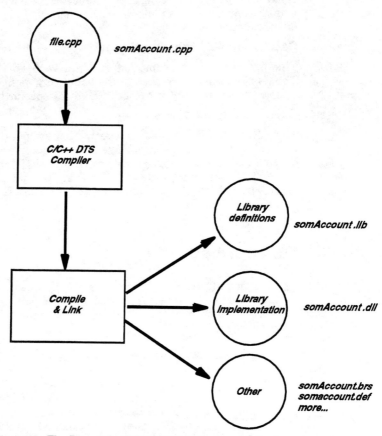

Figure 40. The Direct-To-SOM Implementation Approach

Relationship of Direct-To-SOM to Distributed SOM

DSOM is a technology that handles the creation and destruction of remote objects. Distributed object support provides for easier creation and reuse of SOM objects across platforms and operation systems that are SOM-aware. Combined with IBM's implementation of Direct-To-SOM C++ compilation, support for distributed objects is now greatly simplified and more practical for corporate application developers.

The CORBA-compliant distribution of objects and transparent access of those objects requires the support of IDL to populate the Interface Repository. VisualAge for C++ simplifies the creation of IDL greatly by generating the IDL from the interface description of the C++ class. Figure 41 illustrates the necessary steps in using this Direct-to-SOM development process.

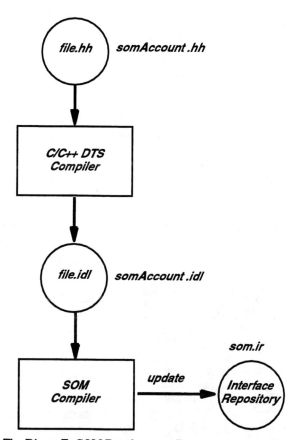

Figure 41. The Direct-To-SOM Development Process

Relationship to C++

Experienced C++ programmers may find that the most surprising difference between SOM and the C++ object model is related to the role of object classes. In C++, a class is a syntactic entity that exists only at compile time; it has no representation outside the source code that defines it. A SOM class, however, is also a SOM object and always exists at run-time. Because SOM classes are run-time objects, they can provide a number of services to client objects at run-time. For example, each SOM class possesses a method named *somSupports-Method* that, when invoked with any string, returns a value representing either true or false, depending on whether the class instances support a method whose name matches the parameter string. Other services supported by a SOM class include the following:

- ❏ Reporting its name to clients
- ❏ Identifying its base classes
- ❏ Indicating whether or not a given SOM object is one of its instances
- ❏ Reporting the size of its instances
- ❏ Reporting the number of methods that its instances support.

All interactions with SOM are through standard procedure calls. Because public instance data are not directly supported, any language that supports external calls can use SOM. However, SOM is most heavily used today with C and C++, mainly because of the support for generating bindings for these languages, and the Direct-To-SOM support provided by some C++ compilers.

Direct-To-SOM C++ Compilers

The capability to generate C++ bindings from an IDL description enables you to create and manipulate SOM objects with any C++ compiler, thereby gaining the advantages of the RRBC support provided by SOM. In addition, those objects can be shared across different C++ implementations or even with different languages such as Smalltalk. In using the C++ bindings, however, you are limited to a subset of the C++ language, which makes the migration of existing C++ applications more difficult. You must also use two languages (IDL and C++) to define and manipulate objects.

Direct-To-SOM (DTS) C++ compilers support and enforce both the C++ and SOM object models, enabling C++ programmers to take advantage of SOM through C++ language syntax and semantics so that the use of SOM is reasonably transparent and efficient. Instead of first describing SOM classes in IDL, the DTS C++ compiler translates C++ syntax to SOM. You can then instruct the compiler to generate IDL from your C++ declaration, or you may find that you do not need to deal with IDL at all and can work exclusively in DTS C++. Finally, because you write C++ directly, you can use C++ features in your SOM classes that were not available before DTS. These features include templates, operators, constructors with parameters, default parameters, static members, public instance data, and more.

Direct-To-SOM Programming

A C++ class is made into a DTS C++ class by inheriting from the class *SOMObject*, which is defined in the header file: som.hh. You can do this explicitly or implicitly through compiler switches or pragmas that insert *SOMObject* as a base class. The access specifiers—private, protected, and public—are supported for SOM classes and enforced following the C+ rules, as are constructors and destructors, and most other C++ constructs.

Once you have defined a DTS class, what can you do with it? You can create SOM objects statically or dynamically, as simple objects, arrays, or embedded members of other classes (or anywhere else that the declaration of a C++ object is valid). Most C++ rules and syntax apply to DTS classes and objects, with some restrictions. Because the size of a SOM object is not known until run-time, compile-time constant expressions such as *sizeof* are treated as run-time constant expressions. Such operators can still be used with SOM objects, but not in contexts that require compile-time evaluation.

A major inhibitor to RRBC with C++ is the fact that so much information about an object is statically compiled into client code—in particular, the location of instance data and virtual function pointers. Data layout and method calling for a DTS C++ class are performed using the SOM Application Programming Interface (API), instead of the native C++ API. When you run a program defining a DTS C++ class, the compiler creates the corresponding SOM class object at run-time and uses it to create and manipulate the object. As a result, unlike a standard C++ object, much of the information about a SOM object and its class—such as the instance size—is not determined until run-time, when the class object is created. This enables class evolution without forcing recompilation of client applications.

The SOM interface does not support direct client access to instance data. C++ instance data members in a DTS class are regrouped into contiguous chunks, according to access, in the order of declaration within the class. This regrouping gives efficient access to data members from client code while enabling RRBC. The location of each chunk is determined at run-time. If the declaration order of public and protected data within a class is not changed, and new members are added after any preexisting members of the same access, this scheme allows new data members to be added without requiring recompilation of any code outside the class (except for friends).

A DTS class also has a release order that, by default, will contain, in the order of declaration, all member functions and static data members introduced by the class, including those with private and protected access. In general, virtual functions that override virtual functions in a base class do not appear in this list, but will appear in the release order for the introducing class. Using the default, you must add any new member functions, or static data members at the end of the class. Instead of relying on declaration order, you can use a pragma to specify the release order. In this case, you can add new release order elements anywhere in the class, but you must add their names to the end of the list.

For DTS classes, instance data and the release order list are created at run-time by SOM and used to manipulate SOM objects, rather than the statically defined compiler constructs used by standard C++. This feature provides for both RRBC and an implementation-independent object model. As long as the list element order does not change and new elements are added to the end of the list, you can add new data members and member functions—including migrating a member function up the class hierarchy—without forcing recompilation of client code.

Accessing SOM Objects Using VisualAge Smalltalk

As described in VisualAge SOMsupport on page 81, the VisualAge SOMsupport feature provides an interface through which VisualAge applications can use objects implemented using SOM. These SOM objects can be developed in any language that has SOM bindings. With this interface, VisualAge applications can create instances of SOM objects and send messages to them. This capability extends to the classes that make up the SOM kernel, meaning that VisualAge applications can interact with the SOM run-time environment.

SOMsupport is implemented through the use of Smalltalk wrapper classes that represent SOM classes. We describe the construction and use of SOM wrapper classes in the following sections.

Constructing SOM Wrapper Classes

VisualAge SOMsupport includes a framework of Smalltalk classes called the SOM Smalltalk Constructor. These classes provide the ability to generate the Smalltalk wrapper classes that represent SOM classes, based on interface definitions that have been compiled from IDL files and stored in the SOM Interface Repository. Figure 42 shows the process of constructing certain wrapper classes from the Interface Repository.

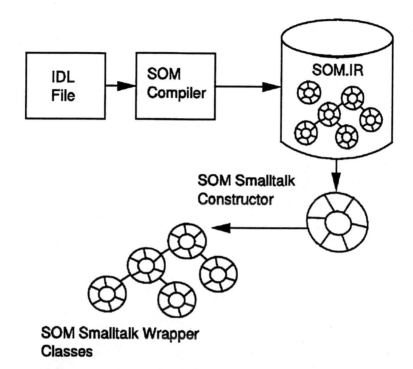

Figure 42. Creating Wrapper Classes from the SOM Interface Repository

Once the wrapper classes are generated, they can be used to interact with the SOM classes.

Using Wrapper Classes

Using VisualAge SOM wrapper classes is very similar to using normal Smalltalk classes. The small differences are mainly in constructing and deleting instances of these classes. We will explain the use of VisualAge SOM wrapper classes in the next chapter and in Chapter 11. Also see *SC34-4518 VisualAge for Smalltalk: User's Guide* and the online reference book *VisualAge for Smalltalk: Features Class and Reference* for more details.

7

A Quick Tour through the Distributed SOM Object Land

This chapter introduces you how to develop a simple distributed SOM object application. We will focus on what needs to be done in the SOM class implementer side as well as the SOM class user side. We will develop our simple class implementation for the server using Visual-Age C++ Version 3, and develop the client with the VisualAge for Smalltalk SOMsupport feature as a class user.

This quick tour should make you more familiar with how to develop a distributed object application using SOMobjects and the VisualAge SOMsupport feature.

Assuming that you have done the necessary analysis and design work for the problem you want to solve, the remaining major procedures to develop a distributed SOM object application are as follows:

❏ Prepare the development and testing environment for SOM class implementation

❏ Develop and test the SOM class implementation as the *class implementer*

❏ Register SOM class information in the appropriate repositories

❏ Generate the SOM wrapper classes using VisualAge for Smalltalk SOMsupport

❏ Develop and test the use of the SOM classes as the *class user*.

Note that once the interface specifications for the SOM classes are finalized, the class implementer and class user can proceed with their development work in parallel.

The next section shows a simple Celsius/Fahrenheit Converter application that we are going to develop.

The Celsius/Fahrenheit converter

The aim is to create a simple application that converts temperature from degrees Celsius to degrees Fahrenheit and vice versa.

The class usage part is developed in the VisualAge Smalltalk environment while the class implementation part is written with VisualAge for C++ Version 3.

Our application consists of two classes:

1. SOMThermometer

   The business domain class SOMThermometer holds and returns its actual temperature value in both Celsius and Fahrenheit. The SOM prefix put in the class name suggests that it is implemented with SOM.

   The SOMThermometer has two attributes[5]: celsius and fahrenheit.

---

[5] Actually one attribute is sufficient in our converter as there is a well-defined relationship between degrees Celsius and degrees Fahrenheit. For easy understanding, we put the degrees as two separate attributes.

- **celsius** is of type *short* and holds the temperature value in Celsius.

- **fahrenheit** is also of type *short* and holds the temperature value in Fahrenheit.

It also has a method called **printString** which will return a formatted string to the caller.

2. SOMThermometerView

The user interface class SOMThermometerView shows the actual temperature value of its underlying thermometer object in both units. It allows the user to change either of the values and immediately updates the other one. Figure 43 shows how the user interface looks.

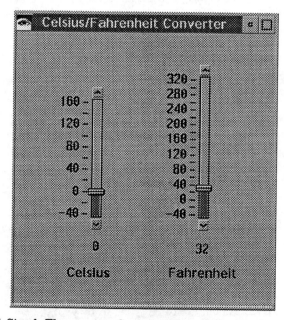

Figure 43. *A Simple Thermometer Converter View*

The SOMThermometer and SOMThermometerView communicate with each other through DSOM. In particular, we use DSOM Workstation and the objects will be running as different processes in the same OS/2 workstation.

Developing the SOMThermometer class

As class implementer, we perform the following tasks to develop the SOMThermometer:

1. Installing the required products
2. Setting up the environment
3. Creating the Interface Definition Language (IDL) for SOMThermometer
4. Generating binding files and updating the Interface Repository for SOMThermometer
5. Creating the SOMThermometer DLL
6. Registering the DSOM alias for SOMThermometer class
7. Creating a test program
8. Testing the SOMThermometer class

Installing the Required Products

To develop theour application in an OS/2 Warp environment, you must install the following software products:

- ❑ OS/2 Warp
- ❑ VisualAge for C++ V3
- ❑ VisualAge for Smalltalk V3 with SOMsupport feature
- ❑ SOMObjects Base Toolkit V2.1[6]

Setting Up the Environment

Now that the required products are successfully installed, the following is what appears in the OS/2 config.sys file as far as SOM is concerned. Note that the settings can be different from those on your machine depending on the install directories of those products. (The texts in bold are to be typed in by you). [7]

```
LIBPATH=C:\OS2\DLL D:\SOM\LIB;...
SET PATH=D:\SOM\BIN;...
SET DPATH=C:\OS2\SYSTEM;D:\SOM\MSG;...
SET SOMIR=D:\SOM\ETC\SOM.IR;C:\OS2\ETC\WPSH.IR;C:\OS2\WPDSERV.IR
```

---

[6] The SOMobjects Base Toolkit is delivered with both the VisualAge for C++ and VisualAge for Smalltalk products. However, the SOMobjects Toolkit supplied with VisualAge for Smalltalk is only for the use of SOM classes. The full set of SOMobjects Base Toolkit is required for class implementer.

[7] A number of other environment variables can be set to facilitate SOM program development and some are required for workgroup DSOM. Refer to the SOM Programming Guide that comes with VisualAge C++ V3 for more details.

```
;D:\THERMO\THERMO.IR
SET SMINCLUDE=.;D:\SOM\INCLUDE;...
SET SOMBASE=D:\SOM
SET SMTMP=D:\SOM\TMP
SET SOMDDIR=D:\SOM\ETC\DSOM
SET INCLUDE=.;D:\SOM\INCLUDE;...
SET LIB=.;D:\SOM\LIB;....
SET SOMDDIR=C:\OS2\ETC\DSOM
SET SMEMIT=xh;xih;xc;def
```

After installing the SOMObjects Toolkit, run the following command to generate the necessary C++ binding files for development :

```
somxh.cmd
```

Creating the IDL for SOMThermometer

The directory d:\thermo serves as the working directory. Edit the file named **thermo.idl** and type the following in the file:

```
#ifndef SOM_THERMO_IDL
#define SOM_THERMO_IDL

#include <somobj.idl>
#include <snglicls.idl>

interface SOMThermometer : SOMObject
{
    attribute short celsius;
    attribute short fahrenheit;

    string printString();

#ifdef __SOMIDL__
    implementation {
        releaseorder: _get_celsius,
        _set_celsius,
                      _get_fahrenheit,
        _set_fahrenheit,
                      printString;

        fahrenheit : noset;
        celsius    : noset;

        dllname            = "thermo.dll";
        memory_management  = corba;
        metaclass          = SOMMSingleInstance;
```

```
            filestem           = thermo;
            passthru C_xih_before = "#include <stdio.h>";
    };
#endif
};

#endif
```

❑ Here **#include <somobj.idl>** is required as SOMThermometer
   will be inherited from **SOMObject**, as shown in the line :

```
interface SOMThermometer : SOMObject
```

❑ In the **interface** definition of SOMThermometer, you can see the
   declarations of the two attributes, namely, celsius and fahrenheit,
   as well as a method printString.

❑ Following the attribute and function declarations, there is an
   implementation section. The implementation section specifies
   information about how the class will be implemented by SOM. [8]

❑ Inside the implementation section you have defined the **release-
   order** of the "getters" and "setters" and the method printString. It
   specifies the order in which the SOM compiler places the methods
   in the data structure. Note that every get and set method of the
   attribute and every method has to be listed here.

❑ The next two lines:

```
        fahrenheit : noset
        celsius    : noset;
```

   inform SOM compiler not to generate default "setters" for the
   attributes celsius and fahrenheit. Usually if we are dealing with
   variables with remote ownership (generally speaking pointers are
   involved) or with special business rules requirement (in our case,
   we want to update one attribute if the other is updated), we will
   define "noset" or "noget" for the corresponding attributes.

❑ Further down we can find several other lines inside the implementation section.

   ➤ **dllname = "thermo.dll";** specifies the name of the library file
      that will contain the class's implementation.

   ➤ **memory_management=corba;** notifies that all methods
      introduced by the class will follow the CORBA specification for
      parameter memory management, except where a particular
      method has an explicit modifier indicating otherwise.

---

[8] Because the implementation section is specific to SOM IDL it is preceded by an "#ifdef
__SOMIDL__" directive and followed by an "#endif" directive.

➤ **metaclass=SOMMSingleInstance;** is used so only one instance of this class runs in the class implementer machine no matter how many connections are to be made on this class for the server machine.

➤ **filestem=thermo** specifies how the SOM compiler will construct file names for the binding files it generates. The default is what you specified explicitly here. With this line, the generated xh, xih and cpp files are all started with the file name "thermo".

➤ **passthru C_xih_before = "#include <stdio.h>";** allows you to specify blocks of code that the SOM compiler will pass into the header files it generates.

To know more about the IDL syntax, refer to the online book **SOM Programming Guide** that comes with VisualAge C++ V3.

Generating Binding Files and Updating the Interface Repository

With the thermo.idl file in hand, you can now generate the required stub files and binding files.

If SMEMIT is set as listed in Setting Up the Environment on page 110, the following commands will generate a number of files. These files include thermo.cpp, thermo.def, thermo.xh and thermo.xih :

```
sc thermo.idl
```

You can update the SOMThermometer class information to the Interface Repository in the same command as well. However, as the interface is usually quite stable, it is not necessary to update it all the time; just issue this command when the interface definition is newly created or changed:

```
sc -u thermo.idl
```

To check whether the update to the Interface Repository is successful or not, issue the following command in an OS/2 command prompt:

```
irdump SOMThermometer
```

Creating the SOMThermometer DLL

To create the SOMThermometer DLL, perform the following steps:

❑ Add codes to the generated source file: thermo.cpp
❑ Create a make file to build the DLL
❑ Make the DLL

1. Adding codes to the generated source file: thermo.cpp

Now use your favorite editor to edit the **thermo.cpp** generated by the SOM Compiler. Type in the text in bold face:

```
/*
 *  This file was generated by the SOM Compiler.
 *  Generated using:
 *      SOM incremental update: 2.43
 */
/*
 *  This file was generated by the SOM Compiler and Emitter Framework.
 *  Generated using:
 *      SOM Emitter emitxtm: 2.42
 */
#ifndef SOM_Module_thermo_Source
#define SOM_Module_thermo_Source
#endif
#define SOMThermometer_Class_Source

#include "thermo.xih"

/*
 *Method from the IDL attribute statement:
 *"attribute short celsius"
 */

SOM_Scope void  SOMLINK _set_celsius(SOMThermometer *somSelf,
                            Environment *ev, short celsius)
{

    SOMThermometerData *somThis = SOMThermometerGetData(somSelf);
    SOMThermometerMethodDebug("SOMThermometer","_set_celsius");

    somThis->celsius = celsius;
    somPrintf("celsius set to %d degrees\n", celsius);

    somThis->fahrenheit = celsius*1.8+32;
}


/*
 *Method from the IDL attribute statement:
 *"attribute short fahrenheit"
 */

SOM_Scope void  SOMLINK _set_fahrenheit(SOMThermometer *somSelf,
                            Environment *ev, short fahrenheit)
{
    SOMThermometerData *somThis = SOMThermometerGetData(somSelf);
    SOMThermometerMethodDebug("SOMThermometer","_set_fahrenheit");

    somThis->fahrenheit = fahrenheit;
    somPrintf("fahrenheit set to %d degrees\n", fahrenheit);

    somThis->celsius=(fahrenheit-32) / 1.8;
}
```

```
SOM_Scope string  SOMLINK printString(SOMThermometer *somSelf,
                                      Environment *ev)
{
    SOMThermometerData *somThis = SOMThermometerGetData(somSelf);
    SOMThermometerMethodDebug("SOMThermometer","printString");

    string myPrintString = (string) SOMMalloc(256);
    sprintf(myPrintString, "%d degrees Celsius, %d degrees Fahrenheit");

    return myPrintString;
}
```

Each method has a SOM_Scope and SOMLINK macro defined. You can ignore them as they are defined for SOM and should be of no interest to you.

However, the following terms should be mentioned:

- **somSelf** is a pointer to the target object (in our case, an instance of the class SOMThermometer) that will respond to the method

- **somThis** is a pointer pointing to the instance variables o the target object.

- **SOMThermometerMethodDebug** is a macro to aid SOM method debugging. By default it will display a message each time when the method is executed, if a trace-level global variable is set.

2. **Creating a make file to build the DLL**

   Edit the following make file :

```
FFIXES: .CPP .DEF .IDL .LIB .SQC .c .OBJ


        @echo " Link::Linker "
        ICC.EXE @<<
           /Tdp
           /Oc /Q /Gm+ /Gd /Ge- /G4
           /B" /nologo"
           /Fe..\BIN\Thermo.DLL
           Thermo.OBJ
           SOMTk.LIB
        Thermo.DEF
<<
        DLLRNAME \FCE\BIN\Thermo.DLL CPPOM30=FCEOM30
        DLLRNAME \FCE\BIN\Thermo.DLL CPPOOB3=FCEOOB3
        DLLRNAME \FCE\BIN\Thermo.DLL CPPODS3I=FCEODS3I


        @echo " Link::Linker "
        ICC.EXE @<<
        /B" /nologo"
        /Fe..\BIN\TESTTHEM.EXE
        TESTTHEM.OBJ
        SOMTk.LIB
```

```
                   Thermo.LIB
         <<
                   DLLRNAME \FCE\BIN\TESTTHEM.EXE CPPOM30=FCEOM30
                   DLLRNAME \FCE\BIN\TESTTHEM.EXE CPPOOB3=FCEOOB3
                   DLLRNAME \FCE\BIN\TESTTHEM.EXE CPPODS3I=FCEODS3I


         Thermo.cpp: Thermo.IDL
                   @echo " Compile::SOM Compiler "
                   SC.EXE -sxc Thermo.IDL
                   @echo " Update Interface Repository"
                   UPD_IR.CMD

         Thermo.OBJ: Thermo.CPP Thermo.xih
                   @echo " Compile::C++ Compiler "
                   ICC.EXE /I. /Oc /Tdp /Q /Gm+ /Gd /Ge- /G4 /C Thermo.CPP

         Thermo.xih: Thermo.xh Thermo.idl
                   @echo " Compile::SOM Compiler "
                   SC.EXE -sxih Thermo.idl

         Thermo.xh:  Thermo.idl
                   @echo " Compile::SOM Compiler "
                   SC.EXE -sxh Thermo.idl

         Thermo.LIB: ..\BIN\Thermo.DLL
                   @echo " Lib::Import Lib "
                   implib.EXE Thermo.LIB ..\BIN\Thermo.DLL

         TEST.OBJ: TestThem.cpp Thermo.xh
                   @echo " Compile::C++ Compiler "
                   ICC.EXE /I. /Oc /Tdp /Q /Gm+ /Gd /Ge+ /G4 /C TestThem.cpp

         Thermo.DEF: Thermo.IDL
                   @echo " Compile::SOM Compiler "
                   SC.EXE -sdef Thermo.idl

         clean:
                   if exist *.OBJ                 del *.OBJ
                   if exist *.xh                  del *.xh
                   if exist *.xih                 del *.xih
                   if exist *.def                 del *.def
                   if exist *.lib                 del *.lib
                   if exist ..\BIN\Thermo.DLL     del ..\BIN\Thermo.DLL
                   if exist ..\BIN\TESTTHEM.EXE   del ..\BIN\TESTTHEM.EXE
```

3. Making the DLL

The last step to build the library is running **nmake** against the make file you just created. Issue the following command in an OS/2 command prompt:

```
nmake /f thermo.mak
```

Upon completion you will have a working **THERMO.DLL**.

Registering the DSOM Alias for SOMThermometer Class

Before SOMThermometer can be used by client applications, it must be registered with DSOM by running the implementation registration utility: **pregimpl**. This will enable DSOM to find and activate the server so that clients can invoke methods on it.

Instead of writing a special server program to load and execute your **thermo.dll**, use the generic SOM-object server program that comes with the toolkit (the **SOMDSRV.EXE**). It is sufficient for most of the general purpose SOM implementations.

To register the DSOM alias :

1. Start the **pregimpl** program by typing the following in an OS/2 command prompt:

   ```
   pregimpl
   ```

   The DSOM implementation window appears.

2. Define to DSOM the **implementation alias** that you want to add (SOMThermometer). Use your mouse to choose the following: Implementations -> Add and the window (Figure 44 on page 118 will be shown).

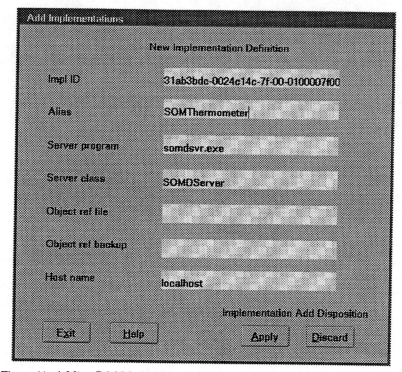

New Implementation Definition

Impl ID	31ab3bdc-0024c14c-7f-00-0100007f00
Alias	SOMThermometer
Server program	somdsvr.exe
Server class	SOMDServer
Object ref file	
Object ref backup	
Host name	localhost

Figure 44. *Adding DSOM alias*

Type in **SOMThermometer** in the **Alias** field. You need not change any other field; the default is sufficient.

Note that the implementation ID generated by the **pregimpl** is a universally unique number for the implementation alias. Also, a host name of **localhost** means the class implementer and the class users are running in same machine, although they are running in different processes.

Press **Apply** when finished.

3. Then we define to dsom the name of the classes (that we registered into the Interface Repository before, in our case we are also using the name SOMThermometer)to be mapped to the implementation alias. We do this by choosing **Classes -> Add** and the window Figure 45 will be shown.

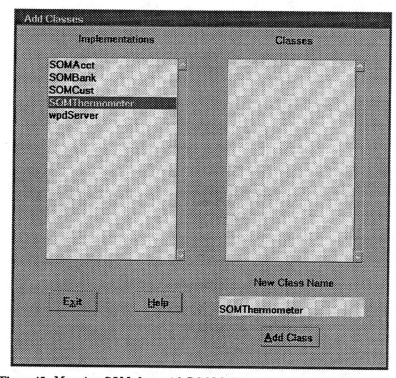

Figure 45. *Mapping SOM class with DSOM alias*

Choose SOMThermometer and type in **SOMThermometer** in the **New Class Name** field. Then press **Add Class** button.

4. Now choose **File -> Save** to save your information and then **File - > Exit** to end the program.

SOMThermometer is available to be used through DSOM now! The next thing to do is to create a small test program to test your SOMThermometer.

Creating a Test Program

Use your editor to edit the file **test.cpp**

```
#include <somd.xh>
#include "thermo.xh"

main(int argc, char *argv[], char *envp[])
{
    Environment ev;
```

```
/* initialization */
SOM_InitEnvironment(&ev);
SOMD_Init(&ev);

SOMThermometerNewClass(0,0);

SOMThermometer *myThermometer = (SOMThermometer *)
    SOMD_ObjectMgr->somdNewObject(&ev, "SOMThermometer", "");

/* testing operations */
somPrintf( "First we set the current temperature to be 30 degrees Celsius\n");
myThermometer->_set_celsius(&ev, 30);

somPrintf( "Now the Fahrenheit reading is %d\n",
myThermometer->_get_fahrenheit(&ev) );
somPrintf( "Now the Celsius reading is %d\n\n",
myThermometer->_get_celsius(&ev) );

/* termination */
((SOMDClientProxy *) SOMThermometer)->somdProxyFree(ev);
SOMD_ObjectMgr->somdDestroyObject(ev, SOMThermometer);

SOMD_Uninit(ev);
SOM_DestroyLocalEnvironment(ev);
}
```

Then build the test program by typing the following lines:

```
icc test.cpp somtk.lib thermo.lib
```

You can also put the test program building procedures into the make file that you created before.

Testing the SOMThermometer Class

Finally, you can test our SOMThermometer class now.

1. Make sure that the thermo.dll is inside one of the directories that LIBPATH= statement in CONFIG.SYS is pointing to. You can either append d:\thermo to the LIBPATH= statement and then reboot the system, or copy (not recommended though) the thermal.dll into any of the pointed directories to achieve that.

2. Start the DSOM daemon : type

   somdd

   in an OS/2 command prompt

3. Run the test program by typing

   test

   in d:\thermo directory

Did you see the correct messages printed out from the test program?

Generating SOM Wrapper for SOMThermometer

To generate the SOM wrapper class for SOMThermometer within VisualAge, first ensure that the SOMsupport feature is loaded. If you haven't done so, start your VisualAge Smalltalk. From the **Smalltalk tools** menu of the System Transcript window select **Load Features**

The displayed prompter shows three options for SOMsupport on OS/2. Select **SOMsupport** which is the base feature. However, you can also choose the **SOMsupport Samples** which illustrate how to use SOM and DSOM objects.

Remember to save the image after loading the SOMsupport feature.

You should also create a new application SOMThermometerApp and put the to-be-generated SOMThermometer wrapper class inside the application.

To wrap the SOMThermometer class with VisualAge, use the Create SOM Wrappers window accessed by selecting **Generate -> SOM Wrappers** from the **Parts** menu. Then choose the SOMThermometer class in the list box and select the **DSOM** radio button. Press **OK** when done.

Alternatively, you can generate the SOM wrapper for SOMThermometer with a bit of Smalltalk programming. Evaluate the following code in a Workspace window:

```
| options aCollection |
options := SOMSmalltalkConstructorOptions new.
options targetApplication: SOMThermometerApp.
aCollection := SOMSmalltalkConstructor
        constructWrappersFor: 'SOMThermometer'
        usingOptions: options.
SOMSmalltalkConstructor generateNew: aCollection.
```

Completing either of the above options adds the SOM wrapper named SOMThermometer to the SOMThermometerApp. You will see the SOMThermometer icon displayed in the parts list for SOMThermometerApp from the VisualAge Organizer.

Developing the SOMThermometerView

Follow these steps to build the VisualAge Smalltalk SOMThermometerView part:

1. Inside the SOMThermometerApp, create a visual part SOMTher-mometerView.

   Use the VisualAge Composition Editor to define the layout as shown in Figure 43 and add a part of the SOMThermometer class to the freeform surface.

2. In the Public Interface Editor for the SOMThermometerView part, define three actions **celsiusChanged** and **fahrenheitChanged** and **initialize**. None of them takes any parameter.

3. Generate the default scripts for the actions

4. In the Script Editor, add an instance variable **lockChange**

```
AbtAppBldrView subclass: #SOMThermometerView
    instanceVariableNames: 'lockChange '
    classVariableNames: ''
    poolDictionaries: ''
```

5. Change the generated code as shown below (texts in underlined bold are method names):

```
initialize
 lockChange := false.


celsiusChanged
 "Celsius slider is changed, perform the necessary update"
 | c f |
 lockChange
 ifFalse: [
  lockChange := true.

  f := (self subpartNamed: 'SOMThermometer1') valueOfAttributeNamed:
   #fahrenheit selector: #'IS_fahrenheit'.
  (self subpartNamed: 'FahrenheitSliderBar') topOrLeftValue: f
        ]

 ifTrue: [
  lockChange := false.
        ]

fahrenheitChanged
 "Fahrenheit slider is changed, perform the necessary update"
 | c f |
 (lockChange)
 ifFalse: [
  lockChange := true.

  c := (self subpartNamed: 'SOMThermometer1') valueOfAttributeNamed:
   #celsius selector: #'IS_celsius'.
  (self subpartNamed: 'CelsiusSliderBar') topOrLeftValue: c.
        ]
 ifTrue: [
  lockChange := false.
        ].
```

6. Define the necessary attribute-to-attribute connections:

- Connect the actual slider values (topOrLeftValue attribute) to their corresponding label parts.
- Connect the actual slider values to the corresponding attributes (celsius and fahrenheit) of the SOMThermometer part.

7. Define the necessary event-to-action connections:

- Connect the topOrLeftValue event of the Celsius slider bar to the action celsiusChanged
- Connect the topOrLeftValue event of the Fahrenheit slider bar to the action fahrenheitChanged.

Figure 46 shows the Composition Editor after all connections have been defined.

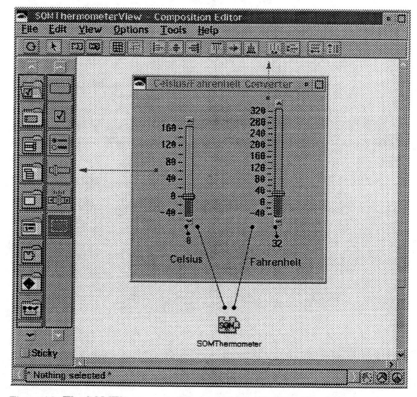

Figure 46. *The SOMThermometerView inside the Composition Editor*

8. Now you are ready to test your application! First ensure that the DSOM daemon (somdd) is still running in the system. Then press the test button in the composition editor to test the view.

9. Try to drag the slider of either the Celsius or the Fahrenheit slider bar and see the effect of the application!

10. You can also see that a background process called **SOMDSRV** is started by the **somdd** daemon and text messages are displayed also.

Experiences

During this quick tour, you developed a distributed object application using DSOM as the middle layer.

You first prepared the necessary environment and then created and tested the class implementer, in our case using C++.

Then you wrapped the SOMThermometer class into VisualAge Smalltalk environment and developed a class user using Smalltalk.

The DSOM daemon **somdd** automatically started the DSOM server **SOMDSRV** for you when the first client request arrived.

As this is only a quick tour, it does not touch on every aspect. However, this experience will allow you to develop your first SOM application using VisualAge Smalltalk and DSOM.

There are, of course, many other considerations that you may be interested to know. See VisualAge SOMsupport on page 81 for more details.

Part 2

Developing a Distributed Object Application

Part 2 describes the development of a distributed object application. The application itself is a simplification of a real-world foreign currency exchange banking application. The initial object-oriented modeling of this application is described in the ITSO redbook, *Object-Oriented Application Development in a Client/Server Environment* (GG24-4227). Part 2 refines the design of the foreign currency exchange application and extends it by using distributed objects, that is, it becomes an object-oriented implementation for both the client and server parts of the application.

8

The Foreign Currency Exchange (FCE) Case Study

The Foreign Currency Exchange (FCE) case study project was first conducted at the ITSO San Jose Center during the winter of 1993. The project had the following goals:

❑ Define a methodology to build real-life object-oriented applications with VisualAge

❑ Apply the proposed methodology to build an object-oriented banking application with VisualAge. The application was designed to run in a Client/Server computing environment.

The results of the project were published in a redbook, *Object-oriented Application Development with VisualAge in a Client/Server Environment* (GG24-4227), which also introduced the Visual Modeling Technique (VMT), an object-oriented application development methodology that supports a visual programming environment like that provided by the VisualAge product.

The FCE application has since then been ported to the latest version of VisualAge Smalltalk and VisualAge C++. It was also used to test drive a number of object-oriented analysis and design tools in a few ITSO residency projects. Please refer to "Related Publications" in the preface for more references.

Requirements Specifications

The bank (see Figure 47) has a number of world-wide branches. It provides its customers with various banking services, such as automated teller machines, credit card, and foreign currency exchange.

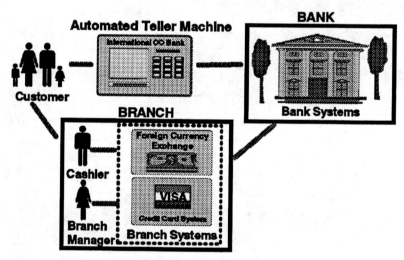

Figure 47. *The International OO Bank Environment*

The FCE application provides a foreign currency exchange service. The service supplies foreign cash and travelers check trading services to customers based on current exchange rates. Customers who have an account in a bank branch are considered bank customers. Customers who do not have an account in any bank branch are considered general customers. Both bank and general customers are eligible to use the exchange services.

The FCE application provides the branch cashiers with country information, for example, country currency name, denominations of both cash and travelers checks, and foreign country currency restrictions.

The cashiers get customer information, create an order, and receive an immediate response regarding the requested stock availability in their drawers and in the local branch. Customer orders can be pending, in process, or completed. Orders become pending only if sufficient stock is not available in the cashier's drawer or in the local branch.

The system manages foreign currencies, customers, orders and payments, and stock availability.

Please refer to Appendix A, "Requirement Specifications," on page 213, for the complete requirements specifications of the sample application.

The Solution Prototype

The previous project team developed a VisualAge solution prototype for the application and ported it to VisualAge Smalltalk Version 3.0. The application prototype was developed using VisualAge Smalltalk with remote data access to a DB2/2 database.

Project Objectives

Extending the work from the previous residency project, this project explored distributed object perspectives in objected-oriented application development. More specifically, the focus was on applying the IBM VisualAge SOM/DSOM support to extend an application involving distributed objects.

In this project, we extended a subset of the FCE application: the customer information management subsystem. Wherever possible, we tried to reuse the analysis work result and the same look-and-feel from the previous project.

Project Iterations

We went through a few iterations for the extension case study, trying out different approaches that would illustrate how to develop distributed object applications with VMT and the implementing technology.

We revisited the requirements study, object-oriented analysis, and object-oriented design of the original FCE case study before proceeding with the development of the application extension.

Incremental Development

This project also practiced building the application incrementally. We had an existing nondistributed FCE application and wanted to add new functions to it using distributed objects. For example, the object classes involved in distribution changes would be moved to a different object space and platform. In other words, we could expect to redesign them. However, those parts of the existing application that were not distributed would remain very much the same with little or no change. The distributed portion of the application thus could be viewed as increments to the existing FCE.[9]

The VisualAge Distributed Feature provides distribution tool support for the design and development of distributed object applications. This support facilitates incremental development. Applications can be developed as local (nondistributed) and then modified to suit a distributed object space environment (see Figure 48 and Figure 49).

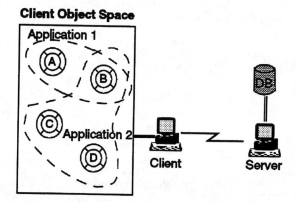

Figure 48. *Incremental Development: Nondistributed*

---

[9] During this project, we developed the customer management *object server*. Concurrently, another residency project team developed the distributed currency management subsystem *active server* separately as a different subproject. The two projects used different technologies and should be viewed as two increments of the original application.

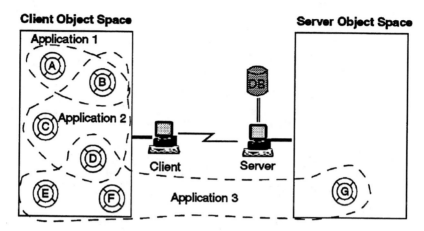

Figure 49. *Incremental Development: Distributed*

Distributed FCE Application Scenarios

In Distributed Object Applications on page 19, we introduced the concepts of *object server*, *active server*, and *peer-to-peer*, as traditional data server takes on these new roles in a distributed object application environment. Let us look at how these new server roles are applicable to scenarios in the FCE application environment.

Customer Management: Object Server

Let us assume that the bank maintains customer and account information in centralized databases located in the bank center system. The branches are remote from the bank center location.

Bank-specific operations are carried out at the central site, that is, the bank. These operations may include certain customer management operations. However, the cashiers sitting in a branch also perform other customer management functions, such as:

❑ Adding a new customer to the list of bank customers
❑ Updating a customer's information
❑ Removing a customer from the list of bank customers.

The required information to perform these functions includes:

❑ A list of customers and related customer information

❑ A list of accounts and related account information.
❑ Certain information about the bank (such as bank name).

Instead of accessing data from cashier client workstations using SQL database query, we can create objects in the bank server that access databases locally and satisfy the client workstations for the required objects. Some reasons why this approach is desirable are:

❑ Database access is required only on the server.

Client workstations do not have to issue queries to access remote databases.

❑ There are only a few objects (the customer and account that reside in the server) that have direct access to the data, thus simplifying data maintenance at the central bank.

❑ Network traffic can be reduced between the branch client workstations and bank server. Thus, the cashiers see a performance improvement of the overall FCE application.

❑ The database software does not have to be installed in each client machine, so the software license cost could be reduced.

The residency project described in this redbook focuses on the development of a distributed customer management solution based on DSOM object servers. There are certain design considerations for distributed objects, which we will discuss in Designing the FCE Application with Distributed Objects on page 143.

Exchange Rate Management: Active Server

The bank center centrally maintains the exchange rate for each currency.

In the previous project, we assumed that the exchange rates for all currencies were updated overnight and remained fixed during the day. The branch cashiers obtained the exchange rate for each currency to perform the foreign exchange transactions.

In our project, to enable the cashiers to use a fluctuating exchange rate for currency trading, a list of all currencies with their corresponding exchange rates was located on a bank server (a center computer at the central site). All clients (the cashier workstations in the branches) had access to the currency information provided by the central site.

The bank server containing the list of currencies was an active server in the sense that it informed all the interested clients when a change occurred. The clients could reflect that change on their corresponding views of the user interface.

See *Developing Distributed Object Application with the VisualAge Smalltalk Distributed Feature (SG24-4521-0)* for more details on the development of the distributed currency management solution.

Currency Trading Between Banks: Peer-to-Peer

By *peer-to-peer* we mean direct communication between two client machines.[10] In the FCE application, a good example of peer-to-peer communication is currency trading between two different banks.

The bank center had to maintain the bank stock and trade with many other banks around the world. We assumed that there was an external system that offered the foreign currency trading facilities across a number of banks. Each bank would be required to pay a fee to use the system. The main requirements for this system were:

❑ Maintain a list of all or most of the existing currencies and the rates each bank assigns to them.

This will help each bank to increase or decrease their own internal exchange rate.

❑ Maintain a list of all trading requests that the member banks send to the system.

A trading request specifies the available currency, the amount, the requested currency, the requested exchange rate, and the bank that originated the request.

❑ Start direct negotiation between banks.

After the initial setup, a connection can be established between a bank and the bank that originally sent in a trading request, without the intervention of the external system. In this way, the banks can directly negotiate the rate, bulk transportation, date, time, and additional considerations.

We did not implement this peer-to-peer scenario in this project.

---

[10] See Peer-to-Peer on page 28.

9

Analyzing the FCE System

In this chapter, we review the analysis work done previously for the nondistributed FCE case study application. We present the modeling result of the original FCE application and the modeling extensions required for the distributed FCE application (developed during this project). The extensions were mainly performed at the design level, because the primary goal of this project was to develop the FCE application with a distributed object architecture.

Object-Oriented Analysis

Analysis can be defined as the process of understanding and describing *what* is the problem to solve. Design is the process of deriving and describing *how* the solution will be implemented. Analysis is an important step, because it helps us to attack the right problem. Without proper analysis, we may build an elegant solution but end up solving the wrong problem.

The analysis phase thus has two main objectives: understanding the problem domain and defining the desired application behavior. Understanding the problem domain requires that, during the analysis phase the analyst, before starting any design and programming activities, gain enough knowledge of the characteristics of the environment and elements that are related to the problem the application is supposed to solve. The analyst should also have an understanding of the scope of the application as defined by user expectations.

Defining (modeling) what the application is supposed to do (as opposed to how it should carry out the desired behavior) requires that design decisions concerning the implementation of the application solution be made at a design phase. In fact, the analysis process and result can be independent of the target implementation environment. For this reason, most of the analysis results from the previous ITSO residency project were reused for this project.

Studying the Requirements for our Case Study

Basically, the general requirements for this project were the same as those of the original FCE case study application (see Appendix A, "Requirement Specifications," on page 213). For easy reference, the assumptions made for the project are repeated here:

- ❑ The branches are located remotely from the bank.
- ❑ Now that the original FCE application is running in a branch, we should retain the same look-and-feel of the application to minimize the impact on the user.
- ❑ The bank manages certain information centrally:
    - ➤ Customers and related customer information
    - ➤ Accounts and related account information
    - ➤ Certain information about the bank (for example, bank name)
- ❑ Bank-specific operations should be carried out at the central site (that is, the bank). These include customer management operations. However, the cashiers in the branch should also be able to perform certain customer management operations, such as:
    - ➤ Adding a person to the list of bank customers
    - ➤ Updating a customer's information
    - ➤ Removing a customer from the list of bank customers

        Other than customer management, the branch handles all other branch-specific transactions, such as order management and branch stock management.
- ❑ The bank currently retains the policy that each customer payment can only be made from one single account in the bank.

In the process of understanding the requirements, it became clear that most of the analysis work from the original FCE case study could be reused, at least for the branch subsystem. The change of implementation technology and platforms for the bank server simply had no effect on our analysis of the branch.

To save space and be friendly to the earth, we will not repeat the entire analysis here. For more information, please refer to *Object-oriented Application Development with VisualAge in a Client/Server Environment* (GG24-4227).

In the sections that follow, we focus on object-oriented analysis related to the customer management functions.

Reviewing the Existing Case Study

This project began with a review of the requirements, work products from analysis and design, and the actual implementation of the existing FCE case study application. Like most projects, we had an existing application to deal with. We decided that making drastic changes to the existing application would not be the best way to "extend" it. However, the existing case study was developed using VMT, which covers all areas of business process modeling, analysis, and design. Thus, we were able to harvest and reuse almost all of the work that had been produced previously.

We were able to reuse some of the existing application code as well as the output from the analysis and design processes. This reuse drastically reduced the amount of work required to complete the new case study.

Use Cases

The use cases for customer management function are repeated here for easy reference. Most use cases for other operations are reusable from the original FCE application.

Customer Management.

❑ Create customer

1. Cashier requests to perform customer management function.
2. System provides a form for the cashier to fill in.
3. Cashier completes the customer information form.
4. Cashier requests the system to perform the create job.
5. System performs the customer create job.
6. System notifies the cashier: job is successful or not.

❏ Update customer

1. Cashier requests to perform customer management function.
2. System provides a list of customers to the cashier.
3. Cashier chooses the customer he/she wants to update.
4. System informs cashier what customer he/she has selected.
5. Cashier requests to perform customer management function on the selected customer.
6. System provides a form to the cashier with customer information on it.
7. Cashier modifies the form with new information.
8. Cashier requests system to perform the update.
9. System performs the customer update job.
10. System notifies the cashier: job is successful or not.

❏ Delete customer

1. Cashier requests to perform customer management function.
2. System provides a list of customers to the cashier.
3. Cashier chooses the customer he/she wants to delete.
4. System informs cashier what customer he/she has selected.
5. Cashier tells the system that he or she wants to delete the selected customer.
6. System deletes the customer from the bank customer list.
7. System notifies the cashier: job is successful or not.

User Interface

We also reused the user interface from the previous project because we wanted to retain the same look-and-feel for the application. Figure 50 shows the main view of the nondistributed FCE application, reused from the previous project.

Figure 50. Main View of the Original FCE Application (Revised)

Clicking on the **Foreign Currency Exchange System** push button opens the toolbar shown in Figure 51. The toolbar contains the push buttons for currency, stock, order, and customer management. It also has a pop-up menu, not shown here, that lets the user log onto the system.

Figure 51. Toolbar of the Original FCE Application (Revised)

Object Model

When analyzing the use cases, we decided to use the object model of the original case study as shown in Figure 52 . Because the analysis process is the same for both cases, we do not repeat the discussion here. However, it is worthwhile to point out that we had grouped some classes into the bank subsystem while other are grouped into the branch subsystem.

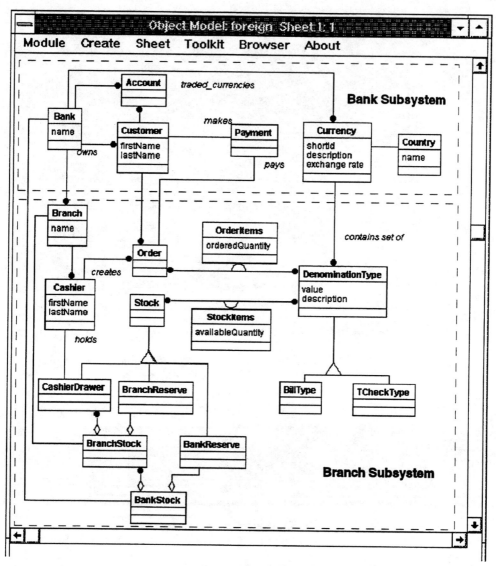

Figure 52. The FCE Object Model with the Bank and Branch Subsystems

Dynamic Model

Figure 53 shows the event trace diagram for customer information update. It is based on the use cases for the customer management functions (see Section Use Cases on page 137). We show only the update customer case here.

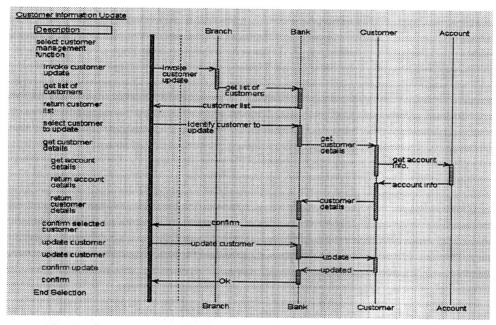

Figure 53. Event Trace Diagram for Customer Information Update

In summary, we reviewed the analysis work done previously for the nondistributed FCE case study application. Most of the analysis results of the original FCE application could be reused to extend the application with a distributed object architecture. The extensions were performed mainly at the design level.

10

Designing the FCE Application with Distributed Objects

This chapter describes the application of VMT to design a distributed object application by extending the Foreign Currency Exchange (FCE) case study.

Object-oriented design encompasses *system design*, *object design*, and *object persistence design* activities.

System design focuses on the design decisions regarding the enabling and implementing of hardware and software platforms. The work products are represented as specifications for system and application architectures. In particular, system design in a Client/Server environment is a complex topic and involves numerous design considerations.

It is not our intent to cover all of these system design issues in this book. The focus however, will be on designing for object distribution, including which objects are to be distributed and how they would be distributed.

In our case study, we followed the VMT design approach. The following sections of this chapter describe how we apply it in designing a distributed object application (the Foreign Currency Exchange).

As Object-oriented design is an iterative process. The design steps listed below, although in a order, are actually carried out iteratively. i.e. They are the deliverables over a number of design iterations.

In the following sections we will first discuss some considerations when designing a distributed object applications. Then we will discuss the points to be taken when performing the system design, follow by the object design and persistence object design activities.

Designing Distributed Object Applications

This section describes general considerations for and approaches to designing distributed object applications.

If we are designing a new application, we must start thinking about object distribution from the very beginning of our application design. This will make life easier as it is quite common we have to perform changes to the application throughout its life. On the other hand, if possible we still should start developing and testing the nondistributed application locally. This can help to isolate the domain of problems when we debug our applications.

After we verified that the overall logic of the nondistributed application works correctly, we can then distribute the application and start testing and tuning the distributed version.

During the object distribution design, the following sources can help us to make decisions on how to divide classes for distribution:

❏ **Requirement specification**

The customer might have specified requirements that are related to the distribution of objects.

❏ **Use cases**

Which use cases will run in which types of workstations or platforms?

❑ **Object model**

Clusters of objects, that is, closely related objects with a high degree of interaction, should remain in the same object space[11] to minimize the message traffic between object spaces. Are there typical "*server*" objects, that is, common objects that are used by many different client workstations at the same time?

❑ **Dynamic model**

Are there interactions between similar kinds of objects within different machines (peer-to-peer requirements)?

❑ **System design**

Are there subsystems to be mapped only to certain object spaces? On which platform does the server system run? Are there LANs that run their own server? Objects can be distributed to platforms currently supported by VisualAge.

❑ **Persistent object design**

Where are the databases and data storage devices located? They should be on the same platform as the object servers, if possible.

The design activities of an object-oriented application can be categorized into three task groups: *system design*, *object design*, and *object persistence design*.

System Design

The outcomes of system design are a high-level *system architecture* and an *application architecture* for the proposed solution. These architectures define the major building blocks of the system (subsystems), the allocation of the subsystems to processes and platforms, and their high-level connectivity.

During system design we must make initial decisions about the placement of objects (putting subsystems into appropriate places) and distribution of processes. We must take a closer look at the system environment in which the application will be running and consider:

❑ Network-related topics

➤ What kind of network is or will be used?
➤ What is the estimated traffic rate between the clients and servers?
➤ Will the bandwidth of the network be able to handle this traffic load?

---

[11] In this book, we use the term *object space* in a generic sense to refer to a separate process or platform where objects run.

❑ Geographical locations and their roles

➤ How many different kinds of locations will there be for servers and clients?

➤ Will there be several layers of servers (department, company, enterprise)?

❑ Security, reliability, and usability topics

➤ What are the security and reliability requirements for servers and clients?

➤ Who has the right to use an object and how is the verification accomplished?

➤ Which servers are responsible for maintaining persistent data?

➤ What is the method of recovery after a system crash?

Here we must also make a decision about which Client/Server enabling technology to use and for what purpose. For example, we can use the VisualAge Distributed Feature to distribute only some objects. Other objects will be local to the client object space or might use some other distribution technique, such as distributed system object model (DSOM).

Choosing the Implementation Technology

VisualAge Smalltalk, with its SOMsupport and Distributed Feature, is a versatile powerful tool for developing the new breed of distributed object applications.

In this section we list some criteria for choosing between the Visual-Age Distributed Feature and SOM/DSOM support. The choice is not an easy one because the two features are based on quite different technologies and approaches.

❑ **Pure Smalltalk programming or language independence**

Which is good and which is not? We believe that this depends on the specific requirements of each customer. Some would prefer to develop an application with a single programming language; in this case, Smalltalk would be the better choice. Others would prefer to have classes written with language-independence so that they can reuse the classes in different languages later on. SOM/DSOM will be more suitable under this circumstance.

In some cases, the legacy systems that customers have may dictate the language they choose when they extend these systems. In other cases, there may be distinct advantages to choosing a particular language to use in the customer's environment. If a customer does not have these requirements, we believe that writing all of the code in plain Smalltalk is a much simpler and more straightforward way of developing object-oriented applications.

❑ **Communication protocols**

Currently, the VisualAge Distributed Feature supports only TCP/IP. However, DSOM supports TCP/IP, NetBIOS, and SPX/IPX. The support of protocol stacks in DSOM is extensible, so customers can even implement their own protocol stack if they choose to.

❑ **Cross-platform requirements**

In the real world, most installations have more than one computer platforms. Applications often must be developed using various languages, and they often run on different platforms. If we want to implement distributed cross-platform, cross-vendor applications, being conforming to CORBA standard of OMG, SOM/DSOM may be a good choice.

SOM/DSOM is a proven technology for facilitating the communication of applications written in different languages. For example, a Smalltalk object application running on the client platform can communicate with C++ SOM objects running on the server machine. Currently, SOM and DSOM are supported in OS/2, AIX, Microsoft Windows, MVS, and other environments.

❑ **Availability of frameworks**

SOM/DSOM provides a number of frameworks that are useful in developing distributed object applications, including the persistence framework for persistence objects.

❑ **Release-to-release binary compatibility**

With SOM/DSOM, in a compilation language environment like C++, client compilations are not required even when the server method implementations change. This eliminates the need to recompile most of the modules should one server method change. Generally, if the changes to the SOM/DSOM objects do not require logic or source code changes in the client programs, those client programs will not have to be recompiled.

❑ **Location transparency**

Location transparency means that the client application objects running on one platform do not have to know the locations of server objects. What client objects must do is communicate with the server objects by sending messages in the same way, regardless of whether the server objects are local or remote.

Location transparency helps the distribution design for applications. VisualAge Distributed Feature and SOM/DSOM both provide a certain level of location transparency support. Using either implementing feature, we can initially develop both the client application and server application on the same machine. After we finished developing and testing the applications locally, we simply moved the server application to another machine. With a few minor adjustments to communication and the DSOM settings, we had the client application communicating with the server application, without code changes to either application.

❑ **Flexibility, scalability, and extensibility**

If we must make any changes to the implemented server environment, including moving it to another platform or rewriting it in another language, the client application would remain unchanged, provided that the interface between the two is not changed. The reverse also applies.

❑ **Distributed tools**

The VisualAge Distributed Feature has many tools that help a developer build distributed applications. Tools like the distributed debugger and distributed event profiler help developers see which messages are going through the network and what is happening in the remote machine. These tools are not available with VisualAge SOMsupport.

Instead, the SOM compiler provides a method-debug routine when it is generating the template functions. SOM class developers can use the method-debug routine for debugging how methods are invoked in a SOM/DSOM environment. However, debugging the business logic still relies on the debugger of the language of choice.

Similarly, if we are using a DSOM object that exists in a remote machine, we must use the corresponding debugger in the other machine. As they may be on a different platform or written in a language different from the client platform. As a result, debugging is more complicated with DSOM than with the VisualAge Distributed Feature.

Subsystem Design and Placement

Recall that we also make decisions for the placement of subsystems during system design, this section describes some general considerations and criteria for the design and placement of them.

In general, subsystems must have clearly defined functions, be fairly independent, and have well-defined interfaces. When a cluster of classes adhere to the above criteria, they become candidates for subsystems. Subsystems are units for distribution because some of the considerations in selecting subsystems also apply to distribution.

The placement of subsystems and some of their internal functioning are influenced by a number of business requirements, most importantly the following: data integrity, data consistency, performance, and availability.

Data Integrity

Managing data remotely is not easy. This does not mean that distributed data cannot be managed without losing integrity. A number of feasible solutions exist, but exploring them here in depth is beyond the scope of this book.

The designer must make the necessary trade-off between the level of data integrity dictated by the business requirement and overhead and associated performance impact costs. For example, even though the same level of integrity can be achieved with less overhead during runtime, more time may be required to start up the application or recover from a system failure.

Data Consistency

Data consistency ensures that data values presented are true values. Consistency is not always needed, but if it is, several different schemes are possible, each with different consequences for the internal functioning and placement of subsystems.

Performance

The placement of subsystems and the size and number of messages passing between them are the major factors in determining response time.

Availability

An application in which all subsystems are 100% dependent on the availability of all parts of the system works only when all subsystems are available.

Subsystems can be designed to have a few dependencies on other subsystems for most of their functions. Therefore, some functions of one subsystem can still be available when other subsystems are not available.

During our system design with VMT, wedecomposed the analysis object model into subsystems and mapped the resulting subsystems to separate VisualAge applications. This is a design strategy for the initial application architecture structure and development work assignment among developers. This division of the business application into a number of VisualAge applications enables a team of developers to proceed with development work concurrently. By partitioning the object model into subsystems, we might find some candidates for object distribution. But, keep in mind that we should minimize object references across processes or a network. We should divide only those subsystems that are loosely coupled and will not interact with each other very often into different object spaces.

Figure 54 shows the application architecture we used in our distributed FCE application.

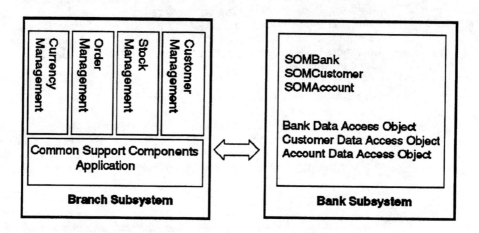

Figure 54. Application Architecture for the Distributed FCE Application

Figure 55 on page 151 shows the system architecture we used in our distributed FCE application.

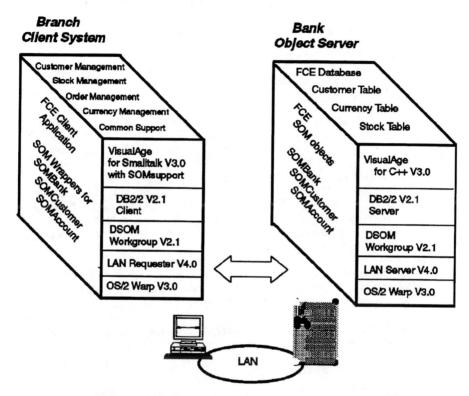

Figure 55. System Architecture for the Extended FCE Application

> The relational database in the branch subsystem contains branch-specific data, such as branch reserve, branch stock, and order information.

> The relational database in the bank subsystem contains customer and account information.

Function Placement (Fat Client or Fat Server?)

> Beside subsystem design and placement, we have to make decisions about the distribution of processes.

> Although we decided to separate the branch and bank subsystems in previous work, there were still some grey areas we had to consider: Where should we put the processing logic? More on the server? (i.e.

class implementer) or more on the client?(i.e. class user). Where should we put the data? The questions are actually closely related. Let us look at the alternatives we have.

❑ *A fat client*

We can have a fat branch client that performs most of the processing for the whole system. In this setup, we leave only the data storage and retrieval functions to be done by the bank server.

❑ *A fat server*

We can have a fat server that performs all processing logic, leaving only the user interface handling to be done on the client side.

In the case of a fat client, as the server (in our case, the bank) does not filter any information it obtains before sending it to the client, there may be excessive and unnecessary traffic generated between the server and client. The problem is even greater in a distributed object environment, because the attributes of an object may be another object (in an aggregate case), and, that object's attributes could even contain other objects.

Thus, a "get attribute" message sent to an object will result in a number of database access requests to or from one or more tables. Performance, in this case, may be seriously affected.

Figure 56 shows how a fat client can cause excessive data access loading in a distributed object environment.

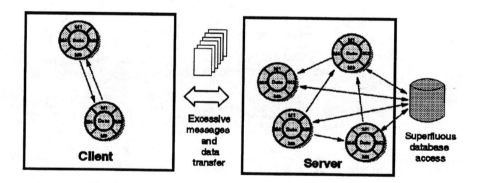

Figure 56. A Fat Client

In the case of a fat server, we have the client depending too much on the server. Again, we could have a performance problem due to the contention created by simultaneous access of the server from multiple clients.

Our approach of functional division processing is somewhere in the middle of the fat client and fat server cases: The branch function is carried out in the branch subsystem, and the bank function is carried out in the bank subsystem.

We adopted this design approach to avoid the problem of excessive database access to support the aggregation relationships between objects. The bank server, instead of performing a "deep" object data retrieval and then sending all actual data across the network, performs a "shallow" object data retrieval. For example, when handling a request for a list of customers, the bank server only returns a list of customers with their account IDs. The actual content of the account is not retrieved until the cashier requests it. This eliminates potential performance problems and reduces network traffic loading.

You may also want to refer to for some more in-depth discussions. Figure 57 shows our approach to maintaining a balanced system.

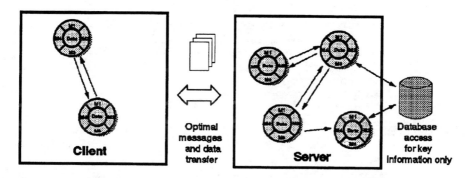

Figure 57. A Balanced System in a Distributed Object Environment

Data Placement

Refer to Introduction to Distributed Systems on page 3 for a general discussion of data placement. In our case, we put the branch-specific data into the branch subsystem machine and the bank-specific data into the bank machine.

We have one more consideration: Should we cache information obtained from the bank into the branch itself? By caching some local data onto the client machine, we reduce network traffic loading, as well as the dependency of the client on the availability of the server.

In our case study, we kept a list of customer objects in the branch. This list was obtained by requesting customers from the bank object. However, this approach raises one more issue: synchronization. What if there are a number of branches and each of them have cached local data (say, account information)? To simplify the case study, we chose not to address the synchronization requirement. If we had chosen to address the synchronization requirement, we could have utilized the Replication Framework provided with the SOMobjects Developer Toolkit.

Other Considerations

For simplicity, we chose to exclude security checks in both applications and use only the database security logon procedures supplied by OS/2. In the case study, all database update requests done on the customer, bank, and account objects were followed immediately by COMMIT statements, that is, for simplicity, all requests during customer management were committed immediately.

If we chose to implement a transaction-based operation during customer management, we could have used the rollback capability provided by the generated data access objects of VisualAge C++. The rollback method could have returned the database to its original state if a problem occurred.

Object Design

The primary goal of object design was to map the semantic classes identified in our analysis object model to solution domain classes (interface classes, application classes, and service classes).

In our case study, the semantic classes became the required SOM/DSOM and VisualAge classes. During object design, we repeated the following steps several times:

❑ Refine object interactions and message flows of the dynamic model.

➤ Evolve event traces with detailed message passing and additional object interactions

➤ Prepare class specifications, methods, and message formats.

❑ Design the details of the SOM/DSOM classes. Define and refine:

➤ The public interface (attributes, actions, events) and methods

➤ The instance methods and variables

➤ The derived attribute policies.

From these as input sources, we produced the IDL files.

❑ Review the design of the VisualAge visual classes for the application's GUI to consider whether the following had to be defined or refined:

➤ The elementary visual class for each application class

➤ Additional composite visual classes, as required

➤ Input data validation

➤ Deferred updates.

In our extension project, very little had to be done to the visual classes because we reused what we had from the previous project.

The object design phase involved the refinement and fleshing out of each object's internal structural and behavioral details, as well as details of object interactions.

Designing the Solution Domain Classes

The set of object classes that makes up a running application is usually much larger than the set of classes identified during the analysis phase. The initial set of semantic application classes identified in the analysis object model represents only the "core" business behavior of the application.

Other solution domain classes must be designed to provide concrete functionality of the application. Interface classes that represent the user interface and "service" classes that provide service functionality, such as input data validation and database access, are some examples of additional classes required for the implementation of the application.

The design of solution domain classes is, as in other processes of object-oriented development, iterative. However, we suggest the following design steps:

1. Map the semantic classes, identified in the object model from analysis to application classes; this is almost straightforward.

2. Add interface and "service" classes to provide user interface and additional functionality, as required.

Object Design for the Server

As discussed in Function Placement (Fat Client or Fat Server?) on page 151, we can have a simple server that handles only data access and retrieval. In fact, for our first cut of the server design, we used this approach (see Figure 58).

Design Object Model for Bank Server System(first cut)

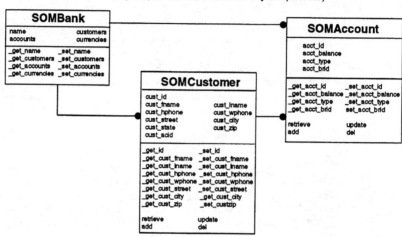

Note:The _gets and_sets to the attributes for SOMBank, SOMCustomer, and SOMAccount
perform direct access to the database.
No logic was added and all codes are generated by the data access server

Figure 58. First Cut of Server Design Object Model

In the second cut, we refined the design for better traceability and maintainability. Instead of directly accessing the database, we created a SOM class that used data access objects to perform data update and retrieval operations. We separated data access logic from business logic to obtain a more portable server. In addition, the SOM classes we created were given attribute names that related more to the business world than the database tables. For example, the customer object with the attribute of firstName was changed from cust_fname. Figure 59. illustrates the object model for the refined design.

Design Object Model for Bank Server System(second cut)

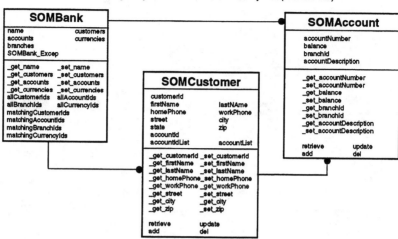

Note: (1) The _gets and_sets to the attributes for SOMBank, SOMCustomer, and SOMAccount use the
corresponding data access server objects to access the database.
(2) All attribute names are the same as those in the original FCE application.
Therefore minimal changes were required for the client application.

Figure 59. Second Cut of Server Design Object Model

Object Design for the Client

The client part of the application contains the user interface, as well as the application logic and data management functions. In all cases, the user interface part adds some function to the model part of the application.

Taking advantage of the SOM/DSOM support of VisualAge Smalltalk Version 3.0, we did not have to change much in the client. In fact, we could reuse most of the original design.

To extend the application, we replaced the Bank class, Customer class, and Account class in the original FCE application object design model with the corresponding SOM wrapper classes (SOMBank, SOMCustomer, and SOMAccount). Thus, other objects, instead of interfacing with the original Customer class, now deal with the SOMCustomer wrapper class. No additional work is required, provided that the SOM wrapper class has the same public interface as the original object class, which it does.

Figure 60 and Figure 61 show the "before" and "after" of the object model diagram.

Module: custom01 Sheet: 1: 1 Panel: (0,0) Time: Wed Jul 03 07:57:29 1996

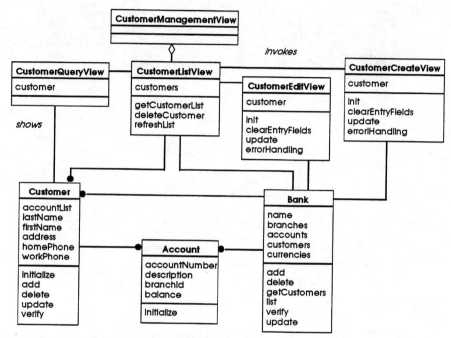

Figure 60. Original Design Object Model with the Customer Class

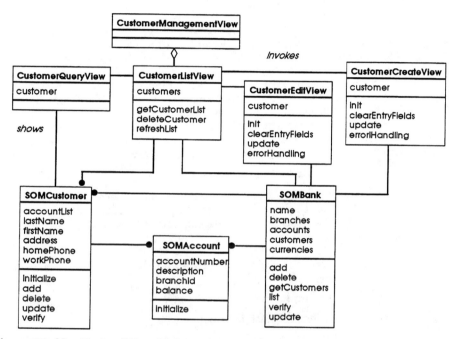

Figure 61. New Design Object Model with the SOMCustomer Class

In fact, the only way other objects know that they are actually distributed across the network is by the different names we deliberately chose for the classes (that is, SOMCustomer instead of Customer; see Figure 64 and Figure 65).

We added a number of service classes for SOM/DSOM support. As defined in CORBA, when the server object has a problem handling a request from a client object, it raises an exception. The exception travels all the way back to the client application, and the client program then takes appropriate actions to handle the exception.

In our case study, for each SOM class we created, we defined an exception associated with it. In the branch machine, when we created a SOM wrapper class, we also created a SOM exception handling class to handle the exception coming back from the DSOM environment.

Designing with VisualAge SOMsupport

In this section, we discuss the aspects of designing with VisualAge SOMsupport from both the client and the server perspectives: implementing the SOM classes to run in the server processes, and using the SOM objects in a client program.

As SOM class implementers, we first identify the SOM classes that are to be distributed. We must define the interface for the SOM classes using a standard Interface Definition Language (IDL). We then implement methods to add the desired behavior for the SOM classes with a programming language for which SOM bindings have been defined. (The current SOMobjects release provides bindings for C and C++). The SOM classes are then compiled into dynamic link libraries (DLLs). We must register their interface and implementation in the SOM Interface Repository (SOMIR), and we must also register them with DSOM before they can be used remotely by a client through DSOM.

To use the SOM classes from a VisualAge client program, we first generate SOM wrapper classes for them using the VisualAge SOMsupport feature. The SOM wrapper classes can then be used as other Smalltalk classes.

There are a number of design emphasis when designing the interfaces for the SOM classes:

❑ Performance implications

❑ Object creation and destruction

❑ Exceptions handling

❑ Reuse considerations

Performance Implications

A properly designed interface for the distributed SOM objects can significantly improve their performance. To illustrate the performance related design issues when creating the interface for SOM classes, consider the following IDL examples for SOMCustomer (SOMCust.idl) and SOMBank (SOMBank.idl):

Interface for SOMCustomer (SOMCust.idl)

```
#include <somobj.idl>

interface SOMAccount;

interface SOMCustomer: SOMObject

{
    attribute string<10> id;
    attribute string<16> firstName;
    attribute string<24> lastName;
    attribute string<8> homePhone;
    attribute string<8> workPhone;
    attribute string<40> street;
    attribute string<16> city;
    attribute string<2> state;
    attribute string<5> zip;

    sequence<SOMAccount> accounts();
};
```

Interface for SOMBank (SOMBank.idl)

```
#include <somobj.idl>

interface SOMCustomer;
typedef sequence<SOMCustomer> customers;

interface SOMBank: SOMObject
{
  attribute customers allCustomers;
  ..
  ..
};
```

In the example, the SOMCustomer interface contains a number of string attributes that belong to a customer, e.g. the customer's first name, last name etc. There is also a member function that SOMCustomer provides for a list of accounts that a customer owns. The SOMBank has an attribute called customers that contains a list of all customers for the bank.

While this represents a natural object thinking in writing the IDL and it works for a small-scale, demo application such as our FCE case study, it imposes a number of performance considerations for use in a high-volume, performance-critical real-life application environment.

First, the attribute allCustomers of SOMBank is an unbounded sequence of customers. Every time this attribute is queried (a get method of this attribute is invoked) the whole list of customers is returned. If the bank has thousands of users, the link between the class users (clients) and the class implementer (server) will be flooded by data, resulting in a long response time.

One way to avoid this performance problem is to return only one attribute: that is, the customerIds of the customers, as shown in the following modified IDL.

```
┌── Interface for SOMBank (SOMBank.idl), revised ──────────────┐
│  #include <somobj.idl>                                        │
│                                                              │
│  typedef sequence<string> customerIds;                       │
│                                                              │
│  interface SOMBank: SOMObject                                │
│  {                                                           │
│     attribute customerIds allCustomerIds;                    │
│     ..                                                        │
│     ..                                                        │
│  };                                                          │
└──────────────────────────────────────────────────────────────┘
```

Here, SOMBank returns only a list of customer IDs instead of a list of the whole customer objects, greatly reducing the network traffic. An even better way is to add some intelligence to the SOMBank class and let it return only a small number of customers (or customer IDs) according to some criteria or business rules. For example, each query or search by customer name could be limited to a maximum of 20 customers, as shown in the following example.

```
┌── Interface for SOMBank (SOMBank.idl), revised ──────────────┐
│  #include <somobj.idl>                                        │
│                                                              │
│  interface SOMBank: SOMObject                                │
│  {                                                           │
│     sequence <string> someCustomerIds(in string criteria);   │
│     ..                                                        │
│     ..                                                        │
│  };                                                          │
└──────────────────────────────────────────────────────────────┘
```

To further improve performance, we can change the attribute declarations for firstName, lastName, and so on, to a structure containing all of them. The design trade-off is between the number of requests and the data traffic over the network per request (one query for the whole data structure versus a request for each attribute) [12]

Object Creation and Destruction

Objects are created and destroyed during the operation of an object application. There are a number of ways to allocate and deallocate objects. It is essential to be careful when defining the SOM IDL file, as the defined relationships between the class users and class implementers will affect the actual coding of the client and server programs, as well as the ownership of memory management for the created objects.

Another design issue is the actual creation and destruction of the SOM objects. In C++, we use the constructors and destructors to create and destroy an object. In DSOM, a factory interface should be defined to deal with the creation of new objects, as recommended by the CORBA Object Lifecycle service of the Common Object Services Specification (COSS). See following example:

```
┌─ Interface for SOMCustomerFactory (SOMFact.idl) ──────────

    #include <somobj.idl>

    interface SOMAccount;

    interface SOMCustomerFactory: SOMObject
    {
        SOMCustomer createCustomerWithName( in string firstName );
        SOMCustomer createCustomerWithId( in string id );

        SOMCustomer findCustomerWithName( in string firstName );
        .. ..
};
```

VisualAge Smalltalk SOMsupport provides object creation and destruction support. Dropping a SOM wrapper onto the free-form surface of the VisualAge Composition editor as a part creating a SOM object at runtime. VisualAge calls the newPart method of the SOM wrapper class, which in turn creates an instance of the SOM class. Alternatively, the client program can also send a Smalltalk message somNew to the wrapper class directly to create an instance.

---

[12] This is a compromise between a pure object-oriented design and performance over a network link.

To destroy a SOM object, the client program sends the SOM wrapper object a Smalltalk message somFree, which then invokes the somFree method of the SOM object to destroy the object and reset the object reference of the wrapper object to nil. Note that the SOM object actually resides outside of the Smalltalk image and thus it will not be garbage collected. When a client program no longer needs a SOM object, it must explicitly destroy it.

To delete a SOM object using VisualAge visual programming, we can connect the closedWidget event of the main view to the somFree action of the SOM object. This will destroy the SOM object when the view closes at runtime.

Exceptions Handling

Another design consideration when designing SOM objects relates to the raising and capturing of exception information. The SOM exception handling capability is a powerful feature that allows a software designer to be explicit about the specific actions to take if an abnormal condition should occur.

By defining the exceptions and associating them with methods in the SOM IDL file, the class designer can easily show the client program designer exactly what will happen if abnormal situations occur when they invoke the method of the class.

This is a powerful tool as it helps to make explicit the range of possible errors that a method might return and also provides greater flexibility for properly describing each error condition.

The SOM Exception is declared in the SOM IDL file, as shown in the next example.

```
┌─── Interface for SOMBank (SOMBank.idl), with exception handling ───┐
│  #include <somobj.idl>                                             │
│                                                                    │
│  exception noCustomer {                                            │
│          string recommendedAction;                                 │
│  }                                                                 │
│                                                                    │
│  exception tooManyCustomers {                                       │
│     sequence <string> customerIds;                                 │
│     long numCustomerIds;                                           │
│  }                                                                 │
│                                                                    │
│  interface SOMBank: SOMObject                                      │
│  {                                                                 │
│     sequence <string> someCustomerIds(in string criteria)          │
│     raises(tooManyCustomers, noCustomer);                          │
│     ..                                                             │
│     ..                                                             │
│  };                                                                │
└────────────────────────────────────────────────────────────────────┘
```

In VisualAge for Smalltalk, the SOMsupport maps SOM exceptions to the Smalltalk ExceptionalEvents, which extends the full power of Smalltalk exception handling to SOM exceptions.

By default, VisualAge Smalltalk will handle the exceptions raised by the SOM object. However, the default handling is designed for a development environment. Thus, it is better to override the default handling for production environment.

Reuse Considerations

When using an object-oriented language, we have three general ways of acquiring the services of other object classes, namely, through inheritance, aggregation, or delegation.

Inheritance. Obtaining services through inheritance is quite straightforward. A subclass inherits all the attributes and operations defined in its superclasses. Thus, all services of the superclasses are made available to the subclass as part of its public interface.

The drawback of this approach is that the subclasses are very dependent on the superclasses, which can cause a lot of recompilation in languages like C++, or force developers to include the complete class hierarchy in languages with late binding, like Smalltalk.

Aggregation. Services can be obtained through aggregation by creating a composite object class that contains the class with the desired services. In most object-oriented languages, the composite (aggregate) object usually contains a reference (object ID) to the contained object rather than containing the object itself. The composite object and contained object are coupled with this aggregation relationship. However, the coupling is not as tight as the inheritance relationship.

Providing the services to the client through aggregation enables one to define a cleaner interface between the server and client. Creating an interface class using aggregation at the server provides even more flexibility. It can hide all function that is not needed. It lessens the dependency on a superclass, therefore causing fewer recompiles, and does not force a lot of classes to be present during run-time for languages with late binding. The drawback is that all methods that are part of the interface must be coded in the composite class.

Delegation. Services can be obtained through delegation by invoking the desired service of another class—by sending it the proper message. A class can invoke the service of any classes with which it has an association relationship. Delegation is the most flexible way in which classes can collaborate with each other with minimum coupling.

Effects of Inheritance and Aggregation

This section discusses the effects of inheritance and aggregation of DSOM classes in a Visualage Smalltalk environment with regard to runtime overhead and development effort.

With SOM, there can be an inheritence relationship between a class written in one language with another class written in a different language. For example, with SOM, we can subclass a server class written in *C++* in a *Smalltalk* environment.

In the case that the subclass is developed using Smalltalk, as Smallalk applies a late bindings concept (method bindings are done at runtime), in order for the child class (subclass) to inherit and reuse code from its DSOM parent class (superclass), all classes of the DSOM parent class inheritance hierarchy tree must be present on the client side as well.

In particular, if the client side is implemented with VisualAge for Smalltalk which applies a SOM wrapper concept, we must generate SOM wrapper classes for not just the DSOM server class itself but all the classes that the DSOM server class inherits from. This means more effort during development phase and also more overhead which affects the run time performance.

The same consideration applies to code reuse by aggregation.

In general, if the client environment is developed using a late binding language, such as Smalltalk, avoid inheritance relationship for a client class with a DSOM wrapper class which has a deep inheritance tree at the server side.

Effects of Extending the SOM Wrapper Classes

This section examines the effects of directly extending the generated SOM wrapper classes in the VisualAge Smalltalk environment. We explored this approach in our case study. From the client application point of view, it only cares about the services that a customer class provides. Therefore, it does not matter how the customer class is actually implemented. Whether the customer class is a SOM-enabled class or native Smalltalk class should not affect the client application. Thus, any customer-specific methods or attributes could be added to the customer class.

If a SOM wrapping process is to occur in the future, the SOM wrapper in VisualAge will make only those modifications that are required. All methods, whether they were added in the Smalltalk environment or obtained from the previous SOM wrapping process, are left untouched if they do not require changes.

Although directly extending SOM wrapper classes is possible, it should be done with caution and only in certain cases because the approach has some negative implications. For example, if you add instance data to a wrapper class, the instance data cannot be made persistent through SOM. Also, by directly extending SOM wrapper classes, the explicit contract between the client and server is broken, as represented by the IDL description of the server interface.

If you are adding real functions as opposed to minor auxiliary functions to assist in the Smalltalk environment, do not directly extend SOM wrapper classes.

Object Persistence Design

Compared with the traditional design for a nondistributed solution, a distributed solution design involves trade-offs when objects are in server object spaces with local access to the database and when objects are in server object spaces without local access to the database. Obviously, when objects have local access, the corresponding persistence manager class should reside in the same object space. When objects do not have local access to the database, we can

❑ Place the corresponding persistence manager class into the object space that has local access to the database and use a shadow of the persistence manager to access its services. This approach places the object and data access within the same object space, but the complete object will be transferred between the object spaces over the network. Since the persistence manager uses instance methods to populate the object's data, the object class must also reside in that object space.

❑ Place the corresponding persistence manager class into the same server object space and use remote database access. This approach places the object class and its persistence manager class within the same object space, but the SQL query and results will be transferred over a network.

❑ Move the object class and the persistence manager into the object space that has local access to the database to minimize the SQL traffic; we use a shadow to access the object. This approach places the object class and its persistence manager class within the same object space with local SQL traffic, but every message to the object instances (and its return value) will be transferred over the network.

When designing distributed applications using SOM/DSOM, we can consider using SOM Persistence Object Service, which conforms to Object Management Group (OMG) CORBA specifications. The next section provides more details.

SOM Support for Persistence

The OMG has adopted a specification for the Persistence Object Service (POS) that provides an industry standard for writing data-store-independent code and for plugging existing data stores into an object storage framework. The adoption of the POS standard by this large industry consortium will likely have a major impact on the way object-oriented storage systems are designed and used in the next few years.

The POS specification ensures that the same client code can be used for storing objects, regardless of whether the object is stored in file systems, relational databases, object-oriented databases, or other data stores. For the first time, programmers have a well-defined interface for storing objects in existing corporate-centric data stores, such as relational databases.

The POS standard also defines the components that must be implemented by data store vendors to support the storage of objects. IBM is currently working on POS plug-in components for DB2, IMS, stream files, and other data stores. This will allow traditional IBM data stores to be used as full-fledged object storage facilities.

There are many advantages to using traditional data store products as object data stores, for both developers and users. Developers now have an industry-defined standard for accessing existing corporate-centric data and storing object data in a format compatible with existing multi-million dollar software investments. Users can exploit mature data store technologies to ensure the reliability and integrity of their data.

The POS standard is designed to support object-oriented databases as well as traditional data store products. This offers application developers the best of all worlds: A single object interface to a multitude of data store products that encompass the best of the past, the present, and the future.

Object to Database Mapping

Each class maps to one (or more) tables. For ease of maintenance the tables are given the same names as the classes from which they were derived.

3. Each base attribute (char, int,...) of a class maps to one column in the table. In the case where an object attribute type is not supported by the database, the database supported type is used in the class.

4. Each object maps to one row in the table.

5. Each attribute of type object or collection of objects is mapped as follows:

    a. 1 : 1 relationship (1 company, 1 address)

    In a 1:1 relationship a column in the owning table points to the table containing the referred object.

    b. 1 : n relationship (1 company, n departments)

    A 1: n relationship is resolved implicitly: within the table containing the n portion (departments) the key of the owning object (company) is used to resolve the relationship

    c. inheritance :

    Inheritance was not mapped into the database schema, that is, each table in the database contains all attributes of all inherited classes, and there is no special table representing the superclass. For example, if 'special company' inherits from 'company' all attributes, the attributes of 'company' and those of 'special company' are contained in one table - the 'special company' table. In the future, if performance allows, mapping inheritance into the tables would be a good approach. The mapping would be resolved by foreign key relationships, where the inheriting table would have a foreign key which is the primary key of its parent table. Data would be retrieved through a join (possibly represented in a view), although updates (since they are not allowed on views or joins) would have to be done separately for each row resulting from inheritance contained in the join. The disadvantage of this approach is that it is slower than the approach where the inheritance of the object model is always collapsed into tables containing the whole inheritance hierarchy. This approach requires possibly multiple updates to circumvent the restriction of not being able to perform updates on joins and views. Additionally join operations tend to be the most time expensive operations in relational database systems. An advantage of this approach is that maintenance of the database would be much easier, because changes in class attributes would not spread across many tables.

Performance Considerations

The following considerations apply when using a relational database management system (RDBMS) for storing persistent objects.

Static SQL

Static SQL has the advantage of being faster than dynamic SQL, because queries are not interpreted (compiled) at run time. If the amount of data processed in relation to the number of queries made is large, the speed advantage of static SQL is negligible.

Dynamic SQL

Dynamic SQL has the advantage of being more flexible, thus allowing for a wide variety of ad-hoc queries. Dynamic SQL has the disadvantage of being slower than static SQL because queries are built and compiled at run time. The fact that queries are compiled at run time can result in speed improvements, because the query optimizer uses the current database state. This tends especially to be true in highly volatile databases. The flexibility of dynamic SQL also tends to reduce the amount of code to be written for the object to database mapping, because all the information necessary for building a select statement can be defined at run time. If the amount of data processed in relation to queries made is small, the speed disadvantage of dynamic SQL is large. Object queries, when defined by the user at run time, can almost always be managed with reasonable programming effort when dynamic SQL is used.

Multiuser Concurrent Access

DSOM provides the mechanism of a server program. The server program, as previously described, is the place where objects are created or restored on behalf of the client. This process (the server program when in execution) acts as a database client to DB2/6000. To have multiple clients access the same database concurrently, each client has its own server process where it can create, store and restore, or delete objects at will. Issuing DB2 transaction API calls, the client can also commit or roll back these changes to the database.

When the SchemaMapper issues a query to read the object's data, it announces a read or write intent for the row(s) it is about to receive from the database. Objects are then materialized from the rows returned by the query. Any locks acquired are held for the time of the logical unit of work (LUW).

Object persistence design, focused on how the persistent data for the objects would be stored and retrieved in the target system. In our case study, we looked at the listed below. However, there was not much which needed to be modified from the original project on these designs :

❑ Model and design server databases

❑ Define the interactions between database objects and model objects

❑ Define the distribution of objects in users images

❑ Define access policies for retrieve update shared data.

Data Storage and Management

We still reuse the database design of the last project. The only thing we did was separated them into two databases.

Refer to appendix FCE Database Definitions on page 229 for the database table definitions.

11

Implementing the Distributed FCE Application

We used the IDL approach to implement the FCE sample application.

Implementing a distributed application whose parts were developed to run on different systems adds to the complexity of the development process.

The synchronization of the development of an application that spans heterogeneous environments is not an easy task. For a small project, team members can synchronize development by keeping one another informed. For a larger project, synchronization of development should be automated with the help of change management tools.

Server Implementation

This section presents the process of implementing a server by using the SOMobjects Developer Toolkit Version 2.1. The process focuses primarily on creating the class interfaces using IDL. The following are the major steps in the process:

1. Write the class description in IDL.
2. Register the classes in the SOM Interface Repository.

   Once the Interface Repository contains the class interface descriptions, implementation of the client can proceed in parallel with creating Smalltalk wrappers for SOM classes (see Section "Generating VisualAge SOM Wrapper Classes for the Client" on page 192). Registration of the class interface descriptions in the Interface Repository is a prerequisite for the SOM support of VisualAge to derive wrapper classes from SOM classes.

3. Generate and implement language bindings for C++ from IDL.
4. Generate C++ program skeleton code from IDL.
5. Create stub DLLs for all required SOM wrapper classes.
6. Generate data access (DAX) objects.
7. Implement the logic of the class methods in C++.
8. Compile the completed class source file.
9. Make SOM class implementation available as a class library.
10. Register class implementation with the DSOM Implementation Repository.

Before you can carry out the individual tasks of the server implementation process, you must prepare the development environment. The environment setup primarily controls the operation of the tools, such as the SOM compiler, but it can also help foster cooperation between the development teams assigned for client and server implementation.

SOM and DSOM require several environment variables to be set before any class is registered in the SOM Interface Repository or DSOM Implementation Repository.

For effective communication between the client development environment and server development environment, a shared file system is recommended. A file system helps ensure that information needed on both sides is consistent. In particular, the shared file system should include:

❑ The SOM Interface Repository

❑ The DSOM Implementation Repository

❑ The IDL files that are ready for client use.

Write Class Description in IDL

At this stage of the development process, the object-oriented design model specifies the classes and their relationships, attributes, and methods. During implementation, more classes are usually needed to keep implementation details separate from the essential classes of the model.

The first cut of the IDL can be derived directly from the object-oriented design model. CASE tools are available that are capable of generating IDL directly from an object-oriented design model. When IDL is to be created without support of any tool, describing the class interface is a straightforward task.

Some issues, such as the relationships between classes and object initialization, deserve special attention.

Class Relationships

Class relationships other than inheritance relationships can be implemented as attributes. The FCE application's design model contains the following class relationships:

❑ One-to-one between Country and Currency

❑ One-to-many between Customer and Account, and between Customer and Order

❑ Aggregation between Order and OrderItem.

The following definitions can be used to represent the relationship in IDL:

One-to-one   A one-to-one relationship can be implemented by defining an attribute that is an object reference in both related classes.

The one-to-one relationship between Country and Currency can be defined as:

```
interface Country
    .
    .
    .
attribute Country currency;
```

One-to-many One-to-many relationships between classes can be reflected in IDL files in two different ways.

The first one-to-many relationship is when the classes have a *structural relationship* that is, several classes are pieces of a "more complex class." In this case, the pieces tend to be referred to quite often during run-time. Hence, those objects should reside in memory, and the classes should be included inside the more complex class. For example, if class A has a one-to-many relationship with class B and class C, the following should be reflected in the IDL definitions of class A:

```
attribute sequence<classB> classBs
attribute sequence<classC> classCs;
```

In the FCE application, the relationship between SOMCustomer and SOMAccounts is a one-to-many relationship. The SOMCustomer has the following declared in its IDL file:

```
attribute<SOMAccount,20> accountList
```

where 20 indicates that each customer can hold at most 20 accounts under his/her name.

The second many-to-one relationship is when the one object *"knows of the many objects"*. In this case, it is sufficient to have the one object hold the many objects' keys rather than having the many objects included in the one object. Thus, if SOMCustomer wants to "know of the SOMAccounts" he/she holds, the IDL file of SOMCustomer could be declared like this:

```
attribute <long, 20> accountIDList
```

Aggregation Aggregation relationships between classes can be reflected in IDL files by defining an attribute that is a collection of objects in the aggregate class. The type of collection chosen depends on the intended use of the contained objects, such as an ordered or sorted sequence requirement. For example, in the FCE application, the Order class contains a number of Order-Items. In the IDL file for the Order class, the definition of the list of order items can be reflected like this:

```
attribute sequence<OrderItem> orderList
```

Object Initialization

SOM provides a somDefaultInit method to initialize instance variables and attributes in a newly created object. It also provides a somDestruct method for cleanup when the SOM object "dies." Both methods are similar to the constructor and destructor of the C++ language.

We recommend that the somDefaultInit and somDestruct methods always be overridden by implementation classes. To override the two methods, make sure that override is specified for them in the implementation section of the SOM IDL files:

```
implementation {
        .
        .
        .
    somDestruct: override;
    somDefaultInit: override;
        .
        .
            }
```

Register Classes in SOM Interface Repository

The SOM Interface Repository provides run-time access to all information in the IDL description of a class of objects.

DSOM, in particular, requires that object classes that will be accessed from another process have their interfaces added to the Interface Repository. It uses the interface information when transforming local method calls on proxies into request messages transmitted to remote objects.

The SOM support of VisualAge also uses information in the Interface Repository to create wrapper classes from it. These wrapper classes, in turn, define the interface of SOM objects to the Smalltalk environment.

The Cashier class is registered in the Interface Repository by using the following command:

```
sc -u -sir csh.idl
```

A class that has not been registered in the Interface Repository causes DSOM to generate a run-time error when an attempt is made to invoke a method of that class.

Generate Language Bindings for C++

Bindings make it easy for programmers to implement and use SOM classes. They define an interface to classes that enables programmers to declare objects and invoke methods in the same way they do for C++ objects.

The SOM compiler generates two different kinds of C++ binding files out of IDL files:

❑ Usage bindings provide the definitions needed to implement a client program using SOM classes. These usage binding files have the extension .xh.

❑ Implementation bindings provide the internal view of SOM classes needed by the class implementer. The implementation binding files have the extension .xih. They include the usage binding files.

Changes made to an IDL file are directly reflected in changes to the generated bindings. Therefore, each time IDL files are changed, the bindings must be regenerated.

The SOM compiler generates both usage and implementation bindings for the class Cashier through the following command:

```
sc -D__PRIVATE__ -D__SOMIDL__ -sxih:xh csh.idl
```

where the macro -D__PRIVATE__ causes the SOM compiler to omit everything marked as private by #ifdef __PRIVATE__ in the IDL. Thus, a public view is generated for use by clients.

-D__SOMIDL__ lets the SOM compiler make use of the implementation-specific definitions in the IDL, such as the release orde of methods and overridings.

-sxih:xh specifies which emitter is going to be invoked by the SOM compiler to produce output. Here, both usage bindings and implementation bindings are requested to be generated.

Generate C++ Program Skeleton Code from IDL

To assist users in implementing classes, the SOM compiler produces a C++ program skeleton file (also known as a template implementation file). This file contains all definitions and method prototypes that are needed for a class implementation, except the actual logic of the methods.

Specify the C++ emitter (xc) on the invocation of the SOM compiler:

```
sc -D__PRIVATE__ -D__SOMIDL__ -sxc .csh.idl
```

Before the business logic is implemented in the skeletons, **stub DLLs** are generated for the client through the C++ compiler. See Section "Creating Stub DLLs" on page 179 for more details.

Creating Stub DLLs

DSOM needs stub DLLs to access the class data structure of objects at run time. Stub DLLs are generated from C++ skeleton files, which are obtained from IDL through the SOM compiler in the server implementation process.

Stub DLLs are obtained through the C++ compiler. No business logic is added to the implementation skeletons. Because stub DLLs do not contain business logic, their *size* is considerably smaller than application DLLs (APP.DLLs).

Generate Data Access (DAX) Objects

SOM object classes require data access capabilities as part of their implemented logic. We can use VisualAge C++ Data Access (DAX) objects to provide SOM objects with the required data access capabilities. The DAX object of each SOM object can be generated by the Data Access Builder which is part of VisualAge C++ Version 3.

With the Data Access Builder, we can graphically create a data access class for each table of the database. In this section, we describe how to generate the SOMCustomer data access object. The procedures for generating data access objects for SOMAccount and SOMBank are very similar.

Before using the DAX builder, you must have the database in place and have the *FCE* userid as the qualifier for the database tables.

1. Open the Data Access Builder from the VisualAge C++ tools folder.
2. Click on the **Create Classes** push button from the Data Access Builder - startup window.
3. The Create classes window appears (see Figure 62 on page 180).
4. Select **CSOODB** and click on the **Connect** push button.
5. Select *FCE.Customer* and click the on **Create classes** push button.

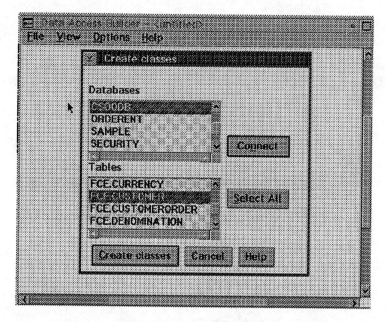

Figure 62. Connecting to the FCE.CUSTOMER Table

6. The Data Access Builder window appears (see Figure 63) with a Customer icon which represents the created customer data access class.

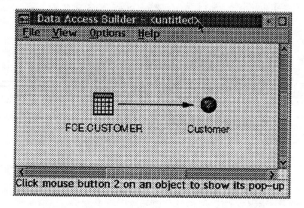

Figure 63. The Data Access Class Created for FCE.CUSTOMER Table.

7. Click on the Customer icon with mouse button 2 and choose **Open settings** to open the Settings notebook (refer to Figure 64 on page 181).

8. Change the Class name of the class from Customer to DaxCust and close the Settings window.

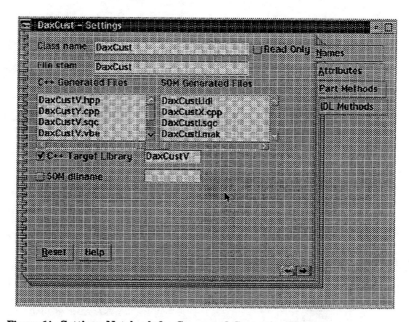

Figure 64. Settings Notebook for Generated Customer Class

9. Click on the DaxCust icon with mouse button 2 from the Data Access Builder window (refer to Figure 65 on page 182) and choose Generate -> Parts to generate the required sources.

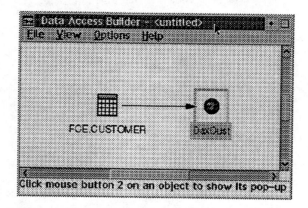

Figure 65. Renamed DaxCust Class

10. Exit the Data Access Builder window and choose *Save* when prompted.

11. The generated .cpp and .hpp files can be found in the \IBM-CPP\WORKING directory.

Adding Business Logic

Figure 66 on page 183 shows the C++ code template of the SOMAccount.CPP function template, which was generated by the SOM compiler.

```
/*
 *  This file was generated by the SOM Compiler and Emitter Framework.
 *  Generated using:  *      SOM Emitter emitxtm: 2.42
 */

#ifndef SOM_Module_somacct_Source
#define SOM_Module_somacct_Source
#endif
#define SOMAccount_Class_Source

#include "somacct.xih"

/*
 *Method from the IDL attribute statement:
 *"attribute string accountNumber"
 */

SOM_Scope string  SOMLINK _get_accountNumber(SOMAccount *somSelf,
                                             Environment *ev)
{
    SOMAccountData *somThis = SOMAccountGetData(somSelf);
    SOMAccountMethodDebug("SOMAccount","_get_accountNumber");

    /* Return statement to be customized: */
    { string retVal;   return (retVal); }
}

/*
 *Method from the IDL attribute statement:
 *"attribute string accountNumber"
 */

SOM_Scope void  SOMLINK _set_accountNumber(SOMAccount *somSelf,
                                           Environment *ev,
                                           string accountNumber)
{
    SOMAccountData *somThis = SOMAccountGetData(somSelf);
    SOMAccountMethodDebug("SOMAccount","_set_accountNumber");

}

/*
 *Method from the IDL attribute statement:
 *"attribute string branchId"
 */

SOM_Scope string  SOMLINK _get_branchId(SOMAccount *somSelf,
                                        Environment *ev)
{
```

Figure 66. (Part 1 of 4) SOMAcct.CPP Function Template Generated by SOM Compiler

```
    SOMAccountData *somThis = SOMAccountGetData(somSelf);
    SOMAccountMethodDebug("SOMAccount","_get_branchId");

    /* Return statement to be customized: */
    { string retVal;  return (retVal); }
}

/*
 *Method from the IDL attribute statement:
 *"attribute string branchId"
 */

SOM_Scope void  SOMLINK _set_branchId(SOMAccount *somSelf,
                              Environment *ev, string branchId)
{
    SOMAccountData *somThis = SOMAccountGetData(somSelf);
    SOMAccountMethodDebug("SOMAccount","_set_branchId");

}

/*
 *Method from the IDL attribute statement:
 *"attribute string accountDescription"

 */

SOM_Scope string  SOMLINK _get_accountDescription(SOMAccount *somSelf,
                                                Environment *ev)
{
    SOMAccountData *somThis = SOMAccountGetData(somSelf);
    SOMAccountMethodDebug("SOMAccount","_get_accountDescription");

    /* Return statement to be customized: */
    { string retVal;  return (retVal); }
}

 /*
 *Method from the IDL attribute statement:
 *"attribute string accountDescription"
 */


SOM_Scope void  SOMLINK _set_accountDescription(SOMAccount *somSelf,
                                          Environment *ev,
                                          string accountDescription)
{
    SOMAccountData *somThis = SOMAccountGetData(somSelf);
    SOMAccountMethodDebug("SOMAccount","_set_accountDescription");
}
```

Figure 66. (Part 2 of 4) SOMAcct.CPP Function Template Generated by SOM Compiler

```
SOM_Scope void  SOMLINK update(SOMAccount *somSelf, Environment *ev)
{
    SOMAccountData *somThis = SOMAccountGetData(somSelf);
    SOMAccountMethodDebug("SOMAccount","update");

}

 SOM_Scope void  SOMLINK add(SOMAccount *somSelf, Environment *ev)
{
    SOMAccountData *somThis = SOMAccountGetData(somSelf);
    SOMAccountMethodDebug("SOMAccount","add");

}

/*
 * Following methods return specific information of this SOMAccount object
 */

SOM_Scope void  SOMLINK del(SOMAccount *somSelf, Environment *ev)
{
    SOMAccountData *somThis = SOMAccountGetData(somSelf);
    SOMAccountMethodDebug("SOMAccount","del");

}

SOM_Scope boolean  SOMLINK isCheckingAccount(SOMAccount *somSelf,
                                             Environment *ev)
{
    SOMAccountData *somThis = SOMAccountGetData(somSelf);
    SOMAccountMethodDebug("SOMAccount","isCheckingAccount");

    /* Return statement to be customized: */
    { boolean retVal;  return (retVal); }
}

SOM_Scope boolean  SOMLINK isSavingsAccount(SOMAccount *somSelf,
                                            Environment *ev)
{
    SOMAccountData *somThis = SOMAccountGetData(somSelf);
    SOMAccountMethodDebug("SOMAccount","isSavingsAccount");

    /* Return statement to be customized: */
    { boolean retVal;  return (retVal); }
}

/*
 * SOM/DSOM specific stuffs
 */
```

Figure 66. (Part 3 of 4) SOMAcct.CPP Function Template Generated by SOM Compiler

```
SOM_Scope boolean  SOMLINK isSuperSavingsAccount(SOMAccount *somSelf,
                                                  Environment *ev)
{
    SOMAccountData *somThis = SOMAccountGetData(somSelf);
    SOMAccountMethodDebug("SOMAccount","isSuperSavingsAccount");

    /* Return statement to be customized: */
    { boolean retVal;  return (retVal); }
}

SOM_Scope void SOMLINK somDestruct(SOMAccount *somSelf, octet doFree,
                                   somDestructCtrl* ctrl)
{
    SOMAccountData *somThis; /* set in BeginDestructor */
    somDestructCtrl globalCtrl;
    somBooleanVector myMask;
    SOMAccountMethodDebug("SOMAccount","somDestruct");
    SOMAccount_BeginDestructor;

    /*
     * local SOMAccount deinitialization code added by programmer
     */

    SOMAccount_EndDestructor;
}


SOM_Scope void SOMLINK somDefaultInit(SOMAccount *somSelf, somInitCtrl* ctrl)
{
    SOMAccountData *somThis; /* set in BeginInitializer */
    somInitCtrl globalCtrl;
    somBooleanVector myMask;
    SOMAccountMethodDebug("SOMAccount","somDefaultInit");
    SOMAccount_BeginInitializer_somDefaultInit;

    SOMAccount_Init_SOMObject_somDefaultInit(somSelf, ctrl);

    /*
     * local SOMAccount initialization code added by programmer
     */
}
```

Figure 66. (Part 4 of 4) SOMAcct.CPP Function Template Generated by SOM Compiler

The SOMAccount.CPP file, with our logic added to it, is shown in the SOMAccnt implementation listing in Appendix E, "SOM Objects Implementation Files," on page 241.

SOMAccount Makefile

The next step is to compile and link the completed class source files to make the SOM class implementation available as a class library. Figure 67 shows the makefile to build the SOMAccount class for the distributed FCE application. The makefiles for building other classes are similar to the makefile for the SOMAccount class.

```
# Created by IBM WorkFrame/2 MakeMake at 20:39:05 on 25 May 1996
#
# The actions included in this make file are:
#   Compile::SOM Compiler
#   Compile::SQL Precompile
#   Compile::C++ Compiler
#   Link::Linker
#   Lib::Import Lib (from def)

.SUFFIXES: .CPP .DEF .IDL .LIB .SQC .c .OBJ

.all: \
    ..\..\BIN\SOMAcct.DLL \
    ..\..\BIN\TestAcct.EXE \
    SOMAcct.LIB

.IDL.cpp:
    @echo " Compile::SOM Compiler "
    SC.EXE -sxc %s
    @echo " Update Interface Repository"
    ..\UPDATEIR %s

.IDL.xih:
    @echo " Compile::SOM Compiler "
    SC.EXE -sxih %s

.IDL.xh:
    @echo " Compile::SOM Compiler "
    SC.EXE -sxh %s

.CPP.OBJ:
    @echo " Compile::C++ Compiler "
    ICC.EXE /I. /Oc /Tdp /Q /Gm+ /Gd /Ge- /G4 /C %s

.c.OBJ:
    @echo " Compile::C++ Compiler "
    ICC.EXE /I. /Oc /Tdc /Q /Gm+ /Gd /Ge- /G4 /C %s

..\..\BIN\SOMAcct.DLL: \
    .\SOMAcct.OBJ \
    .\DaxAcctY.OBJ \
    .\DaxAcctV.OBJ \
    SOMAcct.DEF
    @echo " Link::Linker "
  ICC.EXE @<<
    /Tdp
    /Oc /Q /Gm+ /Gd /Ge- /G4
    /B" /nologo"
    /Fe..\..\BIN\SOMAcct.DLL
    SOMAcct.OBJ
    DaxAcctY.OBJ
    DaxAcctV.OBJ
    SOMTk.LIB
    CPPOOC3I.LIB
    SOMAcct.DEF
```

Figure 67. (Part 1 of 3) Makefile Used to Build SOMAccount Class

```
<<
    DLLRNAME \FCE\BIN\SOMAcct.DLL CPPOM30=FCEOM30
    DLLRNAME \FCE\BIN\SOMAcct.DLL CPPOOB3=FCEOOB3
    DLLRNAME \FCE\BIN\SOMAcct.DLL CPPODS3I=FCEODS3I
..\..\BIN\TestAcct.EXE: \
    TestAcct.OBJ \
    SOMAcct.lib
    @echo " Link::Linker "
    ICC.EXE @<<
    /B" /nologo"
    /Fe..\..\BIN\TestAcct.EXE
    TestAcct.OBJ
    SOMTk.LIB
    SOMAcct.LIB
<<
    DLLRNAME \FCE\BIN\TestAcct.EXE CPPOM30=FCEOM30
    DLLRNAME \FCE\BIN\TestAcct.EXE CPPOOB3=FCEOOB3
    DLLRNAME \FCE\BIN\TestAcct.EXE CPPODS3I=FCEODS3I


SOMAcct.cpp: \
    SOMAcct.IDL

DaxAcctV.c: \
    DaxAcctV.SQC
    @echo " Compile::SQL Precompile "
    sqlprep.EXE DaxAcctV.SQC SOMBANK /B=..\..\BIN\DaxAcctV.BND /P

DaxAcctY.OBJ: \
    DaxAcctY.CPP \
    DaxAcctV.hpp

SOMAcct.OBJ: \
    SOMAcct.CPP \
    SOMAcct.xih

SOMAcct.xih: \
    SOMAcct.xh \
    SOMAcct.idl

SOMAcct.xh: \
    SOMAcct.idl

DaxAcctV.OBJ: \
    DaxAcctV.c

SOMAcct.OBJ: \
    SOMAcct.cpp

SOMAcct.LIB: \
    ..\..\BIN\SOMAcct.DLL
    @echo " Lib::Import Lib "
    implib.EXE SOMAcct.LIB %s

TestAcct.OBJ: \
    TestAcct.cpp \
    SOMAcct.xh
    @echo " Compile::C++ Compiler "
    ICC.EXE /I. /Oc /Tdp /Q /Gm+ /Gd /Ge+ /G4 /C %s
```

Figure 67. (Part 2 of 3) Makefile Used to Build SOMAccount Class

```
clean:
    if exist *.OBJ              del *.OBJ
    if exist *.xh              del *.xh
    if exist *.xih             del *.xih
    if exist *.lib             del *.lib
    if exist ..\..\BIN\SOMAcct.DLL    del ..\..\BIN\SOMAcct.DLL
    if exist ..\..\BIN\TestAcct.EXE   del ..\..\BIN\TestAcct.EXE
    if exist ..\..\BIN\DaxAcctV.bnd   del ..\..\BIN\DaxAcctV.bnd
    if exist DaxAcctV.C        del DaxAcctV.C
    if exist TEMPINC\*.CPP     del TEMPINC\*.CPP
    if exist TEMPINC\*.OBJ     del TEMPINC\*.OBJ
```

Figure 67. (Part 3 of 3) Makefile Used to Build SOMAccount Class

Register Server Objects

Register the server objects to the DSOM repository through the **pregimpl** utility. You can also use the command line utility, regimpl.

1. Add an implementation alias. Select **Add** from the **Implementations** pull-down menu in the DSOM Implementation Registration window (see Figure 68 on page 190). Fill in the **Alias** and **Host name** fields accordingly **Host name** is either the TCP/IP host name on the server machine or "localhost" if you want to put both the bank server and branch client on the same machine.

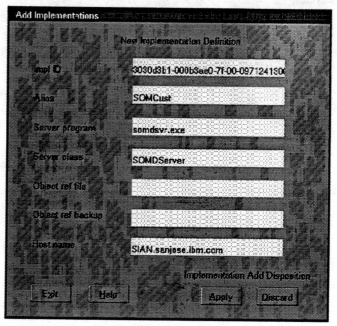

Figure 68. Adding the SOMCust Alias for the DSOM Repository

2. Define the class to DSOM and map the classes to the aliases. Select *Add* from the *Classes* pull-down menu in the DSOM Implementation Registration window (see Figure 69 on page 191). Enter *SOMCustomer* in the New Class Name field for the *SomCust* alias.

3. For a DSOM Workstation, both the client and server run on the same machine. The above procedures are sufficient for them to interoperate.

   For a DSOM WorkGroup, the client and the server run on different machines. For distributed objects to talk over DSOM, their implementation IDs must be identical. To generate identical implementation IDs:

   a. Make the client and server share the same implementation files through a shared file system.

   b. Copy the implementation files from one machine to the other.

The implementation files are located in the directory pointing to the %SOMDDIR% environment variable.

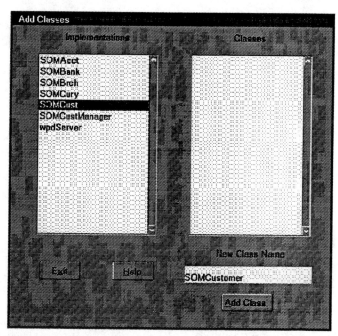

Figure 69. Adding a New Class and Mapping It to the Defined DSOM Alias

Client Implementation

The client part of the application was developed entirely in VisualAge.

The functions implemented in the client were those that enabled the cashier to:

❑ Log onto the system

❑ Query and update customer information.

The connection with the server part of the application was through VisualAge wrapper classes. In our implementation, we extended the SOM wrapper classes (see discussions in Section "Effects of Extending the SOM Wrapper Classes" on page 167 for precautions).

The presentation part of a nondistributed application is dependent on the model classes of that application for its business function and data. This is also true in a distributed application. By using DSOM, these classes are defined in IDL statements. VisualAge SOMsupport can create wrapper classes from compiled IDL statements, which will to be stored in the Interface Repository. Assuming that the Interface Repository exists and is stable enough to be used, the steps for implementing the client code are as follows:

1. Set up the environment to use VisualAge and DSOM as described in Appendix B, "Setting Up the Implementation Platform," on page 221.

2. Create the wrapper classes needed on the client side from the Interface Repository.

3. Create the nonvisual parts by extending the SOM wrapper classes.

4. Add the desired methods and variables and make the interface public with the VisualAge Public Interface Editor.

5. Create the visual parts and composite visual parts and connect them to the other parts of the system.

6. Test and iterate this process.

Generating VisualAge SOM Wrapper Classes for the Client

VisualAge SOMsupport includes a framework of Smalltalk classes called the SOM Smalltalk Constructor. These classes provide the ability to generate the Smalltalk wrapper classes that represent SOM classes based on interface definitions that have been compiled from IDL files and stored in the SOM Interface Repository. Figure 42 on page 105 shows this process.

To generate SOM wrapper classes, you can either use the VisualAge visual interface or Smalltalk programmatic interface. Before generating SOM wrapper classes, ensure that the SOMsupport feature has been loaded into the VisualAge Smalltalk image on the client workstation.

Using the VisualAge Visual Interface

The VisualAge visual interface enables you to create SOM wrapper classes or explore class structures, as defined in the Interface Repository.

To generate SOM wrapper classes through the VisualAge visual interface, follow this procedure for SOMCustomer below. The procedures for SOMBank and SOMAccount are similar.

1. Create an application to hold the SOM objects. We created an application named FCESOMObjects.

2. Click on the Parts container with mouse button 2 (as shown in Figure 70) and select *Generate* and then select *SOM Wrappers*.

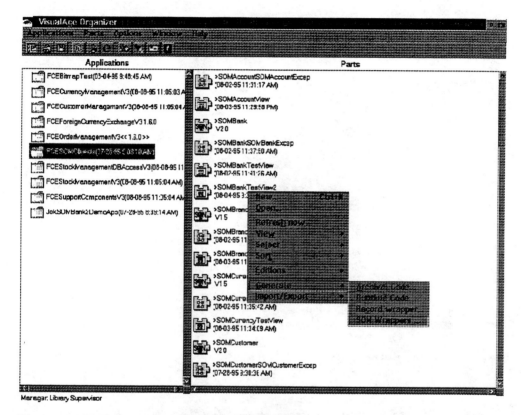

Figure 70. Generating a SOM Wrapper Class (Part 1)

3. The Create SOM Wrappers window appears (Figure 71 on page 194). Scroll down the list box to find the SOMCustomer class.[13] Select SOMCustomer, click on the *DSOM:* radio button, and then press *OK* to generate the SOMWrapper.

Note: If there is an existing SOMCustomer wrapper class, the wrapper generator modifies only what has to be modified and does not change anything that you previously added.

---

[13] VisualAge obtains the information from the Interface Repositories of the system. The information required was added by the SOM Compiler during the SOM compilation phase (that is, an option of -usir was specified when running SC.EXE against the corresponding IDL files).

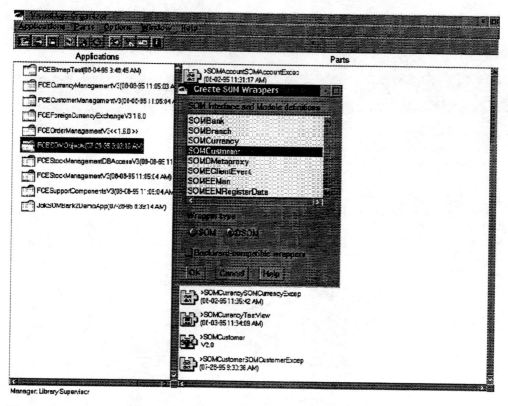

Figure 71. Generating a SOM Wrapper Class (Part 2)

Using the Smalltalk Programmatic Interface

You can also use the programmatic interface to generate SOM wrapper classes by writing Smalltalk code. See the online reference book "VisualAge for Smalltalk: Features Class Guide and References," for details on generating wrapper classes through this interface.

Modifying the FCE Application To Use SOM Objects

This section describes the changes required to extend the FCE application to use SOM objects. The changes involve modification in some visual parts and some Smalltalk coding.

Visual Parts

Figure 72 and Figure 73 on page 196 show the CustomerQueryView before and after modification, respectively. Notice that few changes are required. In fact, a good design and analysis model results in minimal changes to the code of the client platform.

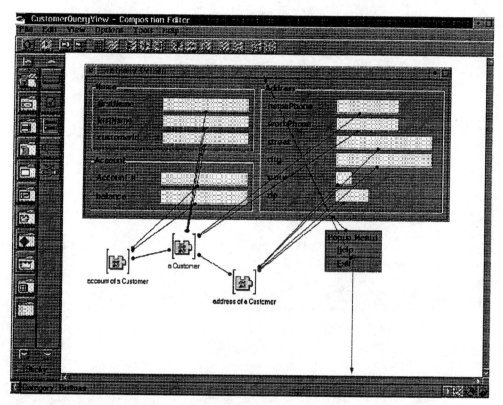

Figure 72. CustomerQueryView Before Modification

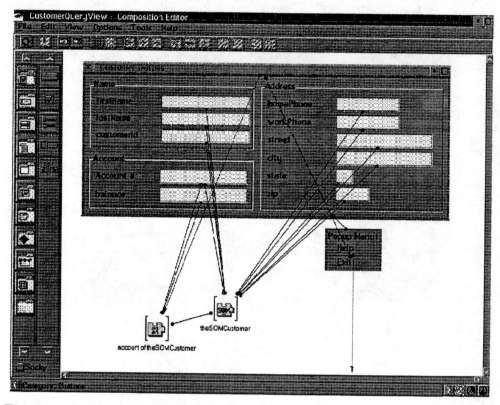

Figure 73. CustomerQueryView After Modification

Script

Figure 74 on page 197 shows the script after modification. Note that we removed all the direct database access logic in the original FCE application and instead obtained customer, bank, and account information from the respective SOM objects.

Notice that the use of the objects to populate the views is the same for both "ordinary" Smalltalk objects and SOM objects. In fact, only the name we used indicates whether it is SOM object or not.

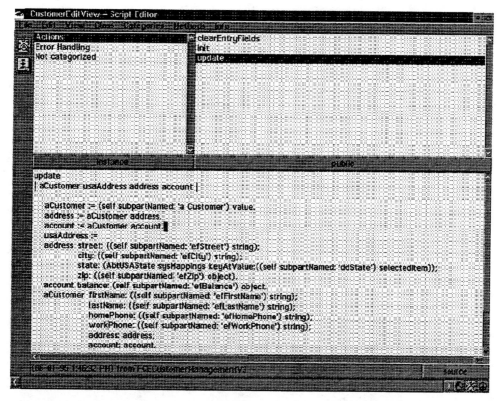

Figure 74. CustomerQueryView and Script After Modification

Considerations for Using VisualAge SOMsupport

This section describes some important points to consider when using VisualAge Smalltalk SOMsupport to develop distributed object applications.

Support of SOM Data Types

SOMsupport Version 3.0 supports basic and composite SOM data types, as well as some SOM-unique data types, and in addition to those specified in the CORBA specification.[14]

Basic Data Types

Figure 75 maps SOM basic data types to their equivalent Smalltalk classes. A Smalltalk wrapper method requires as input, or returns as output, an object of the equivalent Smalltalk class.

```
SOM                     Smalltalk
---------------         -----------------------------------------

boolean                 Boolean (true or false)
char                    Character
float                   Float
double                  Float
short                   Integer (between -2^15 and 2^15-1)
long                    Integer (between -2^31 and 2^31-1)
unsigned short          Integer (between 0 and 2^16-1)
unsigned long           Integer (between 0 and 2^32-1)
octet                   Integer (betwen 0 and 255)
string                  String
```

Figure 75. VisualAge Smalltalk Equivalents of SOM Basic Data Types

Composite Data Types

Figure 76 on page 199 maps SOM composite data types to their equivalent Smalltalk classes. SOMsupport provides special classes for SOM data types that have no direct Smalltalk equivalents.

---

[14] The data representations from SOMsupport Version 2.0 continue to be supported when the Version 2.0 Migration Facility support is loaded. However, combining Version 2.0 data representations with Version 3.0 methods or Version 3.0 data representations with Version 2.0 methods is generally not supported.

```
SOM                    Smalltalk or SOMsupport special     Notes
---------------        --------------------------------    -----
array                  Array                               1
enum                   SOMEnumerator                       2
sequence               OrderedCollection                   3
any                    (see notes)                         4
struct                 LookupTable (implicit)              5
                       unique subclass of Object (explicit)
union                  Smalltalk object whose class        6
                       maps to one of the types
                       in the union (implicit)
                       instance of SOMUnion (explicit)
pointer                (see notes)                         7
self                   (not supported)
foreign                parameters or return values         8
                       with foreign data types that are
                       passed as simple pointers
```

Figure 76. VisualAge Smalltalk Equivalents of SOM Composite Data Types

Notes:

Note 1: SOMsupport does not support multi-dimensional arrays.

Note 2: SOM enumerators map to instances of the Smalltalk SOMEnumerator class. These instances are stored both in the CORBAConstants dictionary, keyed by their fully-qualified names, and in the SOMGlobals pool dictionary, keyed by their Smalltalk names.

Instances of SOMEnumerator support the full range of comparison operations, as described in the OMG Smalltalk mapping specification, including $<$, $<=$, $=$, $>$, and $>=$.

Note 3: The OrderedCollection class has been extended with two instance methods: length and buffer. These methods correspond to the members of the structure used in the C or C++ bindings for sequences.

Note 4: The actual value of *any* determines which Smalltalk class is used. An application can test the class of an incoming *any* to determine what it is. For an outgoing *any* parameter, you can pass any Smalltalk object that maps to a SOM type.

Note 5: Implicit binding takes maximum advantage of the dynamic nature of Smalltalk. It is the least intrusive binding for the Smalltalk programmer. The explicit binding retains the value of the discriminator, and provides greater control for the Smalltalk programmer (see Section "Implicit and Explicit Binding" on page 200 for more details).

- *struct* mapping with implicit binding: A SOM structure maps to LookupTable, a subclass of Dictionary. The key for each structure member is an atom, whose value is the name of the member converted to Smalltalk naming conventions.
- *struct* mapping with explicit binding: If a SOM struct specifies explicit binding, the structure is mapped to a uniquely named subclass of Object. The class name is the fully qualified name of the structure converted to Smalltalk class name syntax.

Note 6: A SOM *union* maps in one of two ways, depending on whether the IDL file specifies explicit or implicit binding for the *union*:

- *union* mapping with implicit binding: The value of the union maps to a Smalltalk object whose class maps to one of the types in the *union*.
- *union* mapping with explicit binding: A SOM *union* maps to an instance of SOMUnion. You then interact with this object to set or retrieve the actual value, or to change the discriminator through the methods provided by the SOMUnion object.

Note 7: In general, Smalltalk handles all necessary pointer conversions so programmers can deal directly with the object representing the data being pointed to on the Smalltalk side.

However, SOMsupport deals with some special cases. For example, some SOM methods accept a NULL pointer as input or can return a NULL pointer. If you specify nil as an input parameter, a NULL pointer is passed to SOM. Likewise, any SOM method that creates an object (such as somNew), returns a NULL pointer if the object cannot be created.

Another special case is associated with parameters or returned values that are specified in IDL as *void**. In this case, the pointer itself is the data, so it must be preserved.

Note 8: SOM foreign data are not fully described in the SOM Interface Repository. Thus, SOMsupport cannot correctly map foreign types to Smalltalk class equivalents. Parameters or return values that have foreign data types are passed in and out of Smalltalk as simple pointers. The SOMsupport application and SOM object implementation must ensure the validity of these pointers by copying data where necessary.

Implicit and Explicit Binding

For the *struct* and *union* data types, SOMsupport recognizes a modifier that controls the type of mapping to Smalltalk objects. Implicit binding is the default; the IDL file is not modified for implicit binding.

To set explicit binding, use the SOM modifier, ssc_explicit_mapping, in the implementation section of the IDL file. For example, the following partial IDL specification sets explicit binding for a union named *foo*:

```
interface FuObject : SOMObject
{
  attribute union foo;
  #ifdef __SOMIDL__
  implementation
  {
    releaseorder : _get_foo, _set_foo;
    ssc_explicit_mapping : foo;
    ...
  };
```

Memory Management

Because SOM objects exist outside the Smalltalk address space, Smalltalk's built-in memory management facilities cannot control the allocation and freeing of memory used for SOM objects. As a result, several special memory management considerations apply to applications that use SOM objects.

Freeing Objects

A Smalltalk object exists as long as it is in use. When an object is no longer referenced by any other object, the Smalltalk system automatically destroys it and frees the memory associated with it.

SOM objects, however, exist outside the Smalltalk image in ordinary system memory. Therefore, when a SOM object is no longer needed, your application must explicitly destroy the object and free the associated memory.

If the SOM object is used in the VisualAge Composition Editor, you can connect the closedWidget event of your main view to the somFree action of any SOM objects in the view. This connection will generate an operation that destroys the SOM object when the view closes.

Passing Pointers

The absolute memory address of a Smalltalk object can change dynamically as the Smalltalk memory-management system reallocates storage. Therefore, Smalltalk objects cannot be referenced by address. This presents a problem when Smalltalk objects are supplied as parameters to SOM method calls because pointers to Smalltalk objects cannot be safely passed outside the Smalltalk environment.

To handle this situation, a wrapper method that takes arguments does not directly pass to SOM objects pointers to Smalltalk objects. Instead, it copies each Smalltalk object's data into SOM memory, where its address remains constant. The wrapper also passes a pointer to the copied data to the SOM method.

This copy persists only for the duration of the method call. Therefore, a SOM object must not cache pointers to this data for reference during subsequent method calls. Instead, it must make its own copy of the data and refer to that copy.

Copying Parameter Values

Any SOM object method that receives parameters from Smalltalk must perform a deep copy of the parameter values. This requirement applies to the local object, as well as the object located on a remote machine. For example, if a SOM object method takes as a parameter a structure containing a string, the method must make a copy of the string, rather than simply copying the pointer value.

The reason for the deep copy is that any pointers passed outside the Smalltalk image are pointers to copies of the original data, and these copies exist only for the duration of the method call. The result of a shallow copy of a pointer, therefore, is a pointer to freed memory.

The default set method implementation generated by the SOM compiler performs only a shallow copy. When implementing a SOM object that you intend to use with SOMsupport, do not use the default SOM set method for any data type that involves indirection, such as pointers and strings, or for structures that contain them. You can control this by specifying the noset modifier in your IDL.

Exception Handling

SOMsupport Version 3.0 maps SOM exceptions to Smalltalk ExceptionalEvents, extending the full power of Smalltalk exception handling to SOM exceptions. Unlike SOMsupport Version 2.0, you do not have to resume from a walkback to clear the SOM exception.

Here is the Smalltalk exception tree for SOM exceptions:

```
ExAll
  'ExCORBASystem'
    '::StExcep::BAD_OPERATION'
    '::StExcep::INITIALIZE'
    '::StExcep::MARSHAL'
    ...
```

```
'ExCORBAUser'
  '::SOMUserClassA::SOMUserException1'
  '::SOMUserClassA::SOMUserException2'
  '::SOMUserClassA::SOMUserException3'
  ...
```

The CORBAConstants dictionary contains these exception definitions, using the fully-qualified exception name as the key. The SOMGlobals pool dictionary contains these exception definitions, using the Small-talk names as the key.

ExCORBASystem and ExCORBAUser serve as the root for their respective subtrees and provide the default SOM exception handlers. These default handlers report a resumable error to the active process. Complete information for both System and User exceptions is provided in the signal arguments.

IDL allows each operation to include information about the kinds of run-time errors that may be encountered. This information is specified in exception definitions that declare the name of the exception, and an optional error structure to be returned if the exception is detected. For example, look at the partial IDL interface specification for SOMCustomer:

```
#include <somobj.idl>
#include <snglicls.idl>
interface SOMCustomer: SOMObject
{
  // exception to be raised on problem.
  exception SOMCustomer_Excep {
        long errCode;
        char reason[81];
  };
  ...
```

SOM exceptions will be handled automatically by the SOMsupport code as described above, unless you specify alternative handling. The default handling is designed for a development environment. You can code a specific exception handler for the raised exception if you want to override default handling for run time (see the online reference book *VisualAge for Smalltalk: Features Class Guide and References* for examples of coding exception handlers).

Redirecting SOM Character Output to Smalltalk

SOM provides a set of APIs that SOM objects can use to create printed output. In VisualAge Version 2.0 SOMsupport, the only way to see this output was to start IBM Smalltalk or VisualAge with STDOUT redirected to a file: abt > stdout.som or ibmst > stdout.som. However, using this mechanism, the output could not be seen until the file closed, which happened when IBM Smalltalk or VisualAge was shut down. Because SOM trace output is usually produced for debugging, having to end an IBM Smalltalk or VisualAge session to see the trace output can have a significant impact on a programmer's productivity. VisualAge V.3 SOMsupport includes a new class, SOMOutChar, to support the character output redirection function.

The easiest way to use this function is to redirect SOM character output to the Transcript:[15]

```
SOMOutChar on: Transcript
```

All output from the SOM print routines now appears on the Transcript until the redirection ends:

```
SOMOutChar close
```

You can also see the SOM trace output in its own window:

```
SOMOutChar on:
  (EtWorkspace new label: 'SOM Trace Output'; open)
```

To make the most effective use of SOMOutChar support, you can wrap your use of output redirection in an exception handler (see the online reference *VisualAge for Smalltalk: Features Class Guide and Reference* for more details about this wrapping technique).

Setting Up an Individual Test Environment

Testing the client part of a distributed application requires that the developer consider whether to test with or without the server part. Although the final integration test must be performed with the complete system, there are times when testing the client without the server is desirable.

Testing the Client Code Without the Server

Many variations are possible for setting up a test environment where server code is not active. One elegant way can be used when the aggregation scheme proposed in this book is followed. When the aggregation is established, if a test class is obtained instead of a wrapper class, a test environment without a server can be established. These test classes must have all methods of the wrapper classes they replace and return values good enough to enable the tests. It may, in fact, be worthwhile to automate this mechanism.

---

[15] When using the SOMOutChar capability, you can get into situations where you get a large volume of output that you do not really want. In such situations, you can execute a system break (Alt+Sys-Req) to stop Smalltalk.

Testing the Client Code With the Server

While testing the client part of an application, instances of SOM wrapper classes are created. This causes DSOM to consult both the Interface Repository, as well as the Implementation Repository, in the course of creating server objects on the server machine and proxies on the client machine.

The Implementation Repository is queried to find the server implementation's host and implementation ID. This implementation ID is passed to the DSOM daemon on the server machine, where it is used to query the Implementation Repository to start the correct server program.

Because the implementation ID must be identical in both queries, the setup of the test environment should ensure that the information used to create the implementation ID is shared between client and server machines. An easy way to ensure consistent information is to share a file system between participating systems. The shared file system keeps the valid copies of both the Interface Repository and Implementation Repository for testing.

Another very important point to remember is to verify the existence of stub DLLs before starting the test, as described in the *SOMObjects Developers Toolkit User's Guide*, and in Section "Creating Stub DLLs" on page 179.

Additional Considerations

Listed below are additional points to consider when using VisualAge Smalltalk SOMsupport to develop distributed object applications.

❑ If you test both the client and server in the same OS/2 machine, you can omit the installation of SOMObjects Toolkit V2.1. The SOMObjects Base Toolkit is sufficient for a DSOM Workstation. Following are applicable points for VisualAge C++ Version 3.0:

➢ VisualAge Smalltalk V3 SOMsupport is shipped with SOMobjects Toolkit at CSD 2.1.2. However, SOMobjects shipped with VisualAge C++ V3 is at CSD 2.1.1. If you do not apply CSD 2.1.2, VisualAge SOM wrapper generation will not work properly.

➢ You will probably have a problem running the DSOM environment because of a missing file, SOMSEC.DLL. You have to obtain the file from SOMObjects Toolkit V2.1 or from workstations that have the file.

➤ You must modify the SOMCORBA.CMD and SOMXH.CMD files in the \IBMCPP\BIN directory, as well as the %SOM-BASE%\INCLUDE reference to the %SOM-BASE%\INCLUDE\SOM directory.

➤ A number of IDL files are located in the \IBMCPP\INCLUDE directory rather than in the \IBMCPP\INCLUDE\SOM directory. You must copy them to the SOM directory to build the corresponding header files before running SOMCORBA.CMD and SOMXH.CMD.

➤ Ensure that SOMCORBA.CMD, followed by SOMXH.CMD, is run before any C++ development is done.

❑ The generated makefiles from Project Smartz did not fit our requirements for building the server DLLs. However, you can use Project Smartz to generate a makefile and manually edit it to suit your requirements (see Section "SOMAccount Makefile" on page 187).

❑ For the FCE application, we commented out the line

```
#pragma library("DaxyyyyV.LIB")
```

in the DaxyyyyV.hpp, where yyyy can be cust, bank, or acct.

❑ If you make any modifications in the IDL file that affect the release order or signature of the interfaces, you must regenerate the corresponding SOM wrapper class in VisualAge Smalltalk. Failure to do so will cause problems in the Smalltalk environment,

❑ Whenever possible, use a simple C or C++ program to test the SOM server objects that you developed. Try not to use VisualAge Smalltalk to test an unstable server program.

❑ If you have a SOM object with sequence as the attribute, take great care when wrapping it in the VisualAge Smalltalk environment. The sequence will be mapped to a Smalltalk OrderedCollection class. However, as the Collection in Smalltalk is unbounded, the maximum value for the sequence is set to 0. If you take the maximum value of the sequence attribute and use it, problems could occur on the server side.

❑ Exercise caution when handling memory pointers on the server side.

12

Looking Ahead

Most object-oriented applications today are either stand-alone applications accessing database servers, or front-ends to legacy applications. However, to unleash the full power of object technology, we must build distributed object applications with interoperability among objects on heterogeneous platforms. The distributed objects can interact if they conform to a universally accepted object architecture. This interaction mechanism is defined by an ORB. CORBA 2.0 defines interoperable ORBs, which enable ORBs from different vendors to interoperate.

IBM has embraced CORBA, the OMG-defined architecture, and has delivered DSOM, a complete CORBA-compliant implementation of an ORB. The SOMObjects Toolkit enables programmers to build DSOM-based distributed applications. However, the complexity of the toolkit requires special skills to build real-world distributed object applications.

The technology is evolving, and the IBM products are starting to provide facilities to ease the implementation of distributed object applications. VisualAge Smalltalk SOMsupport facilitates the use of SOM objects, and the direct-to-SOM compile options of VisualAge C++ compilers help the application programmer concentrate on business logic, and not spend too much time on tedious implementation details.

Other facilities soon to be seen stem from the new SOM frameworks, such as the Persistence Framework, which helps decouple an object application from the complexities of the underlying repository where the persistent objects are stored. Other frameworks will provide transaction and unit of work management.

One of the major requirements for distributed applications is a distributed debugging facility, because today, when errors occur in a distributed system, it is quite difficult to find the faulty software component.

Another requirement is a facility to handle configuration management of source code in a distributed environment when clients and servers use different library systems.

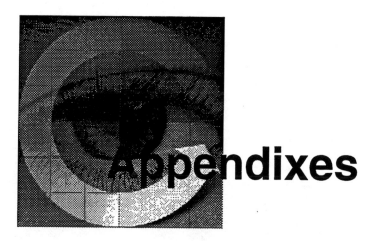

Appendixes

A

Requirement Specifications

This appendix describes the requirements specifications for the Foreign Currency Exchange (FCE) application.

Branch Functions

Because smaller branches do not maintain their own stocks of foreign currency and travelers checks, they can satisfy demand only by ordering from the center on the customer's behalf. Larger branches maintain some stocks, and customer sales and purchases are handled by cashiers allocated to a foreign currency and travelers check "bureau" within the branch.

Functions performed at the branch include:

❑ Customer order management

➢ Customer purchases from branch cashier.

This is the most frequently performed function in this application. Purchases are normally for one currency and one check for the destination country. Payment for this service can be by cash, credit card, local check, or a debit to the customer's account.

Stock levels are reduced, a customer tab is printed, and accounting entries are passed to the accounts application.

Other activities of this function include:

- Check stock levels

- Reduce branch stock level

- Determine currency and/or check denominations (small, mix, large, or specified)

- Obtain exchange rate

- Print tab (duplicate for signature)

- Generate accounting entries (debit currency code and credit dollars branch account)

- Handle multiple currencies

- Handle multiple currencies and checks

- Handle country restrictions, warnings, general information.

➤ Customer sells to branch cashier.

Note: This function is not implemented in the application.

Tourists and travelers returning with excess currency and checks sell or cash in currency and checks to the bank. Notes and checks are checked for forgeries by reference to textual information on legitimate denominations, descriptions, and known forgery defects. Other activities in this function are:

- Obtain exchange rates

- Increase branch stock level

- Print tab (duplicate for signature)

- Handle multiple currencies

- Handle multiple currencies and checks

- Pass accounting entries (debit currency codes and credit dollars branch account).

➤ Customer has order form that cannot be satisfied.

Note: This function is not implemented in the application.

Not all branches stock currencies and checks. Very few branches stock the full range as this would not be economical. All orders that cannot be met by the branch are routed to the center. If payment has been made or the customer has an account with the bank, the currencies or checks will be sent to the customer's address; otherwise, they will be sent to the branch for collection later. Other activities in this function are:

- Handle country restrictions, warnings, general information
- Handle currency and/or check denominations (small, mix, large, or specified)
- Handle multiple currencies
- Handle multiple currencies and checks
- Obtain exchange rate
- Take deposit if noncustomer
- Print tab (duplicate for signature)
- Pass accounting entries (debit currency code and credit dollars branch account).

❏ Cashier management

➤ Cashier stock reconciliation.

At the end of each day, or more frequently, each cashier must verify that the checks and foreign currency in his/her cabinet are equal to the totals held in the system. This is done by viewing the values for each denomination held, within each currency or check.

If these totals cannot be reconciled, the discrepancy is passed to an Overs and Shorts account, and the totals are amended accordingly.

Authority can be granted only by a supervisor.

Activities include:

- Obtain exchange rate for each currency or check
- Display totals of each currency or check and local currency equivalent
- Display totals of each currency or check denomination and local currency equivalent
- Order replenishment stock if minimum stock quantity reached
- Send excess stock to center if maximum stock quantity exceeded
- Display total local currency equivalent
- Raise compensating accounting entries for small losses or gains
- Archive reconciliation

❏ Branch management

Note: Branch management functions are not implemented in the application.

➤ Branch stock replenishment.

At the end of each day, cashier requests are consolidated. Each request can be an order either to replenish stock or to send excess stock. A consolidated branch order is then sent to the center.

➤ General inquiry of branch stocks.

Similar to customer order (branch), but no update intent.

➤ General inquiry of central stocks.

Similar to customer order (center), but no update intent.

➤ Forgery recognition (computer image).

Inquiry only (compare image to real note and verify descriptive information on which faults to look for).

Center Functions

The center is responsible for supplying foreign currency and travelers checks to the branches (outlets) and selling off excess foreign currency received from branches. It does this by dealing on the foreign currency markets, arranging bulk shipments at favorable exchange rates.

Functions performed at the center include:

❏ Bank management

Note: The bank management functions are not implemented in the application.

➤ Process branch order.

Orders from branches are typically for several currencies and checks. All orders are processed in batch mode, bulk quantities are picked, delivery arrangements are made, postal charges are set, stock levels are reduced, and accounting entries are passed between the branch and central accounts.

Branch order functions include:

- Determine currency and/or check denominations (small, mix, large, specified)
- Check stock levels
  - Single currency
  - Single checks

- •Multiple currencies
- •Multiple checks
- •Multiple currencies and checks
- Print picking lists
- Reduce center stock level
- Obtain exchange rate
- Weigh packages and establish postal charges
- Print branch documents
- Pass accounting entries (debit currency code; credit dollars for center account).

➤ Process customer order.

When branches are unable to satisfy any part of a customer order, the whole order is supplied by the center. Purchases are typically for one currency and one check for the destination country.

If payment for this service has been made at the branch, the foreign currency and travelers checks will be mailed to the customer; otherwise, they will be mailed to the branch for collection.

Stock levels are reduced, a customer tab is printed, and accounting entries are passed to the accounts application.

Customer order functions include:

- Handle country restrictions, warnings, general information
- Handle currency and/or check denominations (small, mix, large, or specified)
- Handle check stock levels
- Handle single currency
- Handle single checks
- Handle multiple currencies
- Handle multiple checks
- Handle multiple currencies and checks
- Print picking lists
- Reduce center stock level
- Weigh packages and establish postal charges
- Obtain exchange rate
- Print customer tab

- Pass accounting entries (debit currency code; credit dollars for center account)

➤ Handle branch excess.

Excess foreign currency received from the branches is counted, reconciled with the branch delivery record, and added to central stocks. When a customer does not accept an order sent by the center to the branch for collection, reversing accounting entries for this cancellation or return are passed.

Customer order functions include:

- Add to central stock
- Match value to branch file
- Pass accounting entries
- Reverse entry for cancellations and/or returns.

➤ Reconcile central stock.

At the end of each day, or more frequently, the center verifies that the checks and foreign currency in its stocks are equal to the totals held in the system. This is done by viewing the values for each denomination within each currency or check, and counting the actual stock.

If these totals cannot reconcile, the discrepancy is passed to an Overs and Shorts account, and the totals are amended accordingly.

Authority can be granted only by the senior manager.

Activities include:

- Obtain exchange rate for each currency and/or check
- Display totals of each currency and/or check and local currency equivalent
- Display totals of each currency and/or check denomination and local currency equivalent
- Order replenishment, if minimum stock quantity reached, from other banks (United States and abroad) through foreign note dealers
- Sell excess, if maximum stock quantity is exceeded, to other banks (United States and abroad) through foreign note dealers
- Display total local currency equivalent
- Raise compensating accounting entries for small losses and/or gains
- Archive reconciliation

➤ Maintain branch stock limits.

Periodically, the stock held at each branch is reviewed to check whether the stock minimum and maximum levels are still appropriate. A number of "what if" conditions are used to establish a revised set of limits, including seasonal, period on period, and general demand conditions.

Stock limit processing includes:

- Generally inquire as to whether stock levels are still valid.

    •Seasonal change, period on period demand change, abnormal condition, and so forth.

- Change stock level minimum or maximum

- Add or remove stock type or denomination

➤ Maintain center stock limits.

Similar to branch, but includes issues of bulk transport, international availability, and capacity.

➤ Maintain exchange rates.

Dealers maintain the rates for each currency and check by comparing with other banks' rates, general market rates from Reuters, Telerate, and the like, and by checking general availability.

A different rate may be applied for small and large denominations.

➤ Process miscellaneous transactions.

- Maintain forgery images

- Create, amend, and delete currency images

- Produce customer labels, envelopes, and documents

- Produce branch sack labels and documents.

B

Setting Up the Implementation Platform

This appendix presents the hardware and software prerequisites for developing and implementing the FCE DSOM application.

Recommended Hardware

The following hardware provided acceptable performance for development in our FCE DSOM case study:

☐ Client machine

   ➤ IBM PS/2 486, 50 MHz, 32 MB RAM, 120 MB or more DASD

☐ Server machine

   ➤ IBM PS/2 486, 50 MHz, 32MB RAM, 250 MB or more DASD

Required System Software

The following required software products were installed:

❏ Client machine

> ➤ OS/2 Warp V3
> ➤ TCP/IP OS/2 V2.0
> ➤ VisualAge for Smalltalk OS/2 V3.0
> ➤ SOMObjects WorkGroup Enabler V2.1[17]
> ➤ DB2/2 V1.2 [16]

❏ Server machine

> ➤ OS/2 Warp V3
> ➤ TCP/IP OS/2 V2.0
> ➤ VisualAge C++ for OS/2 V3.0
> ➤ SOMObjects WorkGroup Enabler V2.1[17]
> ➤ DB2/2 V1.2

We used TCP/IP as the means of communication between client and server machines. NetBIOS or IPX can also be used.

Setting Up the Server System

Figure 77 on page 223 shows an overview of how the server application is implemented on the server machine.

---

[17] SOMObjects WorkGroup Enabler is required for DSOM Workgroup (that is, for communication between two machines). If DSOM WorkStation is used, SOMobjects Workgroup Enabler is not required.

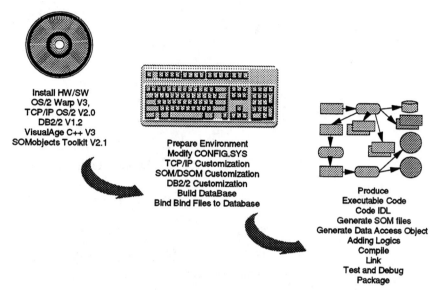

Figure 77. Implementation of Server Application

We carried out the following steps to develop the bank server (see Figure 77 on page 223). For detailed programming code, see SOM Objects Implementation Files on page 241.

1. Prepare environment.

   All of the server files were located in the D:\FCE directory. The subdirectories of the D:\FCE directory were:

   - BIN - contained the actual executable of the servers. (For the client machine, it contained the exported library file of the VisualAge Smalltalk application.)

   - SOMSRV - contained sources of servers.

   - DATABASE - contained exported IXF files and batch programs used to re-create the databases.

2. Install and set up the following required software (refer to the installation manuals accompanying the software):

   - OS/2 Warp V3

   - TCP/IP for OS/2 V2.0

   - DB2/2 V1.2

   - VisualAge C++ for OS/2 V3

   - SOMObjects WorkGroup Enabler V2.1 (for DSOM Workgroup)

- Fixes (for SOM/DSOM, Level SM21001)
- Create a userid FCE with password PASSWORD.

3. Modify CONFIG.SYS file.

   After modifying the CONFIG.SYS file, reboot the machine before performing Step 4.

   a. Add D:\FCE\BIN to the LIBPATH statement:

      ```
      LIBPATH=. C:\OS2;.....;D:\FCE\BIN
      ```

   b. Add D:\FCE\SOMBANK.IR to the SOMIR statement:

      ```
      SET SOMIR=D:\IBMCPP\ETC\SOM.IR D:\FCE\SOMBANK.IR
      ```

   c. If there is a ;SOMIR; statement in the SOMIR environment variable, remove it.

   d. Add the following two environment variables:

      ```
      SET SOMSOCKETS=TCPIPSockets
      SET USER=FCE
      ```

   e. Ensure that the following environment variables are set:

      ```
      SET HOSTNAME=xxxxYYYY
      SET ETC=zzzz
      ```

      where xxxxYYYY is the host name of the client machine, and zzzz is the directory where you can find the HOSTS file.

   f. If the SOMObjects WorkGroup Enabler is installed, you might have to do the following:

      1). Remove the MPTN settings if you use TCP/IP (MPTN should be installed if NetBIOS support is chosen).

      2). Ensure that the SOM\LIB directory of the WorkGroup Enabler is referenced *before* the \IBMCPP\DLL directory in the LIBPATH setting.

      3). Ensure that the SOM\BIN directory of the WorkGroup Enabler is referenced *before* the \IBMCPP\BIN directory in the PATH setting.

   g. Prepare the SOM/DSOM development environment.

      Run the following command from an OS/2 command prompt to build the SOM header files:

      ```
      SOMXH.CMD
      ```

      This command generates header files required for C++ programming.

   h. Build the database in the server machine

      Run the following command file to create the server database:

      ```
      SRVDBV12.CMD
      ```

for DB2/2 V1.2 or

```
SRVDBV21.CMD
```

for DB2/2 V2.1

The command files will build the SOMBANK database in the machine and define the corresponding primary and foreign keys accordingly.

   i. Bind the DaxSQL.BND bind file to the database. DAX-SQL.BND can be found in the \IBMCPP\BND directory:

```
SQLBIND D:\IBMCPP\DAXSQL.BND SOMBANK /G=PUBLIC
```

4. Define the IDL.

We used the following IDLs: SOMBank.IDL, SOMCust.IDL, and SOMAcct.IDL (see Figure 59 on page 157).

For a complete listing of the SOMAcct.IDL file, see SOM IDL Interface Listings on page 235 .

5. Compile the IDL files.

Use the SOM Compiler to compile the IDL files to generate the SOMxxxx.xih and SOMxxxx.cpp files, as well as update the SOM repository file. Refer to Section SOMAccount Makefile on page 11 for information on the makefiles.

6. Build the server stub DLLS (used for client machines).

We can just compile and link the SOM compiler generated stub files. Those files will be distributed to the client platforms if workgroup DSOM is used.

7. Create the data access objects.

Use the Data Access Builder of VisualAge C++ V3 to create the data access objects (see Section Generate Data Access (DAX) Objects on page 6).

8. Modify the generated .CPP files with our logic for the server objects. Refer to SOM Objects Implementation Files on page 241, for details.

Note that when you return information from a pointer, special considerations apply. The SOM object does not just return the pointer. Rather, it allocates a piece of memory, copies the contents of the object to which the pointer points in the allocated memory, and returns it. It is DSOM's responsibility to free the allocated memory, as defined by CORBA. The method does not free the pointer itself.

9. Build the server DLLs.

10. Bind the following bind files for the SOMBANK database:

- DaxAcctV.BND (generated during the build process)
- DaxCustV.BND (generated during the build process)

For example:

```
sqlbind DaxAcctV.BND SOMBANK /G=PUBLIC
```

11. Register the server objects with the DSOM repository.

12. If symbolic names are to be used in the DSOM registration, the %ETC%\HOSTS file must exist, and the addresses of both work-stations must be defined in the file.

The client and server machines must refer to the sample implementation ID. Thus, they have to share either the same set of DSOM implementation files or a drive, or one of the machines has to copy the files from the other.

13. Start the DSOM daemon.

Start an OS/2 command session and type SOMDD. Minimize the session when the SOMDD-Ready message appears.

Setting Up the Client System

We carried out the following steps to develop the branch client work-station system.

1. Install and set up the following software (refer to the installation manuals accompanying the software):

    a. OS/2 Warp V3

    b. TCP/IP for OS/2 V2.0

    c. DB2/2 V1.2

    d. VisualAge for Smalltalk for OS/2 V3.0

    e. SOMObjects WorkGroup Enabler V2.1 (for DSOM Work-Group)

    f. SOMObjects fixes (Level SM21001)

    g. Create a userid FCE.

2. Modify CONFIG.SYS.

    a. Add D:\FCE\BIN to the LIBPATH statement:

```
LIBPATH=. C:\OS2;.....;D:\FCE\BIN
```

VisualAge Smalltalk still requires a stub DLL for the DSOM wrapper object.

    b. Add D:\FCE\SOMBANK.IR to the SOMIR statement:

```
SET SOMIR=D:\IBMCPP\ETC\SOM.IR D:\FCE\SOMBANK.IR
```

In our case study, we copied the SOMBANK.IR file from the server machine. In other situations, for example if the client and server are on different platforms, you might have to take the IDL files on the server and compile them using the SOM Compiler to update the Interface Repository file of the client platform.

c. Remove the ;SOMIR; statement in the SOMIR environment variable, if it exists.

d. Add the following two environment variables:

```
SET SOMSOCKETS=TCPIPSockets
SET USER=FCE
```

e. Ensure that the following environment variables are set:

```
SET HOSTNAME=xxxxYYYY
SET ETC=zzzz
```

f. If the SOMObjects WorkGroup Enabler is installed, you might have to do the following:

1). Remove the MPTN settings if you use TCP/IP (MPTN must is installed if NetBIOS support is chosen).

2). Ensure that the SOM\LIB directory of the SOMObjects WorkGroup Enabler is referenced before the \IBM-CPP\DLL directory in the LIBPATH setting.

3). Ensure that the SOM\BIN directory of the SOMObject Enabler is referenced before the \IBMCPP\BIN directory in the PATH setting.

3. If symbolic names are to be used in the DSOM registration, the %ETC%\HOSTS file must exist, and the addresses of both workstations must be defined in the file.

4. Start the DSOM daemon.

Start an OS/2 command session and type SOMDD. Minimize the session when the SOMDD-Ready message appears.

5. Start VisualAge Smalltalk V3. Ensure that the SOMsupport feature and Database support are loaded are loaded.[18]

6. Create the client program

For our demo you can just import the file D:\FCE\FCED-SOM.DAT which contains all the necessary applications.

---

[18] Although the client platform does not access customer data through the customer database, other part of the client program does require access to data residing in a local database CSOODB.

7. Generate the SOM wrapper classes for each server classes; namely, SOMBank, SOMCustomer, and SOMAccount. Actually this step can be omitted if FCEDSOM.DAT is loaded.

8. Modify the FCE application if necessary (see Section Client Implementation on page 1, for details.)

9. Test the application.[18]

10. Package the application.

C

FCE Database Definitions

This appendix lists the data definition languages that define the tables used in the FCE sample application

The DSOM version of the FCE application uses two databases, namely, CSOODB and SOMBANK.

The CSOODB database contains all the tables listed below and is used by the branch client system. The client program also has code to handle some local processing by accessing this database.

The SOMBANK database contains the CUSTOMER and ACCOUNT tables used by the bank server system.

Data Definition Language for Relational Tables

BRANCH Table

```
CREATE TABLE BRANCH
        (BRCH_ID                CHAR(4)     NOT NULL,
         BRCH_NAME              CHAR(20)    NOT NULL,
         BRCH_STREET            CHAR(40)    NOT NULL,
         BRCH_CITY              CHAR(16)    NOT NULL,
         BRCH_STATE             CHAR(2)     NOT NULL,
         BRCH_ZIP               CHAR(5)     NOT NULL,
         PRIMARY KEY (BRCH_ID)
```

BRANCH RESERVE Table

```
CREATE TABLE BRANCHRESERVE
        (BRSV_ID                CHAR(4)     NOT NULL,
         BRSV_BRID              CHAR(5)     NOT NULL,
         BRSV_TOTAL             FLOAT       NOT NULL,
         PRIMARY KEY (BRSV_ID),
         FOREIGN KEY BRSVBRCH (BRSV_BRID)
             REFERENCES BRANCH ON DELETE RESTRICT)
```

CASHIER Table

```
CREATE TABLE CASHIER
        (CASH_ID                CHAR(6)     NOT NULL,
         CASH_FNAME             CHAR(16)    NOT NULL,
         CASH_LNAME             CHAR(24)    NOT NULL,
         CASH_BRID              CHAR(4)     NOT NULL,
         PRIMARY KEY (CASH_ID)
         FOREIGN KEY CASHBRCH (CASH_BRID)
             REFERENCES BRANCH ON DELETE RESTRICT)
```

CASHIER DRAWER Table

```
CREATE TABLE CASHIERDRAWER
        (CDRW_ID                CHAR(4)     NOT NULL,
         CDRW_CAID              CHAR(6)     NOT NULL,
         CDRW_SIZE              CHAR(9),
         CDRW_SLOTS             INT,
         PRIMARY KEY (CDRW_ID),
         FOREIGN KEY CDRWCASH (CDRW_CAID)
             REFERENCES CASHIER ON DELETE RESTRICT)
```

COUNTRY Table

```
CREATE TABLE COUNTRY
        (CNTY_NAME          CHAR(30)    NOT NULL,
         CNTY_ID            CHAR(3)     NOT NULL,
         PRIMARY KEY (CNTY_NAME)
```

CURRENCY Table

```
CREATE TABLE CURRENCY
        (CURR_ID            CHAR(3)     NOT NULL,
         CURR_NAME          CHAR(16)    NOT NULL,
         CURR_CNTY          CHAR(30)    NOT NULL,
         CURR_XRATE_BUY     DEC(8,4)    NOT NULL,
         CURR_XRATE_SELL    DEC(8,4)    NOT NULL,
         CURR_FORG_INFO     CHAR(40),
         CURR_DESC          CHAR(80),
         PRIMARY KEY (CURR_ID),
         FOREIGN KEY CURRCNTY (CURR_CNTY)
             REFERENCES COUNTRY ON DELETE CASCADE)
```

CUSTOMER ORDER Table

```
CREATE TABLE CUSTOMERORDER
        (CORD_ID            INT         NOT NULL,
         CORD_CREATED       CHAR(8)     NOT NULL,
         CORD_STATUS        CHAR(4)     NOT NULL,
         CORD_TOTAL         FLOAT       NOT NULL,
         CORD_CAID          CHAR(6),
         CORD_CUID          INT         NOT NULL,
         PRIMARY KEY (CORD_ID),
         FOREIGN KEY CORDCASH (CORD_CAID)
             REFERENCES CASHIER ON DELETE SET NULL,
         FOREIGN KEY CORDCUST (CORD_CUID)
             REFERENCES CUSTOMER ON DELETE RESTRICT)
```

DENOMINATION Table

```
CREATE TABLE DENOMINATION
        (DNOM_ID            CHAR(3)     NOT NULL,
         DNOM_TYPE          CHAR(8)     NOT NULL,
         DNOM_VALUE         INT         NOT NULL,
         DNOM_DESC          CHAR(60),
         PRIMARY KEY (DNOM_ID, DNOM_TYPE, DNOM_VALUE),
         FOREIGN KEY DNOMCURR (DNOM_ID)
             REFERENCES CURRENCY ON DELETE CASCADE)
```

ORDERITEM Table

```
CREATE TABLE ORDERITEM
          (ORDI_ORID                INT        NOT NULL,
           ORDI_ID                  CHAR(3)    NOT NULL,
           ORDI_TYPE                CHAR(8)    NOT NULL,
           ORDI_VALUE               INT        NOT NULL,
           ORDI_QTY                 INT        NOT NULL,
           ORDI_FORGN_TOTAL         FLOAT      NOT NULL,
           ORDI_LOCAL_TOTAL         FLOAT      NOT NULL
           PRIMARY KEY (ORDI_ORID, ORDI_ID, ORDI_TYPE, ORDI_VALUE)
```

STOCKITEM Table

```
CREATE TABLE STOCKITEM
          (STKI_DRID                CHAR(4)    NOT NULL,
           STKI_ID                  CHAR(3)    NOT NULL,
           STKI_TYPE                CHAR(8)    NOT NULL,
           STKI_VALUE               INT        NOT NULL,
           STKI_QTY                 INT        NOT NULL,
           STKI_MIN                 INT        NOT NULL,
           STKI_MAX                 INT        NOT NULL
           PRIMARY KEY (STKI_DRID, STKI_ID, STKI_TYPE, STKI_VALUE),
           FOREIGN KEY STKIDNOM (STKI_ID, STKI_TYPE, STKI_VALUE)
           REFERENCES DENOMINATION ON DELETE RESTRICT)
```

Data Definition Language for Relational Tables of Server

ACCOUNT Table

```
CREATE TABLE ACCOUNT
          (ACCT_ID                  CHAR(9)    NOT NULL,
           ACCT_TYPE                CHAR(14)   NOT NULL,
           ACCT_BALANCE             FLOAT      NOT NULL,
           ACCT_BRID                CHAR(4)    NOT NULL,
           PRIMARY KEY (ACCT_ID),
           FOREIGN KEY CUST_ID (CUST_ID) REFERENCES CUSTOMER ON DEL
                                ETE CASCADE
```

CUSTOMER Table

```
CREATE TABLE CUSTOMER
        (CUST_ID              INT          NOT NULL,
         CUST_ACID            CHAR(9),
         CUST_FNAME           CHAR(16)     NOT NULL,
         CUST_LNAME           CHAR(24)     NOT NULL,
         CUST_STREET          CHAR(40)     NOT NULL,
         CUST_CITY            CHAR(16)     NOT NULL,
         CUST_STATE           CHAR(2)      NOT NULL,
         CUST_ZIP             CHAR(5),
         CUST_HPHONE          CHAR(8)      NOT NULL,
         CUST_WPHONE          CHAR(8)      NOT NULL,
         PRIMARY KEY (CUST_ID)
```

D

SOM IDL Interface Listings

Figure 78 through Figure 80 on page 238 contain the interface descriptions, written in IDL, for the SOM classes.

SOMAccount Interface

```
#ifndef D_SOMACCT_IDL
#define D_SOMACCT_IDL

#include <somobj.idl>

// SOMAccount class //
interface SOMAccount: SOMObject {
   // exception to be raised to SOM/DSOM should problem occured
   exception SOMAccount_Excep { long errCode; char reason[81]; };

   // Attributes of SOMAccount    //
   attribute      string<9>      accountNumber;
   attribute      float          balance;
   attribute      string<4>      branchId;
   attribute      string<14>     accountDescription;
   attribute      long           customerId;

   // Storing/updating/adding and removing itself   // from the persistence media, in this demo : DB2/2
   //
   void           retrieve();
   void           update();
   void           add();
   void           del();

   // Specific information available to be queried
   //
   boolean        isCheckingAccount();
   boolean        isSavingsAccount();
   boolean        isSuperSavingsAccount();

   // SOM/DSOM specific stuffs
   #ifdef __SOMIDL__
      implementation {
         releaseorder:
                     _get_accountNumber, _set_accountNumber,
                     _get_balance, _set_balance,
                     _get_branchId, _set_branchId,
                     _get_accountDescription, _set_accountDescription,
                     retrieve, update,
                     add, del,
                     _get_customerId, _set_customerId,
                     isCheckingAccount,
                     isSavingsAccount,
                     isSuperSavingsAccount;

         branchId:           noset,noget;
         accountNumber:      noset,noget;
         accountDescription: noset,noget;

         callstyle = idl;
         dllname = "SOMAcct.dll";

         somDestruct: override;
         somDefaultInit: override;

         memory_management = corba;

         // SOMAcctE.h contains the error code to be put in an exception
         //
         passthru C_xh_after  = "#include <SOMAcctE.h>";

         // Implementation specific header for our application
         //
         passthru C_xih_after = "#include <SOMAcctI.h>";
      };
   #endif
};
#endif
```

Figure 78. SOMAccount Interface

SOMBank Interface

```
#ifndef D_SOMBANK_IDL
#define D_SOMBANK_IDL


#include <somobj.idl>


// forward desclarations //
interface SOMCustomer; interface SOMAccount;
///////////////////////////////////////////////////////////////////
// SOMBank class //
// interface SOMBank: SOMObject
{
    // exception to be rasied on problem. Not implemented yet    //
    exception SOMBank_Excep { long errCode; char reason¢81|; };
    // Attributes of SOMBank   //
    attribute  string  name;
    // One to many association. This is put into here only for simplicity   // purpose.
    // Note that this only works for small implementations like our
    // demo.  Refer to the book for more detail discussions and how
    // to improve them   //
    sequence<SOMCustomer,20> customers();    sequence<SOMAccount>  accounts();


    // return a list of ids instead of the customer itself
    //   sequence<long>    allCustomerIds();
    sequence<string>     allAccountIds();
    // return a list of ids from a dynamic SQL statement   //
    sequence<long>     matchingCustomerIds(in string clause);  sequence<string>   matchingAccountIds(in string clause);


    // SOM specific details   #ifdef __SOMIDL__
        implementation {        releaseorder:  _get_name,        _set_name,
                        customers,                      accounts,
                        allCustomerIds, matchingCustomerIds,                       allAccountIds,  matchingAccountIds;


        name: noset, noget;


        callstyle = idl;
        dllname = "SOMBank.dll";
        somDestruct: override;          somDefaultInit: override;


        memory_management = corba;


        // include the error header file.  Not implemented yet
        //        passthru C_xh_after  = "#include <SOMBankE.h>";


        // include the application implementation header
        //        passthru C_xih_after = "#include <SOMBankI.h>";


    };
#endif };


#endif
```

Figure 79. SOMBank Interface

SOMCustomer Interface

```
#ifndef D_SOMCUST_IDL
#define D_SOMCUST_IDL

#include <somobj.idl>
#include <snglicls.idl>

// forward desclarations
//
interface SOMAccount;

///////////////////////////////////////////////////////////////////
// SOMCustomer class
//
//
interface SOMCustomer: SOMObject
{
  // exception to be rasied on problem. Not implemented yet
  //
  exception SOMCustomer_Excep { long errCode; char reason¢81|; };

  // Attributes of SOMCustomer
  //
  attribute   long        customerId;
  attribute   string<16>  firstName;
  attribute   string<24>  lastName;
  attribute   string<8>   homePhone;
  attribute   string<8>   workPhone;
  attribute   string<40>  street;
  attribute   string<16>  city;
  attribute   string<2>   state;
  attribute   string<5>   zip;

  // Return information of the FIRST checking account this customer owns
  // For simplicity the Smalltalk client of this sample program assumes
  // that each customer has only one account.  We take the first account
  // to "entertain" this client program.
  //
  //
  attribute   SOMAccount  account;
  string      accountNum();
  float       accountBalance();

  // All the functions/attributes in this section is here to support
  // other demo programs, it is not implemented here
  //
  attribute   string<9>  accountId;
  attribute   sequence<string,20> accountIdList;
  attribute   sequence<SOMAccount,20>accountList;


  // One to many association, unbounded.  This is put into here
  // like this only for simplicity purpose.
  // Note that this only works for small implementations like our
  // demo.  Refer to the book for more detail discussions and how
  // to improve them
  //
  sequence<SOMAccount> allAccounts();
  sequence<SOMAccount> allSavingsAccounts();
  sequence<SOMAccount> allCheckingAccounts();
  sequence<SOMAccount> allSuperSavingsAccounts();
  // Storing/updating/adding and removing itself
  // from the persistence media, in this demo : DB2/2
  //
  void        retrieve();
  void        update();
  void        add();
  void        del();
```

Figure 80. (Part 1 of 2) SOMCustomer Interface

```
//# SOM specific details
#ifdef __SOMIDL__
    implementation {
        releaseorder:
                        _get_customerId,  _set_customerId,
                        _get_firstName,     _set_firstName,
                        _get_lastName,    _set_lastName,
                        _get_homePhone,     _set_homePhone,
                        _get_workPhone,   _set_workPhone,
                        _get_street,         _set_street,
                        _get_city,        _set_city,
                        _get_state,          _set_state,
                        _get_zip,         _set_zip,

                        _get_account,  _set_account,
                        _get_accountId,       _set_accountId,
               _get_accountList,  _set_accountList,
             _get_accountIdList, _set_accountIdList,
                        accountNum,    accountBalance,

               allAccounts,
             allSavingsAccounts,
              allCheckingAccounts,
             allSuperSavingsAccounts,

                        accounts,
                        retrieve,
                        update,
                        add,
                        del;

        firstName:      noset,noget;
        lastName:         noset,noget;         homePhone:    noset,noget;
        workPhone:        noset,noget;         street:       noset,noget;
        city:             noset,noget;         state:        noset,noget;
        zip:              noset,noget;         account:      noset,noget;
        accountId:        noset,noget;

        allAccounts:       object_owns_result;
        allSavingsAccounts:    object_owns_result;
        allCheckingAccounts:   object_owns_result;
        allSuperSavingsAccounts: object_owns_result;

     _get_accountList: object_owns_result;
     _set_accountList: object_owns_parameters="_accountList";
     _get_accountIdList: object_owns_result;
     _set_accountIdList: object_owns_parameters="_accountIdList";

        callstyle = idl;
        dllname = "SOMCust.dll";

        somDestruct: override;
        somDefaultInit: override;

        memory_management = corba;

        // SOMCustE.h contains the error code to be put in an exception
        //
        passthru C_xh_after  = "#include <SOMCUSTE.h>";

        // Implementation specific header for our application
        //
        passthru C_xih_after = "#include <SOMCUSTI.h>";
    };
  #endif
};

#endif
```

Figure 80. (Part 2 of 2) SOMCustomer Interface

E

SOM Objects Implementation Files

Figure 81 through Figure 83 on page 253 list the files used to implement the SOM objects with the template files generated by the SOM compiler.

SOMAccount Implementation

```
/*
 *  This file was generated by the SOM Compiler and Emitter Framework.
 *  Generated using:
 *      SOM Emitter emitxtm: 2.42
 */

#ifndef SOM_Module_somacct_Source
#define SOM_Module_somacct_Source
#endif
#define SOMAccount_Class_Source
#define SOMMSingleInstance_Class_Source

#include "SOMAcct.xih"

/*
 *Method from the IDL attribute statement:
 *"attribute string accountNumber"
 */

SOM_Scope string  SOMLINK _get_accountNumber(SOMAccount *somSelf,
                                             Environment *ev)
{
    SOMAccountData *somThis = SOMAccountGetData(somSelf);
    SOMAccountMethodDebug("SOMAccount","_get_accountNumber");

    // if attribute is not set before, return an empty string
    //
    if (somThis->accountNumber == NULL) {
      somThis->accountNumber = (string) SOMMalloc(2);
      somThis->accountNumber[0] =' ';
      somThis->accountNumber[1] ='\0';
    }

    string accountNumber = (string) SOMMalloc(strlen(somThis->accountNumber)+1);
    strcpy(accountNumber, somThis->accountNumber);
    somPrintf("Message from SOMAccount : accountNumber=%s\n", somThis->accountNumber);
    return accountNumber;
}
/*
 *Method from the IDL attribute statement:
 *"attribute string accountNumber"
 */

SOM_Scope void  SOMLINK _set_accountNumber(SOMAccount *somSelf,  Environment *ev
,
                                           string accountNumber)
{
    SOMAccountData *somThis = SOMAccountGetData(somSelf);
    SOMAccountMethodDebug("SOMAccount","_set_accountNumber");

    if (accountNumber != NULL) {
      if (somThis->accountNumber != NULL) SOMFree(somThis->accountNumber);
      somThis->accountNumber = (string) SOMMalloc(strlen(accountNumber)+1);
      strcpy(somThis->accountNumber, accountNumber);
      somPrintf("Message from SOMAccount : accountNumber set to %s\n", somThis->accountNumber);
    }
    else {
      // should raise exception here, for simplicity we ignore it
    }
}
```

Figure 81. (Part 1 of 6) SOMAccount Implementation

```
/*
 *Method from the IDL attribute statement:
 *"attribute string branchId"
 */

SOM_Scope string  SOMLINK _get_branchId(SOMAccount *somSelf,
                                        Environment *ev)
{
    SOMAccountData *somThis = SOMAccountGetData(somSelf);
    SOMAccountMethodDebug("SOMAccount","_get_branchId");

    // if attribute is not set before, return an empty string
    //
    if (somThis->branchId == NULL) {
        somThis->branchId = (string) SOMMalloc(2);
        somThis->branchId[0] = ' ';
        somThis->branchId[1] = '\0';
    }

    string branchId = (string) SOMMalloc(strlen(somThis->branchId)+1);
    strcpy(branchId, somThis->branchId);
    somPrintf("Message from SOMAccount : branch id=%s\n", somThis->branchId);
    return branchId;
}

/*
 *Method from the IDL attribute statement:
 *"attribute string branchId"
 */

SOM_Scope void  SOMLINK _set_branchId(SOMAccount *somSelf,  Environment *ev,
                                      string branchId)
{
    SOMAccountData *somThis = SOMAccountGetData(somSelf);
    SOMAccountMethodDebug("SOMAccount","_set_branchId");

    if (branchId != NULL) {
        if (somThis->branchId != NULL) SOMFree(somThis->branchId);
        somThis->branchId = (string) SOMMalloc(strlen(branchId)+1);
        strcpy(somThis->branchId, branchId);
        somPrintf("Message from SOMAccount : branch id set to %s\n", somThis->branchId);
    }
    else {
        // should raise exception here
    }
}


/*
 *Method from the IDL attribute statement:
 *"attribute string accountDescription"
 */

/*
 * Following methods handle the storing/updating/adding and removing itself
 * from the persistence media. In our case, DB2/2
 */

SOM_Scope string  SOMLINK _get_accountDescription(SOMAccount *somSelf,
                                                  Environment *ev)
{
    SOMAccountData *somThis = SOMAccountGetData(somSelf);
    SOMAccountMethodDebug("SOMAccount","_get_accountDescription");

    // if attribute is not set before, return an empty string
    //
    if (somThis->accountDescription == NULL) {
        somThis->accountDescription = (string) SOMMalloc(2);
        somThis->accountDescription[0] = ' ';
        somThis->accountDescription[1] = '\0';
    }
```

Figure 81. (Part 2 of 6) SOMAccount Implementation

```
       string accountDescription = (string) SOMMalloc(strlen(somThis->accountDescription)+1);
       strcpy(accountDescription, somThis->accountDescription);
       somPrintf("Message from SOMAccount : account description=%s\n", somThis->accountDescription);
       return accountDescription;
}

/*
 *Method from the IDL attribute statement:
 *"attribute string accountDescription"
 */


SOM_Scope void  SOMLINK _set_accountDescription(SOMAccount *somSelf,
                                        Environment *ev, string accountDescription)
{
       SOMAccountData *somThis = SOMAccountGetData(somSelf);
       SOMAccountMethodDebug("SOMAccount","_set_accountDescription");

       if (accountDescription != NULL) {
          if (somThis->accountDescription != NULL) SOMFree(somThis->accountDescription);
          somThis->accountDescription = (string) SOMMalloc(strlen(accountDescription)+1);
          somPrintf("Message from SOMAccount : account description set to %s\n", somThis->accountDescription);
          strcpy(somThis->accountDescription, accountDescription);
       }
       else {
          // should raise exception here
       }

}

/*
 * Following methods handle the querying/storing/updating/adding and removing itself
 * from the persistence media. In our case, DB2/2
 */

SOM_Scope void  SOMLINK retrieve(SOMAccount *somSelf,  Environment *ev)
{
       SOMAccountData *somThis = SOMAccountGetData(somSelf);
       SOMAccountMethodDebug("SOMAccount","retrieve");

       // data access object specifically used to access DB2/2
       DaxAcct DAXAccountObject;

       // retrieve a customer from database with the customer id
       try {
         DAXAccountObject.setAcct_id( somThis->accountNumber );
         DAXAccountObject.retrieve();
         somPrintf("Message from SOMAccount : account information retrieved\n");

       }
       catch (IException &exc) {

         // should set exception to client program
         // Not implemented in our demo
         //

         somSelf->_set_balance(ev,0.0);
         somSelf->_set_branchId(ev,"N/A");
         somSelf->_set_accountDescription(ev,"Not Found");
         somSelf->_set_customerId(ev,0);
         somPrintf("Message from SOMAccount : account information retrieve failed\n
");

         return;
       }
```

Figure 81. (Part 3 of 6) SOMAccount Implementation

```
        somSelf->_set_balance(ev,DAXAccountObject.acct_balance());
        somSelf->_set_branchId(ev,DAXAccountObject.acct_brid());
        somSelf->_set_accountDescription(ev,DAXAccountObject.acct_type());
        somSelf->_set_customerId(ev,DAXAccountObject.cust_id());

}

SOM_Scope void  SOMLINK update(SOMAccount *somSelf, Environment *ev)
{
    SOMAccountData *somThis = SOMAccountGetData(somSelf);
    SOMAccountMethodDebug("SOMAccount","update");

    DaxAcct DAXAccountObject;

    // update the customer with the current id
    try {
        DAXAccountObject.setAcct_id      (somThis->accountNumber );
        DAXAccountObject.setAcct_balance (somThis->balance       );
        DAXAccountObject.setAcct_brid    (somThis->branchId      );
        DAXAccountObject.setAcct_type    (somThis->accountDescription);
        DAXAccountObject.setCust_id      (somThis->customerId    );
        DAXAccountObject.update();

        // we commit immediately, it's a demo anyway
        //
        DSObject.commit();
        somPrintf("Message from SOMAccount : account updated\n");

    }
    catch (IException &exc) {
        // should set exception to client program
        // Not implemented in our demo
        //
    }

}

SOM_Scope void  SOMLINK add(SOMAccount *somSelf, Environment *ev)
{
    SOMAccountData *somThis = SOMAccountGetData(somSelf);
    SOMAccountMethodDebug("SOMAccount","add");

    DaxAcct DAXAccountObject;

    try {
        DAXAccountObject.setAcct_id      (somThis->accountNumber   );
        DAXAccountObject.setAcct_balance (somThis->balance   );
        DAXAccountObject.setAcct_brid    (somThis->branchId   );
        DAXAccountObject.setAcct_type    (somThis->accountDescription );
        DAXAccountObject.setCust_id      (somThis->customerId   );
        DAXAccountObject.add();

        // we commit immediately, it's a demo anyway
        //
        DSObject.commit();
        somPrintf("Message from SOMAccount : account added\n");

    }
    catch (IException &exc) {
        // should set exception to client program
        // Not implemented in our demo
        //
    }

}

SOM_Scope void  SOMLINK del(SOMAccount *somSelf, Environment *ev)
{
    SOMAccountData *somThis = SOMAccountGetData(somSelf);
    SOMAccountMethodDebug("SOMAccount","del");
```

Figure 81. (Part 4 of 6) SOMAccount Implementation

```
        DaxAcct DAXAccountObject;

        try {
            DAXAccountObject.setAcct_id     ( somThis->accountNumber );
            DAXAccountObject.del();

            // we commit immediately, it's a demo anyway
            //
            DSObject.commit();
            somPrintf("Message from SOMAccount : account removed\n");

        }
        catch (IException &exc) {
            // should set exception to client program
            // Not implemented in our demo
            //
        }
}

/*
 * Following methods return specific information of this SOMAccount object
 */

SOM_Scope boolean  SOMLINK isCheckingAccount(SOMAccount *somSelf,
                                             Environment *ev)
{
    SOMAccountData *somThis = SOMAccountGetData(somSelf);
    SOMAccountMethodDebug("SOMAccount","isCheckingAccount");

    if ( strncmp(somThis->accountDescription, "checking", strlen("checking"))==0
) {
        return true;
    }
    else {
        return false;
    }

}

SOM_Scope boolean  SOMLINK isSavingsAccount(SOMAccount *somSelf,
                                            Environment *ev)
{
    SOMAccountData *somThis = SOMAccountGetData(somSelf);
    SOMAccountMethodDebug("SOMAccount","isSavingsAccount");

    if ( strncmp(somThis->accountDescription, "savings", strlen("savings") )==0
) {
        return true;
    }
    else {
        return false;
    }
}
SOM_Scope boolean  SOMLINK isSuperSavingsAccount(SOMAccount *somSelf,
                                                 Environment *ev)
{
    SOMAccountData *somThis = SOMAccountGetData(somSelf);
    SOMAccountMethodDebug("SOMAccount","isSuperSavingsAccount");

    if ( strncmp(somThis->accountDescription, "Super Saving", strlen("Super Saving") )==0 ) {
        return true;
    }
    else {
        return false;
    }
}

/*
 * SOM/DSOM specific stuffs
 */
```

Figure 81. (Part 5 of 6) SOMAccount Implementation

```
/*
 * SOM_Scope void SOMLINK somDestruct(SOMAccount *somSelf, octet doFree,
 *                                    somDestructCtrl* ctrl)
 */


/*
 * The prototype for somDestruct was replaced by the following prototype:
 */
SOM_Scope void SOMLINK somDestruct(SOMAccount *somSelf, octet doFree,
                                   som3DestructCtrl* ctrl)
{
    SOMAccountData *somThis; /* set in BeginDestructor */
    somDestructCtrl globalCtrl;
    somBooleanVector myMask;
    SOMAccountMethodDebug("SOMAccount","somDestruct");
    SOMAccount_BeginDestructor;


    /*
     * local SOMAccount deinitialization code added by programmer
     */


    SOMAccount_EndDestructor;
}


/*
 * SOM_Scope void SOMLINK somDefaultInit(SOMAccount *somSelf, somInitCtrl* ctrl)
 */

/*
 * The prototype for somDefaultInit was replaced by the following prototype:
 */
SOM_Scope void SOMLINK somDefaultInit(SOMAccount *somSelf, som3InitCtrl* ctrl)
{
    SOMAccountData *somThis; /* set in BeginInitializer */
    somInitCtrl globalCtrl;
    somBooleanVector myMask;
    SOMAccountMethodDebug("SOMAccount","somDefaultInit");
    SOMAccount_BeginInitializer_somDefaultInit;

    SOMAccount_Init_SOMObject_somDefaultInit(somSelf, ctrl);


    /*
     * local SOMAccount initialization code added by programmer
     */
}
SOMEXTERN void SOMLINK SOMInitModule( long majorVersion,
                                      long minorVersion,
                                      string className)
{
    SOMAccountNewClass(0,0);


    /*
     * local dTstCust initialization code added by programmer
     */
    try {
      DSObject.connect("SOMBANK", "FCE", "PASSWORD");
    }
    catch (IException &exc) {
      somPrintf("Failed: Exception occurs\n");
      somPrintf("Error id: %ld\n", exc.errorId());

      for (unsigned long i = 0; i < exc.textCount(); i++)
        somPrintf("Error Text: %s\n", exc.text(i) );
      somPrintf("Error Class: %s\n", exc.name());
    }
```

Figure 81. (Part 6 of 6) SOMAccount Implementation

SOMBank Implementation

```
/*
 *  This file was generated by the SOM Compiler and Emitter Framework.
 *  Generated using:
 *      SOM Emitter emitxtm: 2.42
 */

#ifndef SOM_Module_sombank_Source
#define SOM_Module_sombank_Source
#endif
#define SOMBank_Class_Source
#define SOMMSingleInstance_Class_Source

#include "SOMBank.xih"


/*
 *Method from the IDL attribute statement:
 *"attribute string name"
 */

SOM_Scope string  SOMLINK _get_name(SOMBank *somSelf,  Environment *ev)
{
    SOMBankData *somThis = SOMBankGetData(somSelf);
    SOMBankMethodDebug("SOMBank","_get_name");
    // if attribute is not set before, return an empty string
    //
    if (somThis->name == NULL) {
        somThis->name = (string) SOMMalloc(2);
        strcpy(somThis->name," ");
    }

    string name = (string) SOMMalloc(strlen(somThis->name)+1);
    strcpy(name, somThis->name);
    return name;
}

/*
 *Method from the IDL attribute statement:
 *"attribute string name"
 */

SOM_Scope void  SOMLINK _set_name(SOMBank *somSelf,  Environment *ev,
                                          string name)
{
    SOMBankData *somThis = SOMBankGetData(somSelf);
    SOMBankMethodDebug("SOMBank","_set_name");

    if (name!=NULL) {
        if (somThis->name != NULL) SOMFree(somThis->name);
        somThis->name = (string) SOMMalloc(strlen(name)+1);
        strcpy(somThis->name, name);
    }
}

SOM_Scope _IDL_SEQUENCE_SOMCustomer  SOMLINK customers(SOMBank *somSelf,
                                                Environment *ev)
{
    SOMBankData *somThis = SOMBankGetData(somSelf);
    SOMBankMethodDebug("SOMBank","customers");

    // customer list to be returned
    _IDL_SEQUENCE_SOMCustomer    customerList;

    // Other preparations
    //
    DaxCust            *cursorCustomer;
    IVSequence<DaxCust *>::Cursor cursor(*(DAXCustMgrObject.items()));
```

Figure 82. (Part 1 of 6) SOMBank Implementation

```
        // number of total customers
        //
        int numElements;

        // a refresh takes a whole new list of customers

        //
        DAXCustMgrObject.refresh();
        numElements = DAXCustMgrObject.items()->numberOfElements();

        // now prepare the customerList for inserting element
        //
        sequenceMaximum(customerList) = numElements;
        customerList._buffer = (SOMCustomer **)SOMMalloc(sizeof(SOMCustomer *) * numElements);
        sequenceLength(customerList) = 0;

        // the actual logic of inserting found customer into the return list
        for (cursor.setToFirst(); cursor.isValid(); cursor.setToNext()) {
            cursorCustomer = DAXCustMgrObject.items()->elementAt(cursor);
            // looks complicated here, but just setting each attribe on
            // the list of return customer, based on what found from the database
            // access object.

            sequenceElement(customerList, sequenceLength(customerList)) = new SOMCustomer();
            sequenceElement(customerList, sequenceLength(customerList))->_set_customerId(ev,cursorCustomer->cust_id());
            sequenceElement(customerList, sequenceLength(customerList))->_set_firstName(ev,cursorCustomer->cust_fname());
            sequenceElement(customerList, sequenceLength(customerList))->_set_lastName(ev,cursorCustomer->cust_lname());
            sequenceElement(customerList, sequenceLength(customerList))->_set_street(ev,cursorCustomer->cust_street());
            sequenceElement(customerList, sequenceLength(customerList))->_set_city(ev,cursorCustomer->cust_city());
            sequenceElement(customerList, sequenceLength(customerList))->_set_state(ev,cursorCustomer->cust_state());
            sequenceElement(customerList, sequenceLength(customerList))->_set_zip(ev,cursorCustomer->cust_zip());
            sequenceElement(customerList, sequenceLength(customerList))->_set_homePhone(ev,cursorCustomer->cust_hphone());
            sequenceElement(customerList, sequenceLength(customerList))->_set_workPhone(ev,cursorCustomer->cust_wphone());

        ++sequenceLength(customerList);
        }

    return (customerList);
}

SOM_Scope _IDL_SEQUENCE_SOMAccount  SOMLINK accounts(SOMBank *somSelf,
                                                     Environment *ev)
{
    SOMBankData *somThis = SOMBankGetData(somSelf);
    SOMBankMethodDebug("SOMBank","accounts");

    // account list to be returned
    //
    _IDL_SEQUENCE_SOMAccount accountList;

    // Other preparations
    //
    DaxAcct *cursorAccount;
    IVSequence<DaxAcct *>::Cursor cursor(*(DAXAcctMgrObject.items()));

    // number of total accounts
    //
    int numElements;

    // a refresh takes a whole new list of accounts
    // Again, it is only workable for small demo like this
    // More restrictions should be applied to reduce network traffic
    // loading if a production environment is in place
    //
    DAXAcctMgrObject.refresh();

    numElements = DAXAcctMgrObject.items()->numberOfElements();

    // now prepare the accountList for inserting element
    //
    sequenceMaximum(accountList) = numElements;
    accountList._buffer = (SOMAccount **)SOMMalloc(sizeof(SOMAccount *) * numElements);
    sequenceLength(accountList) = 0;
```

Figure 82. (Part 2 of 6) SOMBank Implementation

```
            // the actual logic of inserting found customer into the return list.
            //
            for (cursor.setToFirst(); cursor.isValid(); cursor.setToNext()) {

                cursorAccount = DAXAcctMgrObject.items()->elementAt(cursor);
                // looks complicated here, but just setting each attribe on
                // the list of return account, based on what found from the database
                // access object.
                //
                sequenceElement(accountList, sequenceLength(accountList)) = new SOMAccount();
                sequenceElement(accountList, sequenceLength(accountList))->_set_accountNumber(ev,cursorAccount->acct_id());
                sequenceElement(accountList, sequenceLength(accountList))->_set_balance(ev,cursorAccount->acct_balance());
                sequenceElement(accountList, sequenceLength(accountList))->_set_branchId(ev,cursorAccount->acct_brid());
                sequenceElement(accountList, sequenceLength(accountList))->_set_accountDescription(ev,cursorAccount->acct_type());
                ++sequenceLength(accountList);
            }

            // return the list
            return (accountList);
}

/*
 * SOM_Scope _IDL_SEQUENCE_long  SOMLINK allCustomerIds(SOMBank *somSelf,
 *                                                    Environment *ev)
 */

SOM_Scope _IDL_SEQUENCE_long  SOMLINK allCustomerIds(SOMBank *somSelf, Environment *ev)
{
    SOMBankData *somThis = SOMBankGetData(somSelf);
    SOMBankMethodDebug("SOMBank","allCustomerIds");

    // list of all customer ids to be returned
    //
    _IDL_SEQUENCE_long matchCustomerIds;

    // total number of customers
    //
    int            numElements;

    // refresh to get the new total list
    // Again, it is only workable for small demo like this
    // More restrictions should be applied to reduce network traffic
    // loading if a production environment is in place
    //

    DAXCustMgrObject.refresh();

    // prepare to construct the list
    //
    numElements = DAXCustMgrObject.items()->numberOfElements();
    sequenceMaximum(matchCustomerIds) = numElements;
    matchCustomerIds._buffer =
        (long *)SOMMalloc(sizeof(long *) * numElements);

    // actual logic of list insertion
    //
    sequenceLength(matchCustomerIds) = 0;
    for (int counter=1; counter<=numElements; counter++) {
        sequenceElement(matchCustomerIds,counter-1) =
            DAXCustMgrObject.items()->elementAtPosition(IPosition(counter))->cust_id();
        ++sequenceLength(matchCustomerIds);
    } /* endfor */
    return matchCustomerIds;
}


/*
 * The prototype for allAccountIds was replaced by the following prototype:
 */
SOM_Scope _IDL_SEQUENCE_string  SOMLINK allAccountIds(SOMBank *somSelf, Environment *ev)
{
    SOMBankData *somThis = SOMBankGetData(somSelf);
    SOMBankMethodDebug("SOMBank","allAccountIds");

    // list of all account ids to be returned
```

Figure 82. (Part 3 of 6) SOMBank Implementation

```
//
_IDL_SEQUENCE_string matchAccountIds;

// total number of accounts
//
int                numElements;

// refresh to get the new total list
// Again, it is only workable for small demo like this
// More restrictions should be applied to reduce network traffic
// loading if a production environment is in place

//
DAXAcctMgrObject.refresh();

// prepare to construct the list
//
numElements = DAXAcctMgrObject.items()->numberOfElements();
sequenceMaximum(matchAccountIds) = numElements;
matchAccountIds._buffer =
      (string *)SOMMalloc(sizeof(string *) * numElements);
sequenceLength(matchAccountIds) = 0;

// actual logic of list insertion
//
for (int counter=1; counter<=numElements; counter++) {

    sequenceElement(matchAccountIds,counter-1) =
      (string) SOMMalloc(strlen(DAXAcctMgrObject.items()->elementAtPosition(IPosition(counter))->acct_id())+1);

    strcpy(sequenceElement(matchAccountIds,counter-1),
      DAXAcctMgrObject.items()->elementAtPosition(IPosition(counter))->acct_id());

    ++sequenceLength(matchAccountIds);
} /* endfor */
return matchAccountIds;
}

/*
* This is put in here to accept a SQL statement
* (as the clause) and with the clause we can ask the corresponding
* data access manager object to retrieve a list of objects which satisfy
* the SQL statement.  Dynamic SQL statement is used.
* Note: this function is not implemented yet.  The TOTAL list of objects
* will be returned, and the clause simply get ignored.
* For how to use the data access manager object for the dynamic SQL search
* please refer to the generated DAX program stubs
*/ SOM_Scope _IDL_SEQUENCE_long  SOMLINK matchingCustomerIds(SOMBank *somSelf,
                                                   Environment *ev,
                                                   string clause)

{
    SOMBankData *somThis = SOMBankGetData(somSelf);
    SOMBankMethodDebug("SOMBank","matchingCustomerIds");

    // Preparations
    //
    _IDL_SEQUENCE_long matchCustomerIds;

    // Again, it is only workable for small demo like this
    // More restrictions should be applied to reduce network traffic
    // loading if a production environment is in place
    //
    DAXCustMgrObject.refresh();

    int numElements = DAXCustMgrObject.items()->numberOfElements();

    sequenceMaximum(matchCustomerIds) = numElements;
    matchCustomerIds._buffer =
          (long *)SOMMalloc(sizeof(long *) * numElements);

    sequenceLength(matchCustomerIds) = 0;
    for (int counter=1; counter<=numElements; counter++) {
      sequenceElement(matchCustomerIds,counter-1) =
          DAXCustMgrObject.items()->elementAtPosition(IPosition(counter))->cust_id();
```

Figure 82. (Part 4 of 6) SOMBank Implementation

```
            ++sequenceLength(matchCustomerIds);
      }
      return matchCustomerIds;
}

/*
 *  This is put in here to accept a SQL statement
 *  (as the clause) and with the clause we can ask the corresponding
 *  data access manager object to retrieve a list of objects which satisfy
 *  the SQL statement.  Dynamic SQL statement is used.
 *  Note: this function is not implemented yet.  The TOTAL list of objects
 *  will be returned, and the clause simply get ignored.
 *  For how to use the data access manager object for the dynamic SQL search
 *  please refer to the generated DAX program stubs
 */
/*

 * SOM specific details
 */

SOM_Scope _IDL_SEQUENCE_string  SOMLINK matchingAccountIds(SOMBank *somSelf,
                                                            Environment *ev,
                                                            string clause)
{
    SOMBankData *somThis = SOMBankGetData(somSelf);
    SOMBankMethodDebug("SOMBank","matchingAccountIds");

    // Preparations
    //
    _IDL_SEQUENCE_string matchAccountIds;
    int                  numElements;

    // Again, it is only workable for small demo like this
    // More restrictions should be applied to reduce network traffic
    // loading if a production environment is in place
    //
    DAXAcctMgrObject.refresh();

    numElements = DAXAcctMgrObject.items()->numberOfElements();
    sequenceMaximum(matchAccountIds) = numElements;
    matchAccountIds._buffer =
        (string *)SOMMalloc(sizeof(string *) * numElements);
    sequenceLength(matchAccountIds) = 0;

    for (int counter=1; counter<=numElements; counter++) {
        sequenceElement(matchAccountIds,counter-1) =
            (string) SOMMalloc(strlen(DAXAcctMgrObject.items()->elementAtPosition(IPosition(counter))->acct_id())+1);
        strcpy(sequenceElement(matchAccountIds,counter-1),
            DAXAcctMgrObject.items()->elementAtPosition(IPosition(counter))->acct_id());
        ++sequenceLength(matchAccountIds);
    }

    return matchAccountIds;

}


SOM_Scope void SOMLINK somDestruct(SOMBank *somSelf, octet doFree,
                                    somDestructCtrl* ctrl)
{
    SOMBankData *somThis; /* set in BeginDestructor */
    somDestructCtrl globalCtrl;
    somBooleanVector myMask;
    SOMBankMethodDebug("SOMBank","somDestruct");
    SOMBank_BeginDestructor;

    /*
     * local SOMBank deinitialization code added by programmer
     */

    SOMBank_EndDestructor;
    somPrintf("Message from SOMBank : %d is destructed\n", somSelf);
}
```

Figure 82. (Part 5 of 6) SOMBank Implementation

```
SOM_Scope void SOMLINK somDefaultInit(SOMBank *somSelf, somInitCtrl* ctrl)
{
    SOMBankData *somThis; /* set in BeginInitializer */
    somInitCtrl globalCtrl;
    somBooleanVector myMask;
    SOMBankMethodDebug("SOMBank","somDefaultInit");
    SOMBank_BeginInitializer_somDefaultInit;

    SOMBank_Init_SOMObject_somDefaultInit(somSelf, ctrl);

    somThis->name = (string)SOMMalloc(strlen("ITSO SOM BANK") + 1 );
    strcpy(somThis->name, "ITSO SOM BANK");
    somPrintf("Message from SOMBank : %d connection request accepted\n");
}


SOMEXTERN void SOMLINK SOMInitModule( long majorVersion,
                                      long minorVersion,
                                      string className)


{
    SOMBankNewClass(0,0);

    // connect itself with the CSOODB database
    try {
      DSObject.connect("SOMBANK", "FCE", "PASSWORD");
    } catch (IException &exc) {
      somPrintf("Failed: Exception occurs\n");
      somPrintf("Error id: %ld\n", exc.errorId());
      for (unsigned long i = 0; i < exc.textCount(); i++)
        somPrintf("Error Text: %s\n", exc.text(i) );
      somPrintf("Error Class: %s\n", exc.name());
    }
}
```

Figure 82. (Part 6 of 6) SOMBank Implementation

SOMCustomer Implementation

```
/*
 *  This file was generated by the SOM Compiler.
 *  Generated using:
 *      SOM incremental update: 2.42
 */


/*
 *  This file was generated by the SOM Compiler and Emitter Framework.
 *  Generated using:
 *      SOM Emitter emitxtm: 2.42
 */

#ifndef SOM_Module_somcust_Source
#define SOM_Module_somcust_Source
#endif
#define SOMCustomer_Class_Source

#include "SOMCust.xih"
```

Figure 83. (Part 1 of 16) SOMCustomer Implementation

```
/*
*Method from the IDL attribute statement:
*"attribute string firstName"
*/

SOM_Scope string  SOMLINK _get_firstName(SOMCustomer *somSelf,
                                         Environment *ev)
{
    SOMCustomerData *somThis = SOMCustomerGetData(somSelf);
    SOMCustomerMethodDebug("SOMCustomer","_get_firstName");

    // if attribute is not set before, return an empty string
    //
    if (somThis->firstName == NULL) {
        somThis->firstName = (string) SOMMalloc(2);
        somThis->firstName[0] =' ';
        somThis->firstName[1] ='\0';
    }

    string firstName = (string) SOMMalloc(strlen(somThis->firstName)+1);
    strcpy(firstName, somThis->firstName);
    somPrintf("Message from SOMCustomer : firstName=%s\n", somThis->firstName);
    return firstName;
}


/*
*Method from the IDL attribute statement:
*"attribute string firstName"
*/

SOM_Scope void  SOMLINK _set_firstName(SOMCustomer *somSelf,
                                       Environment *ev, string firstName)
{
    SOMCustomerData *somThis = SOMCustomerGetData(somSelf);
    SOMCustomerMethodDebug("SOMCustomer","_set_firstName");

    if (firstName!=NULL) {
        if (somThis->firstName != NULL) SOMFree(somThis->firstName);
        somThis->firstName = (string) SOMMalloc(strlen(firstName)+1);
        strcpy(somThis->firstName, firstName);
    }
    else {
        // exception should be raised here
        // not implemented in our demo
    }

}


/*
*Method from the IDL attribute statement:
*"attribute string lastName"
*/

SOM_Scope string  SOMLINK _get_lastName(SOMCustomer *somSelf,
                                        Environment *ev)
{
    SOMCustomerData *somThis = SOMCustomerGetData(somSelf);
    SOMCustomerMethodDebug("SOMCustomer","_get_lastName");

    // if attribute is not set before, return an empty string
    //
    if (somThis->lastName == NULL) {
        somThis->lastName = (string) SOMMalloc(2);
        somThis->lastName[0] =' ';
        somThis->lastName[1] ='\0';
    }
```

Figure 83. (Part 2 of 16) SOMCustomer Implementation

```
    string lastName = (string) SOMMalloc(strlen(somThis->lastName)+1);
    strcpy(lastName, somThis->lastName);
    somPrintf("Message from SOMCustomer : lastName=%s\n", somThis->lastName);
    return lastName;
}


/*
 *Method from the IDL attribute statement:
 *"attribute string lastName"
 */


SOM_Scope void  SOMLINK _set_lastName(SOMCustomer *somSelf, Environment *ev,
                                      string lastName)
{
    SOMCustomerData *somThis = SOMCustomerGetData(somSelf);
    SOMCustomerMethodDebug("SOMCustomer","_set_lastName");


    if (lastName!=NULL) {
        if (somThis->lastName != NULL) SOMFree(somThis->lastName);
        somThis->lastName = (string) SOMMalloc(strlen(lastName)+1);
        strcpy(somThis->lastName, lastName);
    }
    else {
        // should raise exception here
        // not implemented in our demo
    }
}


/*
 *Method from the IDL attribute statement:
 *"attribute string homePhone"
 */

SOM_Scope string  SOMLINK _get_homePhone(SOMCustomer *somSelf,
                                         Environment *ev)
{
    SOMCustomerData *somThis = SOMCustomerGetData(somSelf);
    SOMCustomerMethodDebug("SOMCustomer","_get_homePhone");


    // if attribute is not set before, return an empty string
    //
    if (somThis->homePhone == NULL) {
        somThis->homePhone = (string) SOMMalloc(2);
        somThis->homePhone[0] =' ';
        somThis->homePhone[1] ='\0';
    }


    string homePhone = (string) SOMMalloc(strlen(somThis->homePhone)+1);
    strcpy(homePhone, somThis->homePhone);
    somPrintf("Message from SOMCustomer : homePhone=%s\n", somThis->homePhone);
    return homePhone;
}


/*
 *Method from the IDL attribute statement:
 *"attribute string homePhone"
 */

SOM_Scope void  SOMLINK _set_homePhone(SOMCustomer *somSelf,
                                       Environment *ev, string homePhone)
{
    SOMCustomerData *somThis = SOMCustomerGetData(somSelf);
    SOMCustomerMethodDebug("SOMCustomer","_set_homePhone");


    if (homePhone!=NULL) {
        if (somThis->homePhone != NULL) SOMFree(somThis->homePhone);
        somThis->homePhone = (string) SOMMalloc(strlen(homePhone)+1);
        strcpy(somThis->homePhone, homePhone);
    }
```

Figure 83. (Part 3 of 16) SOMCustomer Implementation

```
        else {
            // should raise exception here
            // not implemented in our demo
        }
}


/*
 *Method from the IDL attribute statement:
 *"attribute string workPhone"
 */

SOM_Scope string  SOMLINK _get_workPhone(SOMCustomer *somSelf,
                                         Environment *ev)
{
    SOMCustomerData *somThis = SOMCustomerGetData(somSelf);
    SOMCustomerMethodDebug("SOMCustomer","_get_workPhone");

    // if attribute is not set before, return an empty string
    //
    if (somThis->workPhone == NULL) {
        somThis->workPhone = (string) SOMMalloc(2);
        somThis->workPhone[0] =' ';
        somThis->workPhone[1] ='\0';
    }

    string workPhone = (string) SOMMalloc(strlen(somThis->workPhone)+1);
    strcpy(workPhone, somThis->workPhone);
    somPrintf("Message from SOMCustomer : workPhone=%s\n", somThis->workPhone);
    return workPhone;
}


/*
 *Method from the IDL attribute statement:
 *"attribute string workPhone"
 */

SOM_Scope void  SOMLINK _set_workPhone(SOMCustomer *somSelf,
                                       Environment *ev, string workPhone)
{
    SOMCustomerData *somThis = SOMCustomerGetData(somSelf);
    SOMCustomerMethodDebug("SOMCustomer","_set_workPhone");

    // if attribute is not set before, return an empty string
    //
    if (workPhone!=NULL) {
        if (somThis->workPhone != NULL) SOMFree(somThis->workPhone);
        somThis->workPhone = (string) SOMMalloc(strlen(workPhone)+1);
        strcpy(somThis->workPhone, workPhone);
    }
    else {
        // should raise exception here
        // not implemented in our demo
    }


}


/*
 *Method from the IDL attribute statement:
 *"attribute string street"
 */

SOM_Scope string  SOMLINK _get_street(SOMCustomer *somSelf,  Environment *ev)
{
    SOMCustomerData *somThis = SOMCustomerGetData(somSelf);
    SOMCustomerMethodDebug("SOMCustomer","_get_street");

    // if attribute is not set before, return an empty string
```

Figure 83. (Part 4 of 16) SOMCustomer Implementation

```
    //.
    if (somThis->street == NULL) {
       somThis->street = (string) SOMMalloc(2);
       somThis->street[0]=' ';
       somThis->street[1]='\0';
    }

    string street = (string) SOMMalloc(strlen(somThis->street)+1);
    strcpy(street, somThis->street);
    somPrintf("Message from SOMCustomer : street=%s\n", somThis->street);
    return street;
}



/*
 *Method from the IDL attribute statement:
 *"attribute string street"
 */

SOM_Scope void  SOMLINK _set_street(SOMCustomer *somSelf, Environment *ev,
                                    string street)
{
    SOMCustomerData *somThis = SOMCustomerGetData(somSelf);
    SOMCustomerMethodDebug("SOMCustomer","_set_street");


    if (street!=NULL) {
       if (somThis->street != NULL) SOMFree(somThis->street);
       somThis->street = (string) SOMMalloc(strlen(street)+1);
       strcpy(somThis->street, street);
    }
    else {
       // should raise exception here
       // not implemented in our demo
    }
}



/*
 *Method from the IDL attribute statement:
 *"attribute string city"
 */

SOM_Scope string  SOMLINK _get_city(SOMCustomer *somSelf, Environment *ev)
{
    SOMCustomerData *somThis = SOMCustomerGetData(somSelf);
    SOMCustomerMethodDebug("SOMCustomer","_get_city");


    // if attribute is not set before, return an empty string
    //
    if (somThis->city == NULL) {
       somThis->city = (string) SOMMalloc(2);
       somThis->city[0]=' ';
       somThis->city[1]='\0';
    }

    string city = (string) SOMMalloc(strlen(somThis->city)+1);
    strcpy(city, somThis->city);
    somPrintf("Message from SOMCustomer : city=%s\n", somThis->city);
    return city;
}



/*
 *Method from the IDL attribute statement:
 *"attribute string city"
 */
```

Figure 83. (Part 5 of 16) SOMCustomer Implementation

```
SOM_Scope void SOMLINK _set_city(SOMCustomer *somSelf,  Environment *ev,
                                  string city)
{
    SOMCustomerData *somThis = SOMCustomerGetData(somSelf);
    SOMCustomerMethodDebug("SOMCustomer","_set_city");


    // if attribute is not set before, return an empty string
    //
    if (city!=NULL) {
        if (somThis->city != NULL) SOMFree(somThis->city);
        somThis->city = (string) SOMMalloc(strlen(city)+1);
        strcpy(somThis->city, city);
    }
    else {
        // should raise exception here
        // not implemented in our demo
    }
}



/*
*Method from the IDL attribute statement:
*"attribute string state"
*/


SOM_Scope string  SOMLINK _get_state(SOMCustomer *somSelf,  Environment *ev)
{
    SOMCustomerData *somThis = SOMCustomerGetData(somSelf);
    SOMCustomerMethodDebug("SOMCustomer","_get_state");

    // if attribute is not set before, return an empty string
    //
    if (somThis->state == NULL) {
        somThis->state = (string) SOMMalloc(2);
        somThis->state[0] =' ';
        somThis->state[1] ='\0';
    }

    string state = (string) SOMMalloc(strlen(somThis->state)+1);
    strcpy(state, somThis->state);
    somPrintf("Message from SOMCustomer : state=%s\n", somThis->state);
    return state;
}



/*
*Method from the IDL attribute statement:
*"attribute string state"
*/

SOM_Scope void  SOMLINK _set_state(SOMCustomer *somSelf,  Environment *ev,
                                    string state)
{
    SOMCustomerData *somThis = SOMCustomerGetData(somSelf);
    SOMCustomerMethodDebug("SOMCustomer","_set_state");


    if (state!=NULL) {
        if (somThis->state != NULL) SOMFree(somThis->state);
        somThis->state = (string) SOMMalloc(strlen(state)+1);
        strcpy(somThis->state, state);
    }
    else {
        // should raise exception here
        // not implemented in our demo
    }
}
```

Figure 83. (Part 6 of 16) SOMCustomer Implementation

```
/*
*Method from the IDL attribute statement:
*"attribute string zip"
*/


/*
* Return information of the FIRST checking account this customer owns
* For simplicity the Smalltalk client of this sample program assumes
* that each customer has only one account.  We take the first account
* to "entertain" this client program.
*
*/


/*
* Return information of the FIRST checking account this customer owns
* For simplicity the Smalltalk client of this sample program assumes
* that each customer has only one account.  We take the first account
* to "entertain" this client program.
*
*
*/

SOM_Scope string  SOMLINK _get_zip(SOMCustomer *somSelf, Environment *ev)
{
    SOMCustomerData *somThis = SOMCustomerGetData(somSelf);
    SOMCustomerMethodDebug("SOMCustomer","_get_zip");

    // if attribute is not set before, return an empty string
    //
    if (somThis->zip == NULL) {
       somThis->zip = (string) SOMMalloc(2);
       somThis->zip¢0|=' ';
       somThis->zip¢1|='\0';
    }

    string zip = (string) SOMMalloc(strlen(somThis->zip)+1);
    strcpy(zip, somThis->zip);
    somPrintf("Message from SOMCustomer : zip=%s\n", somThis->zip);
    return zip;
}


/*
*Method from the IDL attribute statement:
*"attribute string zip"
*/


/*
* Return information of the FIRST checking account this customer owns
* For simplicity the Smalltalk client of this sample program assumes
* that each customer has only one account.  We take the first account
* to "entertain" this client program.
*
*/


/*
* Return information of the FIRST checking account this customer owns
* For simplicity the Smalltalk client of this sample program assumes
* that each customer has only one account.  We take the first account
* to "entertain" this client program.
*
*
*/
SOM_Scope void  SOMLINK _set_zip(SOMCustomer *somSelf, Environment *ev,
                          string zip)
```

Figure 83. (Part 7 of 16) SOMCustomer Implementation

```
{
    SOMCustomerData *somThis = SOMCustomerGetData(somSelf);
    SOMCustomerMethodDebug("SOMCustomer","_set_zip");


    if (zip!=NULL) {
        if (somThis->zip != NULL) SOMFree(somThis->zip);
        somThis->zip = (string) SOMMalloc(strlen(zip)+1);
        strcpy(somThis->zip, zip);
    }
    else {
        // should raise exception here
        // not implemented in our demo
    }


}


/*
*Method from the IDL attribute statement:
**"attribute SOMAccount* account"
*/

SOM_Scope SOMAccount*  SOMLINK _get_account(SOMCustomer *somSelf,
                                                 Environment *ev)
{
    SOMCustomerData *somThis = SOMCustomerGetData(somSelf);
    SOMCustomerMethodDebug("SOMCustomer","_get_account");

    if (somThis->account==NULL) {
        // Preparations
        //
        DaxAcctManager          DAXAcctMgrObject;
        DaxAcct         *cursorAccount;
        IVSequence<DaxAcct *>::Cursor cursor(*(DAXAcctMgrObject.items()));
        char            selectArg[256];

        // format the select clause and pass to the account manager.
        // Note that we only find the checking account owned by this coustomer
        //
        sprintf(selectArg, "CUST_ID=%d and ACCT_TYPE='%s'", somThis->customerId, "checking");
        DAXAcctMgrObject.select(selectArg);

        int numAccounts = DAXAcctMgrObject.items()->numberOfElements();
        if (numAccounts >= 1) {

            // Note that if this customer has more than 1 checking accounts
            // the first one will be returned, it's a demo anyway
            //
            cursor.setToFirst();
            cursorAccount = DAXAcctMgrObject.items()->elementAt(cursor);
            somThis->account = new SOMAccount();

            somThis->account->_set_accountNumber(ev,cursorAccount->acct_id());
            somThis->account->_set_balance(ev, cursorAccount->acct_balance());
            somThis->account->_set_branchId(ev,cursorAccount->acct_brid());
            somThis->account->_set_accountDescription(ev,cursorAccount->acct_type());
            somThis->account->_set_customerId(ev,cursorAccount->cust_id());
        }
        else {
            // Account not found, instead of raising an exception for simplicity
            // purpose we just pass back a dummy account
            //
            somThis->account = new SOMAccount();
            somThis->account->_set_accountNumber(ev, " ");
            somThis->account->_set_balance(ev, 0.0);
            somThis->account->_set_accountDescription(ev,"Not Found");
            somThis->account->_set_branchId(ev, "N/A");
            somThis->account->_set_customerId(ev,somThis->customerId);
        }
    }
    return somThis->account;
}
```

Figure 83. (Part 8 of 16) SOMCustomer Implementation

```
/*
 *Method from the IDL attribute statement:
 *"attribute SOMAccount* account"
 */

SOM_Scope void  SOMLINK _set_account(SOMCustomer *somSelf,
                                                Environment *ev,
                                                SOMAccount* account)
{
    SOMCustomerData *somThis = SOMCustomerGetData(somSelf);
    SOMCustomerMethodDebug("SOMCustomer","_set_account");

    if (somThis->account==NULL) {
        somThis->account = new SOMAccount();
    }
    somThis->account->_set_accountNumber(ev,account->_get_accountNumber(ev));
    somThis->account->_set_balance(ev,account->_get_balance(ev));
    somThis->account->_set_branchId(ev,account->_get_branchId(ev));
    somThis->account->_set_accountDescription(ev,account->_get_accountDescription(ev));
    somThis->account->_set_customerId(ev,account->_get_customerId(ev));
}


/*
 *Method from the IDL attribute statement:
 *"attribute string accountId"
 */

SOM_Scope string  SOMLINK _get_accountId(SOMCustomer *somSelf,
                                                Environment *ev)
{
    SOMCustomerData *somThis = SOMCustomerGetData(somSelf);
    SOMCustomerMethodDebug("SOMCustomer","_get_accountId");
    return somSelf->_get_account(ev)->_get_accountNumber(ev);
}

/*
 *Method from the IDL attribute statement:
 *"attribute string accountId"
 */

SOM_Scope void  SOMLINK _set_accountId(SOMCustomer *somSelf,
                                                Environment *ev, string accountId)
{
    SOMCustomerData *somThis = SOMCustomerGetData(somSelf);
    SOMCustomerMethodDebug("SOMCustomer","_set_accountId");
    somSelf->_get_account(ev)->_set_accountNumber(ev, accountId);
}

SOM_Scope string  SOMLINK accountNum(SOMCustomer *somSelf,
                                                Environment *ev)
{
    SOMCustomerData *somThis = SOMCustomerGetData(somSelf);
    SOMCustomerMethodDebug("SOMCustomer","accountNum");
    return somSelf->_get_account(ev)->_get_accountNumber(ev);
}


/*
 * One to many association, unbounded.  This is put into here
 * like this only for simplicity purpose.
 * Note that this only works for small implementations like our
 * demo.  Refer to the book for more detail discussions and how
 * to improve them
 *
 */

/*
 * All the functions/attributes in this section is here to support
 * other demo programs, it is not implemented here
 *
 */
```

Figure 83. (Part 9 of 16) SOMCustomer Implementation

```
SOM_Scope float SOMLINK accountBalance(SOMCustomer *somSelf,
                                       Environment *ev)
{
    SOMCustomerData *somThis = SOMCustomerGetData(somSelf);
    SOMCustomerMethodDebug("SOMCustomer","accountBalance");

    return somSelf->_get_account(ev)->_get_balance(ev);
}

SOM_Scope _IDL_SEQUENCE_SOMAccount SOMLINK allAccounts(SOMCustomer *somSelf,
                                                       Environment *ev)
{
    SOMCustomerData *somThis = SOMCustomerGetData(somSelf);
    SOMCustomerMethodDebug("SOMCustomer","allAccounts");

    // Preparations
    //
    _IDL_SEQUENCE_SOMAccount    returnAccountList;
    DaxAcctManager              DAXAcctMgrObject;
    DaxAcct                     *cursorAccount;
    IVSequence<DaxAcct *>::Cursor cursor(*(DAXAcctMgrObject.items()));
    char                        selectArg[100];


    // format the select clause and pass to the account manager.
    // Note that we only find the checking account owned by this coustomer
    //
    sprintf(selectArg, "CUST_ID=%d", somThis->customerId );
    DAXAcctMgrObject.select(selectArg);

    int numAccounts = DAXAcctMgrObject.items()->numberOfElements();

    returnAccountList._buffer = (SOMAccount **) SOMMalloc(sizeof(SOMAccount *) * numAccounts );
    sequenceLength(returnAccountList) = 0;

    // Put the found accounts into the returning list
    //
    int counter = 0;
    for (cursor.setToFirst(); cursor.isValid(); cursor.setToNext()) {
        cursorAccount = DAXAcctMgrObject.items()->elementAt(cursor);
        sequenceElement(returnAccountList, counter) = new SOMAccount();


        sequenceElement(returnAccountList,counter)->_set_accountNumber(ev,cursorAccount->acct_id());
        sequenceElement(returnAccountList,counter)->_set_balance(ev, cursorAccount->acct_balance());
        sequenceElement(returnAccountList,counter)->_set_branchId(ev,cursorAccount->acct_brid());
        sequenceElement(returnAccountList,counter)->_set_accountDescription(ev,cursorAccount->acct_type());
        sequenceElement(returnAccountList,counter)->_set_customerId(ev,cursorAccount->cust_id());


        ++counter;
        ++sequenceLength(returnAccountList);
    }

    return returnAccountList;
}

SOM_Scope _IDL_SEQUENCE_SOMAccount SOMLINK allSavingsAccounts(SOMCustomer *somSelf,
                                                              Environment *ev)
{
    SOMCustomerData *somThis = SOMCustomerGetData(somSelf);
    SOMCustomerMethodDebug("SOMCustomer","allSavingsAccounts");

    // Preparations
    //
    _IDL_SEQUENCE_SOMAccount    returnAccountList;
    DaxAcctManager              DAXAcctMgrObject;
    DaxAcct                     *cursorAccount;
    IVSequence<DaxAcct *>::Cursor cursor(*(DAXAcctMgrObject.items()));
    char                        selectArg[100];
```

Figure 83. (Part 10 of 16) SOMCustomer Implementation

```
// format the select clause and pass to the account manager.
// Note that we only find the checking account owned by this coustomer
//
sprintf(selectArg, "CUST_ID=%d", somThis->customerId );
sprintf(selectArg, "CUST_ID=%d and ACCT_TYPE='%s'",
                  somThis->customerId, "savings");
DAXAcctMgrObject.select(selectArg);

int numAccounts = DAXAcctMgrObject.items()->numberOfElements();

returnAccountList._buffer = (SOMAccount **) SOMMalloc(sizeof(SOMAccount *) * numAccounts );
sequenceLength(returnAccountList) = 0;

// Put the found accounts into the returning list
//
int counter = 0;
for (cursor.setToFirst(); cursor.isValid(); cursor.setToNext()) {
   cursorAccount = DAXAcctMgrObject.items()->elementAt(cursor);
   sequenceElement(returnAccountList, counter) = new SOMAccount();

   sequenceElement(returnAccountList,counter)->_set_accountNumber(ev,cursorAccount->acct_id());
   sequenceElement(returnAccountList,counter)->_set_balance(ev, cursorAccount->acct_balance());
   sequenceElement(returnAccountList,counter)->_set_branchId(ev,cursorAccount->acct_brid());
   sequenceElement(returnAccountList,counter)->_set_accountDescription(ev,cursorAccount->acct_type());
   sequenceElement(returnAccountList,counter)->_set_customerId(ev,cursorAccount->cust_id());


   ++counter;
   ++sequenceLength(returnAccountList);
}


return returnAccountList;

}

SOM_Scope _IDL_SEQUENCE_SOMAccount  SOMLINK allCheckingAccounts(SOMCustomer *somSelf,
                                                    Environment *ev)

{

   SOMCustomerData *somThis = SOMCustomerGetData(somSelf);
   SOMCustomerMethodDebug("SOMCustomer","allaccounts");


   // Preparations
   //
   _IDL_SEQUENCE_SOMAccount    returnAccountList;
   DaxAcctManager              DAXAcctMgrObject;
   DaxAcct            *cursorAccount;
   IVSequence<DaxAcct *>::Cursor cursor(*(DAXAcctMgrObject.items()));
   char               selectArg[100];


   // format the select clause and pass to the account manager.
   // Note that we only find the checking account owned by this coustomer
   //
   sprintf(selectArg, "CUST_ID=%d", somThis->customerId );
   sprintf(selectArg, "CUST_ID=%d and ACCT_TYPE='%s'",
                  somThis->customerId, "checking");
   DAXAcctMgrObject.select(selectArg);
   int numAccounts = DAXAcctMgrObject.items()->numberOfElements();


   returnAccountList._buffer = (SOMAccount **) SOMMalloc(sizeof(SOMAccount *) * numAccounts );
   sequenceLength(returnAccountList) = 0;

   // Put the found accounts into the returning list
   //
   int counter = 0;
   for (cursor.setToFirst(); cursor.isValid(); cursor.setToNext()) {
      cursorAccount = DAXAcctMgrObject.items()->elementAt(cursor);
      sequenceElement(returnAccountList, counter) = new SOMAccount();
```

Figure 83. (Part 11 of 16) SOMCustomer Implementation

```
        sequenceElement(returnAccountList,counter)->_set_accountNumber(ev,cursorAccount->acct_id());
        sequenceElement(returnAccountList,counter)->_set_balance(ev, cursorAccount->acct_balance());
        sequenceElement(returnAccountList,counter)->_set_branchId(ev,cursorAccount->acct_brid());
        sequenceElement(returnAccountList,counter)->_set_accountDescription(ev,cursorAccount->acct_type());
        sequenceElement(returnAccountList,counter)->_set_customerId(ev,cursorAccount->cust_id());


        ++counter;
        ++sequenceLength(returnAccountList);
    }
    return returnAccountList;
}


/*
 * Storing/updating/adding and removing itself
 * from the persistence media, in this demo : DB2/2
 *
 */


SOM_Scope _IDL_SEQUENCE_SOMAccount  SOMLINK allSuperSavingsAccounts(SOMCustomer*somSelf,
                                                     Environment *ev)
{
    SOMCustomerData *somThis = SOMCustomerGetData(somSelf);
    SOMCustomerMethodDebug("SOMCustomer","allSuperSavingsAccounts");


    // Preparations
    //
    _IDL_SEQUENCE_SOMAccount    returnAccountList;
    DaxAcctManager              DAXAcctMgrObject;
    DaxAcct                     *cursorAccount;
    IVSequence<DaxAcct *>::Cursor cursor(*(DAXAcctMgrObject.items()));
    char                selectArg[100];


    // format the select clause and pass to the account manager.
    // Note that we only find the checking account owned by this coustomer
    //
    sprintf(selectArg, "CUST_ID=%d", somThis->customerId );
    sprintf(selectArg, "CUST_ID=%d and ACCT_TYPE='%s'",
                somThis->customerId, "Super Saving");
    DAXAcctMgrObject.select(selectArg);

    int numAccounts = DAXAcctMgrObject.items()->numberOfElements();

    returnAccountList._buffer = (SOMAccount **) SOMMalloc(sizeof(SOMAccount *) * numAccounts );
    sequenceLength(returnAccountList) = 0;
    // Put the found accounts into the returning list
    //
    int counter = 0;
    for (cursor.setToFirst(); cursor.isValid(); cursor.setToNext()) {
        cursorAccount = DAXAcctMgrObject.items()->elementAt(cursor);
        sequenceElement(returnAccountList, counter) = new SOMAccount();

        sequenceElement(returnAccountList,counter)->_set_accountNumber(ev,cursorAccount->acct_id());
        sequenceElement(returnAccountList,counter)->_set_balance(ev, cursorAccount->acct_balance());
        sequenceElement(returnAccountList,counter)->_set_branchId(ev,cursorAccount->acct_brid());
        sequenceElement(returnAccountList,counter)->_set_accountDescription(ev,cursorAccount->acct_type());
        sequenceElement(returnAccountList,counter)->_set_customerId(ev,cursorAccount->cust_id());


        ++counter;
        ++sequenceLength(returnAccountList);
    }


    return returnAccountList;
}
/*
 * retrieve information about myself, based on the customerId I have
 */
SOM_Scope void SOMLINK retrieve(SOMCustomer *somSelf, Environment *ev)
{
```

Figure 83. (Part 12 of 16) SOMCustomer Implementation

```
    SOMCustomerData *somThis = SOMCustomerGetData(somSelf);
    SOMCustomerMethodDebug("SOMCustomer","retrieve");

    DaxCust DAXCustomerObject;

    // retrieve a customer from database with the customer id
    try {
       DAXCustomerObject.setCust_id( somThis->customerId );
       DAXCustomerObject.retrieve();
       somSelf->_get_account(ev)->_set_accountNumber(ev, DAXCustomerObject.cust_acid());
       somSelf->_get_account(ev)->retrieve(ev);


    }
    catch (IException &exc) {
       // should set exception to client program
       // Not implemented in our demo
       //
       somSelf->_set_firstName(ev," ");
       somSelf->_set_lastName(ev," ");
       somSelf->_set_homePhone(ev," ");
       somSelf->_set_workPhone(ev," ");
       somSelf->_set_street(ev," ");
       somSelf->_set_city(ev," ");
       somSelf->_set_state(ev," ");
       somSelf->_set_zip(ev," ");
       return;
    }


    somSelf->_set_firstName(ev,DAXCustomerObject.cust_fname());
    somSelf->_set_lastName(ev,DAXCustomerObject.cust_lname());
    somSelf->_set_homePhone(ev,DAXCustomerObject.cust_hphone());
    somSelf->_set_workPhone(ev,DAXCustomerObject.cust_wphone());
    somSelf->_set_street(ev,DAXCustomerObject.cust_street());
    somSelf->_set_city(ev,DAXCustomerObject.cust_city());
    somSelf->_set_state(ev,DAXCustomerObject.cust_state());
    somSelf->_set_zip(ev,DAXCustomerObject.cust_zip());
}
/*
 * update my information to the persistance storage
 */

SOM_Scope void  SOMLINK update(SOMCustomer *somSelf,  Environment *ev)
{
    SOMCustomerData *somThis = SOMCustomerGetData(somSelf);
    SOMCustomerMethodDebug("SOMCustomer","update");

    DaxCust DAXCustomerObject;
    DaxAcct DAXAccountObject;


    // update the customer with the current id
    try {
       DAXCustomerObject.setCust_id    (somThis->customerId);

       DAXCustomerObject.setCust_fname (somThis->firstName );
       DAXCustomerObject.setCust_lname (somThis->lastName  );
       DAXCustomerObject.setCust_hphone(somThis->homePhone );
       DAXCustomerObject.setCust_wphone(somThis->workPhone );
       DAXCustomerObject.setCust_street(somThis->street    );
       DAXCustomerObject.setCust_city  (somThis->city      );
       DAXCustomerObject.setCust_state (somThis->state     );
       DAXCustomerObject.setCust_zip   (somThis->zip       );
       DAXCustomerObject.setCust_acid  (somSelf->_get_account(ev)->_get_accountNumber(ev) );
       // Assume successful transaction for both operations,
       // it's a demo anyway
       //
       if ( strcmp(somSelf->_get_account(ev)->_get_accountNumber(ev),"N/A")!=0 )
{
          somSelf->_get_account(ev)->update(ev);
       }
       DAXCustomerObject.update();
```

Figure 83. (Part 13 of 16) SOMCustomer Implementation

```
        // we commit immediately, it's a demo anyway
        //
        DSObject.commit();
        somPrintf("Message from SOMCustomer : customer updated\n");


    } catch (IException &exc) {
        // should set exception to client program
        // Not implemented in our demo
        //
    }


}

/*
 *  add myself to the customer list
 */

SOM_Scope void  SOMLINK add(SOMCustomer *somSelf, Environment *ev)
{
    SOMCustomerData *somThis = SOMCustomerGetData(somSelf);
    SOMCustomerMethodDebug("SOMCustomer","add");

    DaxCust DAXCustomerObject;
    DaxAcct DAXAccountObject;


    // put all necessary information to the data access object
    //
    DAXCustomerObject.setCust_id     (somThis->customerId);
    DAXCustomerObject.setCust_fname  (somThis->firstName );
    DAXCustomerObject.setCust_lname  (somThis->lastName  );
    DAXCustomerObject.setCust_hphone (somThis->homePhone );
    DAXCustomerObject.setCust_wphone (somThis->homePhone );
    DAXCustomerObject.setCust_street (somThis->street    );
    DAXCustomerObject.setCust_city   (somThis->city      );
    DAXCustomerObject.setCust_state  (somThis->state     );
    DAXCustomerObject.setCust_zip    (somThis->zip       );
    DAXCustomerObject.setCust_acid   (somSelf->_get_account(ev)->_get_accountNumber(ev) );

    // Set the default account for it first.  As the client program
    // of this demo only handle one checking account, we hard code it
    // in here for simplicity purpose
    //
    DAXAccountObject.setCust_id(somThis->customerId);
    DAXAccountObject.setAcct_id(somSelf->_get_account(ev)->_get_accountNumber(ev));
    DAXAccountObject.setAcct_type("checking");
    DAXAccountObject.setAcct_brid("AAAA");
    DAXAccountObject.setAcct_balance(0.0);

    // add a customer to the database
    try {


        DAXCustomerObject.add();
        DAXAccountObject.add();

        // we commit immediately, it's a demo anyway
        //
        DSObject.commit();
    }
    catch (IException &exc) {
        // should set exception to client program
        // Not implemented in our demo
        //
    }

}

/*
 *  delete myself from the customer list.  Also all accounts belonged to me
 *  will be deleted
 */
SOM_Scope void  SOMLINK del(SOMCustomer *somSelf, Environment *ev)
{
```

Figure 83. (Part 14 of 16) SOMCustomer Implementation

```
    SOMCustomerData *somThis = SOMCustomerGetData(somSelf);
    SOMCustomerMethodDebug("SOMCustomer","remove");

    DaxCust DAXCustomerObject;

    try {

       DAXCustomerObject.setCust_id( somThis->customerId );
       DAXCustomerObject.del();

       // Note: corresponding accounts will be deleted in cascade

       // commit immediately, this is a demo anyway.
       //
       DSObject.commit();
    }
    catch (IException &exc) {
       // should set exception to client program
       // Not implemented in our demo
       //
    }

}
/*
 * SOM_Scope void SOMLINK somDestruct(SOMCustomer *somSelf, octet doFree,
 *                                    somDestructCtrl* ctrl)
 */

/*
 * The prototype for somDestruct was replaced by the following prototype:
 */
SOM_Scope void SOMLINK somDestruct(SOMCustomer *somSelf, octet doFree,
                                   som3DestructCtrl* ctrl)
{
    SOMCustomerData *somThis; /* set in BeginDestructor */
    somDestructCtrl globalCtrl;
    somBooleanVector myMask;
    SOMCustomerMethodDebug("SOMCustomer","somDestruct");
    SOMCustomer_BeginDestructor;

    /*
     * local SOMCustomer deinitialization code added by programmer
     */

    SOMCustomer_EndDestructor;
}
/*
 * SOM_Scope void SOMLINK somDefaultInit(SOMCustomer *somSelf, somInitCtrl* ctrl
)
 */
/*
 * The prototype for somDefaultInit was replaced by the following prototype:
 */
SOM_Scope void SOMLINK somDefaultInit(SOMCustomer *somSelf, som3InitCtrl* ctrl)
{
    SOMCustomerData *somThis; /* set in BeginInitializer */
    somInitCtrl globalCtrl;
    somBooleanVector myMask;
    SOMCustomerMethodDebug("SOMCustomer","somDefaultInit");
    SOMCustomer_BeginInitializer_somDefaultInit;

    SOMCustomer_Init_SOMObject_somDefaultInit(somSelf, ctrl);

    /*
     * local SOMCustomer initialization code added by programmer
     */

}
```

Figure 83. (Part 15 of 16) SOMCustomer Implementation

```
SOMEXTERN void SOMLINK SOMInitModule( long majorVersion,
                                      long minorVersion,
                                      string className)


{
    SOMCustomerNewClass(0,0);
    SOMAccountNewClass(0,0);


    /*
     * local dTstCust initialization code added by programmer
     */
    try {

        DSObject.connect("SOMBANK", "FCE", "PASSWORD");

    } catch (IException &exc) {

        somPrintf("Failed: Exception occurs\n");
        somPrintf("Error id: %ld\n", exc.errorId());

        for (unsigned long i = 0; i < exc.textCount(); i++)
            somPrintf("Error Text: %s\n", exc.text(i) );

        somPrintf("Error Class: %s\n", exc.name());
    }
}
```

Figure 83. (Part 16 of 16) SOMCustomer Implementation

List of Abbreviations

API	Application Programming Interface
BOA	Basic Object Adapter
CRC	Class-Responsibility-Collaboration
CORBA	Common Object Request Broker Architecture
CUA	Common User Access
DCE	Distributed Computing Environment
DFS	Distributed File System (an OSF DCE component)
DLL	Dynamic Link Library (OS/2)
DRDA	Distributed Relational Database Architecture
DSOM	Distributed System Object Model
DTP	Distributed Transaction Processing
DTS	Direct-To-SOM
ESIOP	Environment-Specific Inter-ORB Protocol
FCE	Foreign Currency Exchange
FIFO	First-In First-Out
GIOP	General Inter-ORB Protocol
GSS	Generic Security Services
GUI	Graphical User Interface
IBM	International Business Machines Corporation
IDL	Interface Definition Language
IIOP	Internet Inter-ORB Protocol
IOP	Inter-ORB Protocol
IP	Internet Protocol
IPC	Inter-Process Communication
IPMD	IBM Presentation Manager Debugger
ITSO	International Technical Support Organization
LAN	Local Area Network
LIFO	Last-In First-Out
NCS	NetWork Computing System
NFS	NetWork File System
NetSP	Network Security Program
OMA	Object Management Architecture
OMG	Object Management Group
OMT	Object Modeling Technique
OOSE	Object-Oriented Software Engineering
ORB	Object Request Broker
OSF	Open Systems Foundation
OSI	Open Systems Interconnection
OTS	Object Transaction Service
PDS	Persistent Data Store
PID	Persistent Identifier
POM	Persistent Object Manager
POS	Persistence Object Service (SOM)
PM	Presentation Manager (OS/2)
RDBMS	Relational Database Management System
RDD	Responsibility Driven Design
RPC	Remote Procedure Call
SOM	System Object Model
SPI	Service Provider Interface
TLS	Two-Level Store (OMG Persistence Service)
TP	Transaction Program/Process (OSI)
UNO	Universal Networked Objects (CORBA 2.0)
VMT	Visual Modeling Technique

Bibliography

[Booch94]   Grady Booch. *Object-Oriented Analysis and Design with Applications, Benjamin / Cummins, 1994.*

[Fang96]   W. Fang, S. Guyet, R. Haven, M. Vilmi and E. Eckmann. *VisualAge for Smalltalk Distributed: Developing Distributed Object Applications*, Prentice Hall, 1996.

[Jacob92]   Ivar Jacobson, Magnus Christerson, Patrik Jonsson, and Gunnar Övergaard. *Object-Oriented Software Engineering: A Use Case Driven Approach*, Addison-Wesley Publishing Company, 1992.

[Mowbr95]   Thomas Mowbray and Ron Zahavi. *The Essential CORBA, Systems Integration Using Distributed Objects*, John Wiley & Sons, Inc, 1995.

[Otte96]   Randy Otte, Paul Patrick, and Mark Roy. *Understanding CORBA*, Prentice Hall, 1996.

[Orfali94]   Robert Orfali, Dan Harkey. *Client / Server Survival Guide with OS / 2*, Van Nostrand Reinhold, 1994.

[Rumba91]   J. Rumbaugh, M. Blaha, W. Premerlani, F. Eddy, and W. Lorenson. *Object-Oriented Modeling and Design*, Prentice Hall, 1991.

[Tkach96]   D. Tkach, W. Fang, and A. So. *Visual Modeling Technique: Object Technology with Visual Programming*, Addison–Wesley, 1996.

[Wirfs90]   R. Wirfs-Brock, B. Wilkerson, and L. Wiener. *Designing Object-Oriented Software*, Prentice Hall, 1990.

Index

A

active server 27, 132
aggregation 153, 165, 166
analysis
    object-oriented 135
application
    design of distribution 144
    VisualAge application 148
architecture
    application 145

B

binding files 178
bridge
    full bridge 41
    half bridge 41

C

CICS OS/2 23
class
    attributes 175
    description in IDL 175
    relationships 175
client
    design considerations 157
    functions 191
    implementation 191
client/server
    evolution of 22
    styles 5
common object request broker
  architecture 29
computing 4
CORBA 29, 209
    CORBA 1.1 34, 72
    CORBA 1.2 38
    CORBA 2.0 37
    CORBA 2.0 interoperability
      protocols 42
    CORBA 2.0 specification 38
    CORBA2-compliant 39
    CORBA2/C 38

CORBA2/CORE 38
CORBA2/C++ 38
CORBA2/IIOP 38
CORBA2/Interoperable 38
CORBA2/Smalltalk 38
CORBA-compliant 56, 75, 209
CORBA-defined data types 55
CORBAservices 33
IDL 47, 54, 55
interface repository 55
link between CORBA and DCE 55
OTS 29
standard 69
C++ 174

D

data
    centralized 10
    partitioned 13
    replicated 11
delegation 166
design
    object 143
    object-oriented 135
    system 143
    system design 145
distributed
    application 5
    file system 8
    operating system 8
    programming language 8
    systems 9
    toolkit 8
distributed object applications
    active server 27
    applicability of 24
    object server 25
    peer-to-peer 28
distributed object computing 19, 23
    benefits 23
    standards 29
distributed objects 21
distributed relational database
  architecture 25
distributed SOM
    architecture 63
    daemon 61

VMT , See visual modeling technique

W

wrapper classes 191, 192, 193, 194, 205,
   206, 207

X

X/Open Distributed Transaction
   Processing 29

LICENSE AGREEMENT AND LIMITED WARRANTY

READ THE FOLLOWING TERMS AND CONDITIONS CAREFULLY BEFORE OPENING THIS DISK PACKAGE. THIS LEGAL DOCUMENT IS AN AGREEMENT BETWEEN YOU AND PRENTICE-HALL, INC. (THE "COMPANY"). BY OPENING THIS SEALED DISK PACKAGE, YOU ARE AGREEING TO BE BOUND BY THESE TERMS AND CONDITIONS. IF YOU DO NOT AGREE WITH THESE TERMS AND CONDITIONS, DO NOT OPEN THE DISK PACKAGE. PROMPTLY RETURN THE UNOPENED DISK PACKAGE AND ALL ACCOMPANYING ITEMS TO THE PLACE YOU OBTAINED THEM FOR A FULL REFUND OF ANY SUMS YOU HAVE PAID.

1.   **GRANT OF LICENSE:** In consideration of your payment of the license fee, which is part of the price you paid for this product, and your agreement to abide by the terms and conditions of this Agreement, the Company grants to you a nonexclusive right to use and display the copy of the enclosed software program (hereinafter the "SOFTWARE") on a single computer (i.e., with a single CPU) at a single location so long as you comply with the terms of this Agreement. The Company reserves all rights not expressly granted to you under this Agreement.

2.   **OWNERSHIP OF SOFTWARE:** You own only the magnetic or physical media (the enclosed disks) on which the SOFTWARE is recorded or fixed, but the Company retains all the rights, title, and ownership to the SOFTWARE recorded on the original disk copy(ies) and all subsequent copies of the SOFTWARE, regardless of the form or media on which the original or other copies may exist. This license is not a sale of the original SOFTWARE or any copy to you.

3.   **COPY RESTRICTIONS:** This SOFTWARE and the accompanying printed materials and user manual (the "Documentation") are the subject of copyright. You may not copy the Documentation or the SOFTWARE, except that you may make a single copy of the SOFTWARE for backup or archival purposes only. You may be held legally responsible for any copying or copyright infringement which is caused or encouraged by your failure to abide by the terms of this restriction.

4.   **USE RESTRICTIONS:** You may not network the SOFTWARE or otherwise use it on more than one computer or computer terminal at the same time. You may physically transfer the SOFTWARE from one computer to another provided that the SOFTWARE is used on only one computer at a time. You may not distribute copies of the SOFTWARE or Documentation to others. You may not reverse engineer, disassemble, decompile, modify, adapt, translate, or create derivative works based on the SOFTWARE or the Documentation without the prior written consent of the Company.

5.   **TRANSFER RESTRICTIONS:** The enclosed SOFTWARE is licensed only to you and may not be transferred to any one else without the prior written consent of the Company. Any unauthorized transfer of the SOFTWARE shall result in the immediate termination of this Agreement.

6.   **TERMINATION:** This license is effective until terminated. This license will terminate automatically without notice from the Company and become null and void if you fail to comply with any provisions or limitations of this license. Upon termination, you shall destroy the Documentation and all copies of the SOFTWARE. All provisions of this Agreement as to warranties, limitation of liability, remedies or damages, and our ownership rights shall survive termination.

7.   **MISCELLANEOUS:** This Agreement shall be construed in accordance with the laws of the United States of America and the State of New York and shall benefit the Company, its affiliates, and assignees.

8.   **LIMITED WARRANTY AND DISCLAIMER OF WARRANTY:** The Company warrants that the SOFTWARE, when properly used in accordance with the Documentation, will operate in substantial conformity with the description of the SOFTWARE set forth in the Documentation. The Company does not warrant that the SOFTWARE will meet your requirements or that the operation of the SOFTWARE will be uninterrupted or error-free. The Company warrants that the

media on which the SOFTWARE is delivered shall be free from defects in materials and workmanship under normal use for a period of thirty (30) days from the date of your purchase. Your only remedy and the Company's only obligation under these limited warranties is, at the Company's option, return of the warranted item for a refund of any amounts paid by you or replacement of the item. Any replacement of SOFTWARE or media under the warranties shall not extend the original warranty period. The limited warranty set forth above shall not apply to any SOFTWARE which the Company determines in good faith has been subject to misuse, neglect, improper installation, repair, alteration, or damage by you. EXCEPT FOR THE EXPRESSED WARRANTIES SET FORTH ABOVE, THE COMPANY DISCLAIMS ALL WARRANTIES, EXPRESS OR IMPLIED, INCLUDING WITHOUT LIMITATION, THE IMPLIED WARRANTIES OF MERCHANTABILITY AND FITNESS FOR A PARTICULAR PURPOSE. EXCEPT FOR THE EXPRESS WARRANTY SET FORTH ABOVE, THE COMPANY DOES NOT WARRANT, GUARANTEE, OR MAKE ANY REPRESENTATION REGARDING THE USE OR THE RESULTS OF THE USE OF THE SOFTWARE IN TERMS OF ITS CORRECTNESS, ACCURACY, RELIABILITY, CURRENTNESS, OR OTHERWISE.

IN NO EVENT, SHALL THE COMPANY OR ITS EMPLOYEES, AGENTS, SUPPLIERS, OR CONTRACTORS BE LIABLE FOR ANY INCIDENTAL, INDIRECT, SPECIAL, OR CONSEQUENTIAL DAMAGES ARISING OUT OF OR IN CONNECTION WITH THE LICENSE GRANTED UNDER THIS AGREEMENT, OR FOR LOSS OF USE, LOSS OF DATA, LOSS OF INCOME OR PROFIT, OR OTHER LOSSES, SUSTAINED AS A RESULT OF INJURY TO ANY PERSON, OR LOSS OF OR DAMAGE TO PROPERTY, OR CLAIMS OF THIRD PARTIES, EVEN IF THE COMPANY OR AN AUTHORIZED REPRESENTATIVE OF THE COMPANY HAS BEEN ADVISED OF THE POSSIBILITY OF SUCH DAMAGES. IN NO EVENT SHALL LIABILITY OF THE COMPANY FOR DAMAGES WITH RESPECT TO THE SOFTWARE EXCEED THE AMOUNTS ACTUALLY PAID BY YOU, IF ANY, FOR THE SOFTWARE.

SOME JURISDICTIONS DO NOT ALLOW THE LIMITATION OF IMPLIED WARRANTIES OR LIABILITY FOR INCIDENTAL, INDIRECT, SPECIAL, OR CONSEQUENTIAL DAMAGES, SO THE ABOVE LIMITATIONS MAY NOT ALWAYS APPLY. THE WARRANTIES IN THIS AGREEMENT GIVE YOU SPECIFIC LEGAL RIGHTS AND YOU MAY ALSO HAVE OTHER RIGHTS WHICH VARY IN ACCORDANCE WITH LOCAL LAW.

ACKNOWLEDGMENT

YOU ACKNOWLEDGE THAT YOU HAVE READ THIS AGREEMENT, UNDERSTAND IT, AND AGREE TO BE BOUND BY ITS TERMS AND CONDITIONS. YOU ALSO AGREE THAT THIS AGREEMENT IS THE COMPLETE AND EXCLUSIVE STATEMENT OF THE AGREEMENT BETWEEN YOU AND THE COMPANY AND SUPERSEDES ALL PROPOSALS OR PRIOR AGREEMENTS, ORAL, OR WRITTEN, AND ANY OTHER COMMUNICATIONS BETWEEN YOU AND THE COMPANY OR ANY REPRESENTATIVE OF THE COMPANY RELATING TO THE SUBJECT MATTER OF THIS AGREEMENT.

Should you have any questions concerning this Agreement or if you wish to contact the Company for any reason, please contact in writing at the address below.

Robin Short
Prentice Hall PTR
One Lake Street
Upper Saddle River, New Jersey 07458